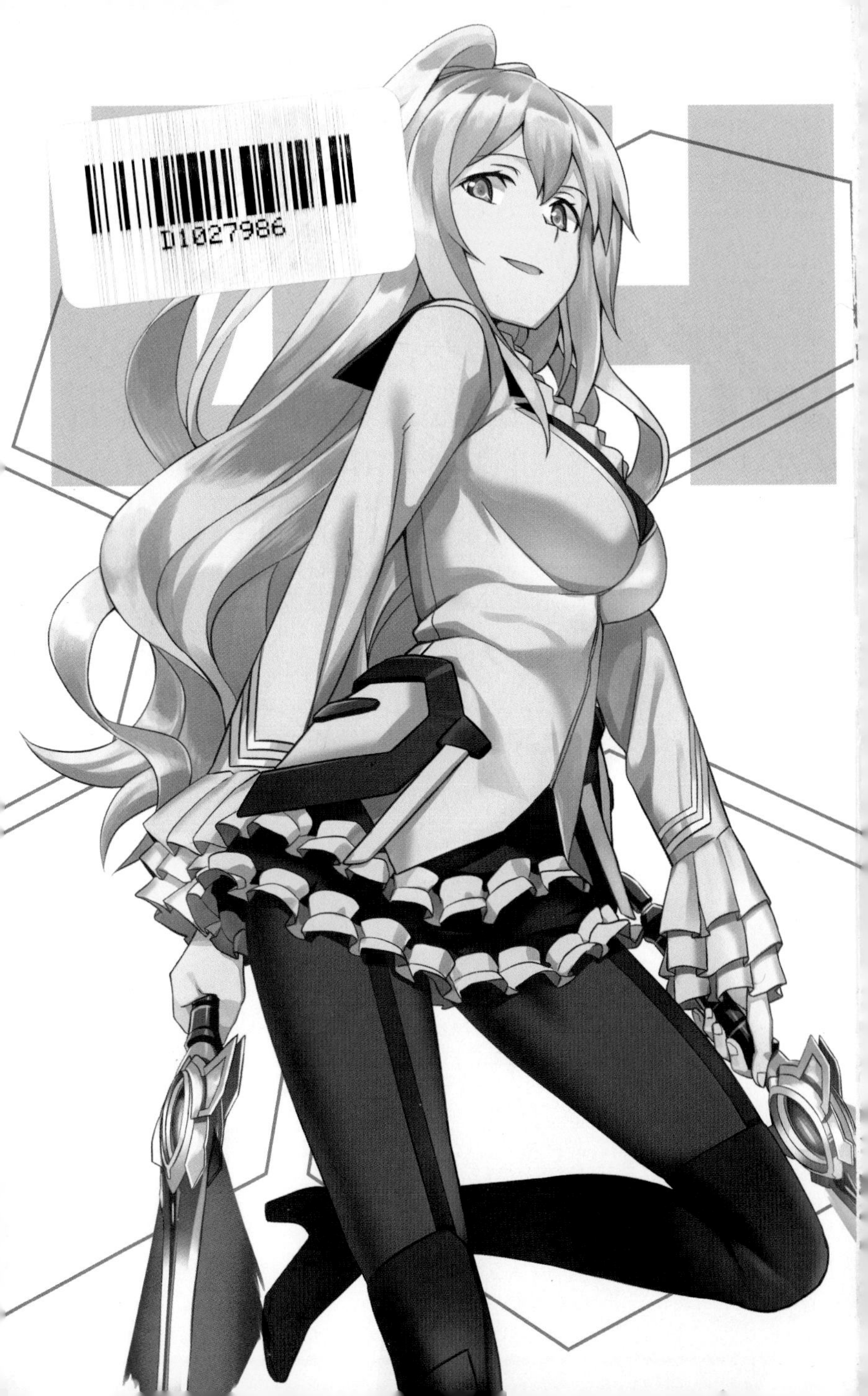

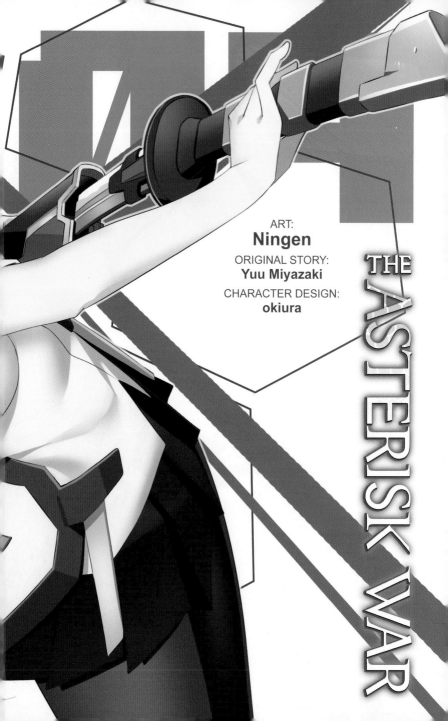

ART:
Ningen

ORIGINAL STORY:
Yuu Miyazaki

CHARACTER DESIGN:
okiura

THE ASTERISK WAR

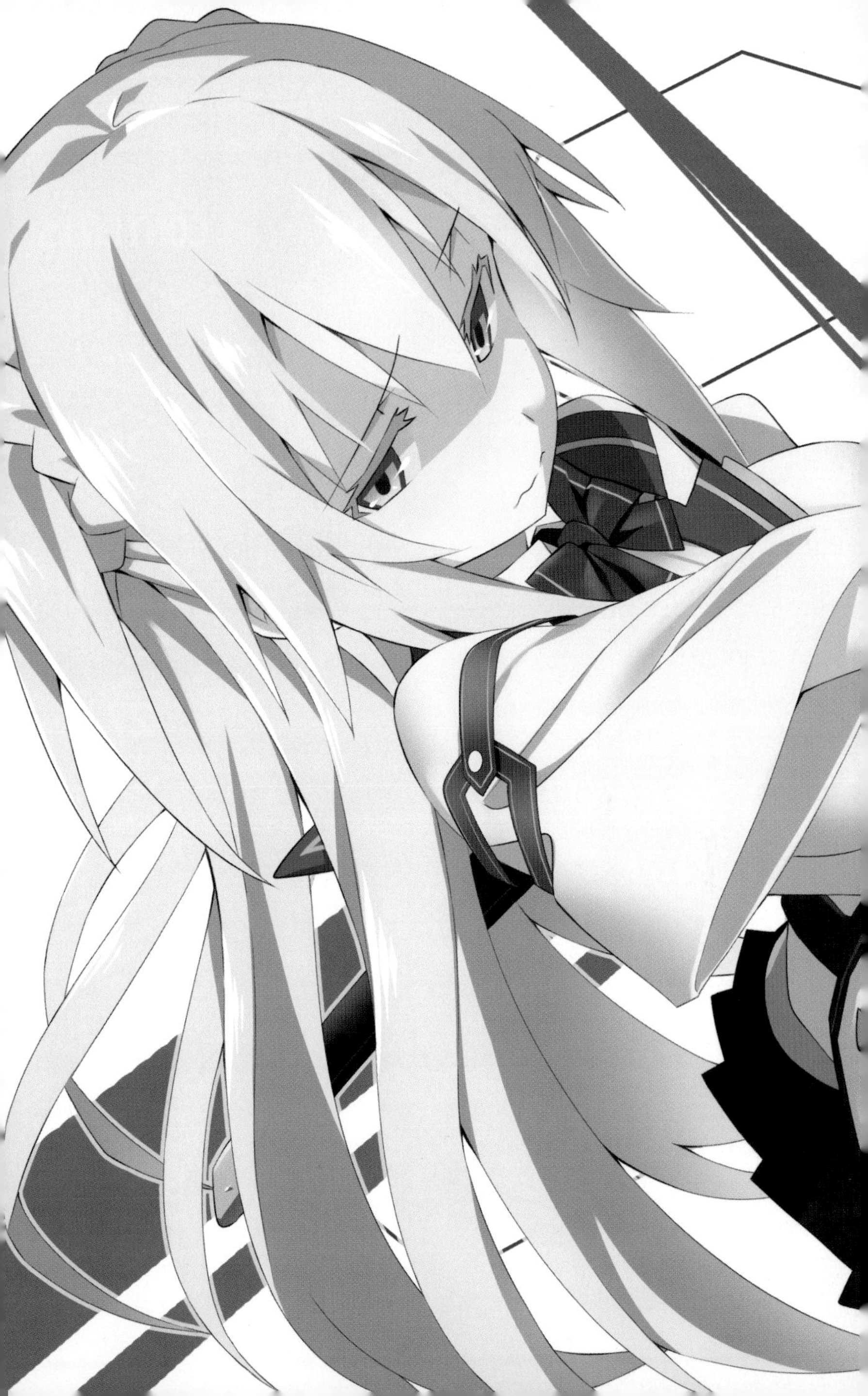

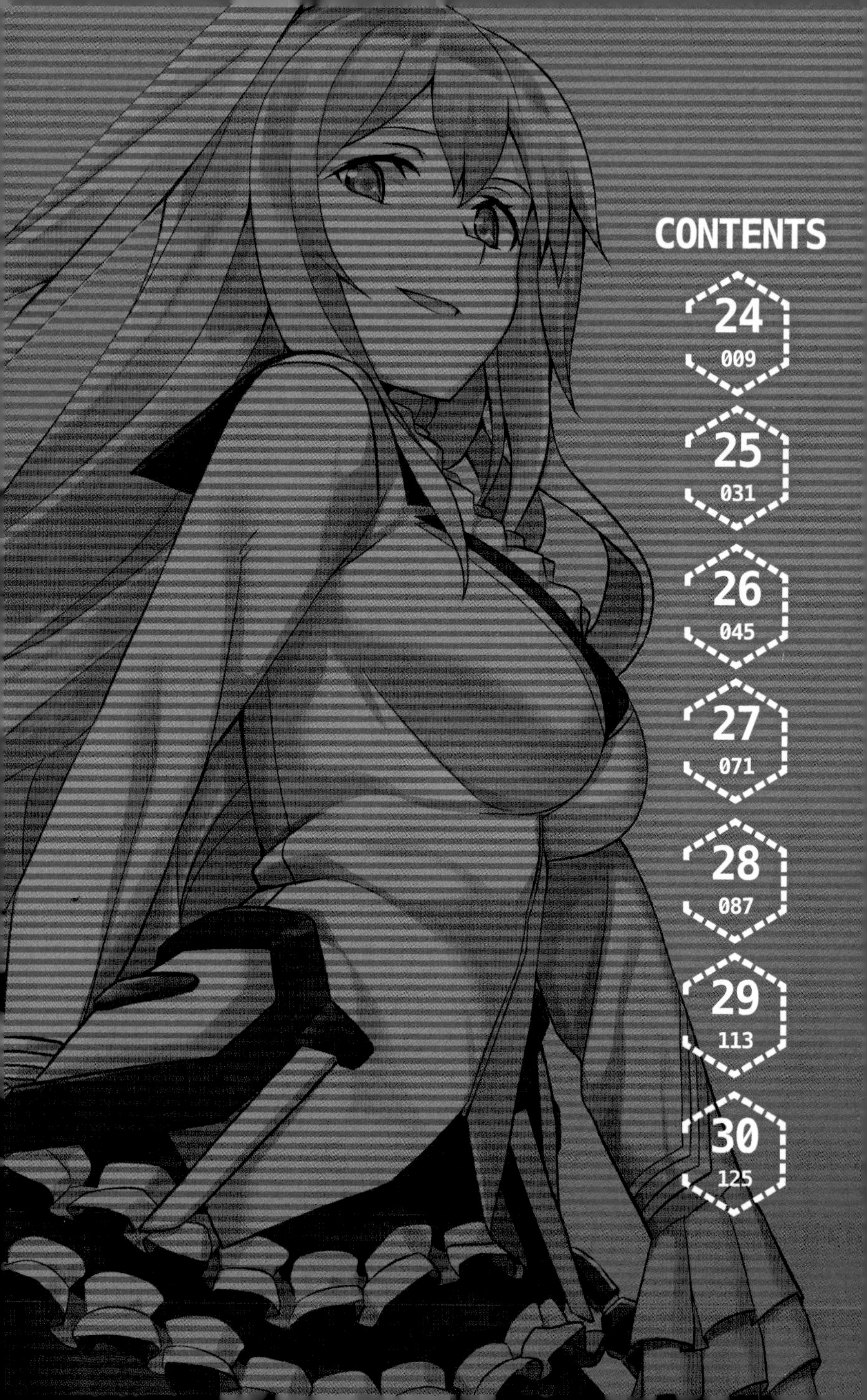

CONTENTS

MURDERER
IN THE STREETS, KILLER
IN THE SHEETS!

THE ASTERISK WAR 04

Ningen
Original Story: Yuu Miyazaki
Character Design: okiura

Translation: Melissa Tanaka   Lettering: Phil Christie

THE ASTERISK WAR
© Ningen 2016
© Yuu Miyazaki 2016
First published in Japan in 2016 by KADOKAWA CORPORATION, Tokyo.
English translation rights arranged with KADOKAWA CORPORATION, Tokyo, through TUTTLE-MORI AGENCY, Inc., Tokyo.

English translation © 2017 by Yen Press, LLC

Yen Press
1290 Avenue of the Americas
New York, NY 10104

Visit us at yenpress.com
facebook.com/yenpress
twitter.com/yenpress
yenpress.tumblr.com
instagram.com/yenpresss

First Yen Press Edition: June 2017

Yen Press is an imprint of Yen Press, LLC.
The Yen Press name and logo are trademarks of Yen Press, LLC.

The publisher is not responsible for websites (or their content) that are not owned by the publisher.

Library of Congress Control Number: 2016936539

ISBNs: 978-0-316-47173-2 (paperback)
         978-0-316-47360-6 (ebook)

10 9 8 7 6 5 4 3 2 1

BVG

Printed in the United States of America

Karino Takatsu, creator of
SERVANT x SERVICE, presents:

My Monster Girl's Too Cool For You

Burning adoration melts her heart...literally!

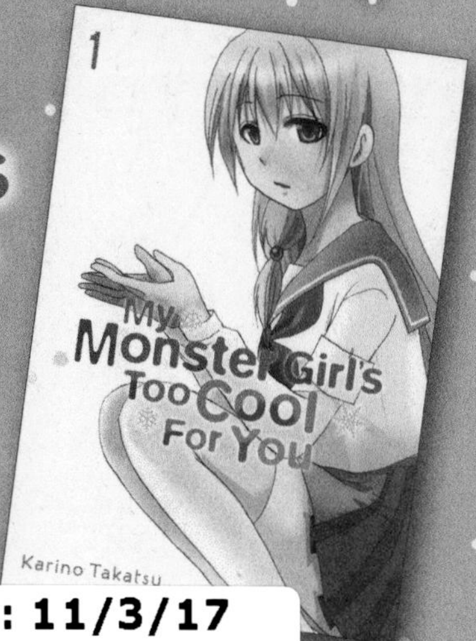
1
My Monster Girl's Too Cool For You
Karino Takatsu

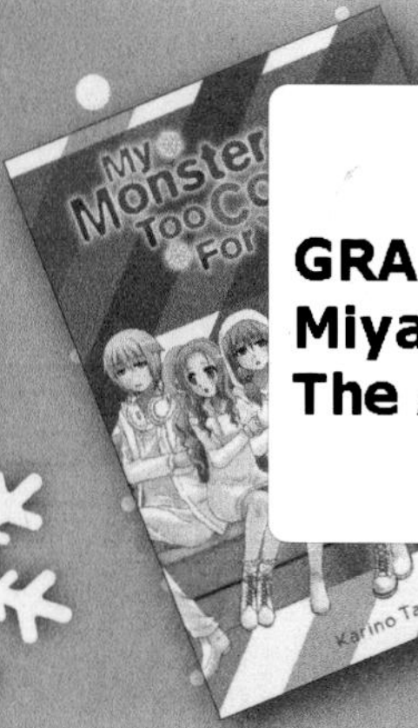
My Monster Girl's Too Cool For You
Karino Takatsu

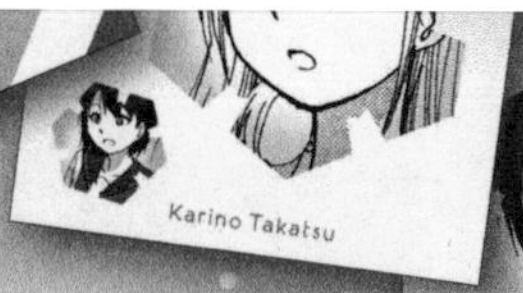
Karino Takatsu

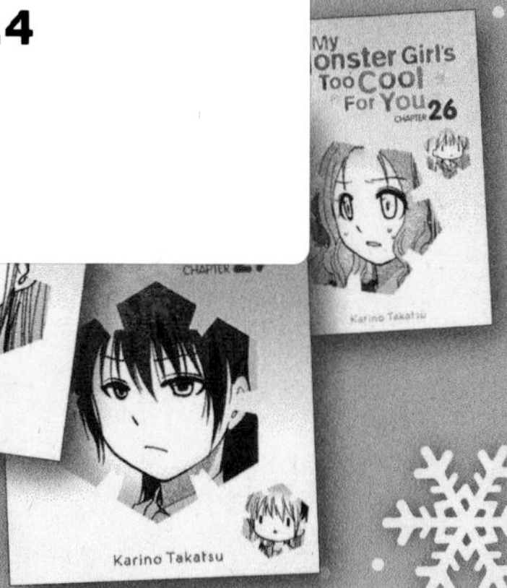
My Monster Girl's Too Cool For You
CHAPTER 26
Karino Takatsu
Karino Takatsu

In a world where *youkai* and humans attend school together, a boy named Atsushi F... falls for snow *youkai* ...onate feelings melt Muku's heart...c ...e of an interspecies romanti... ...over heels for is now available!!

Read new installments of this series every month at the same time as Japan!

CHAPTERS AVAILABLE NOW AT E-TAILERS EVERYWHERE!

Yen Press
YenPress.com

The legends foretold of six heroes awakening to save the world...

BUT IT NEVER SPECIFIED WHAT TO DO WITH SEVEN!

The manga adaptation of the super-popular light novel series!

When the world is threatened with destruction, six chosen heroes will rise to save it. One of them is Adlet Meyer, who calls himself "the strongest man in the world." But when he answers the call to assemble with the other heroes and face the darkness, there are not six heroes but seven. Who is the traitor in their midst?

ROKKA: Braves of the Six Flowers

Yen Press
www.yenpress.com

Read the light novel that inspired the hit anime series!

Re:ZeRo
-Starting Life in Another World-

Also be sure to check out the manga series!
AVAILABLE NOW!

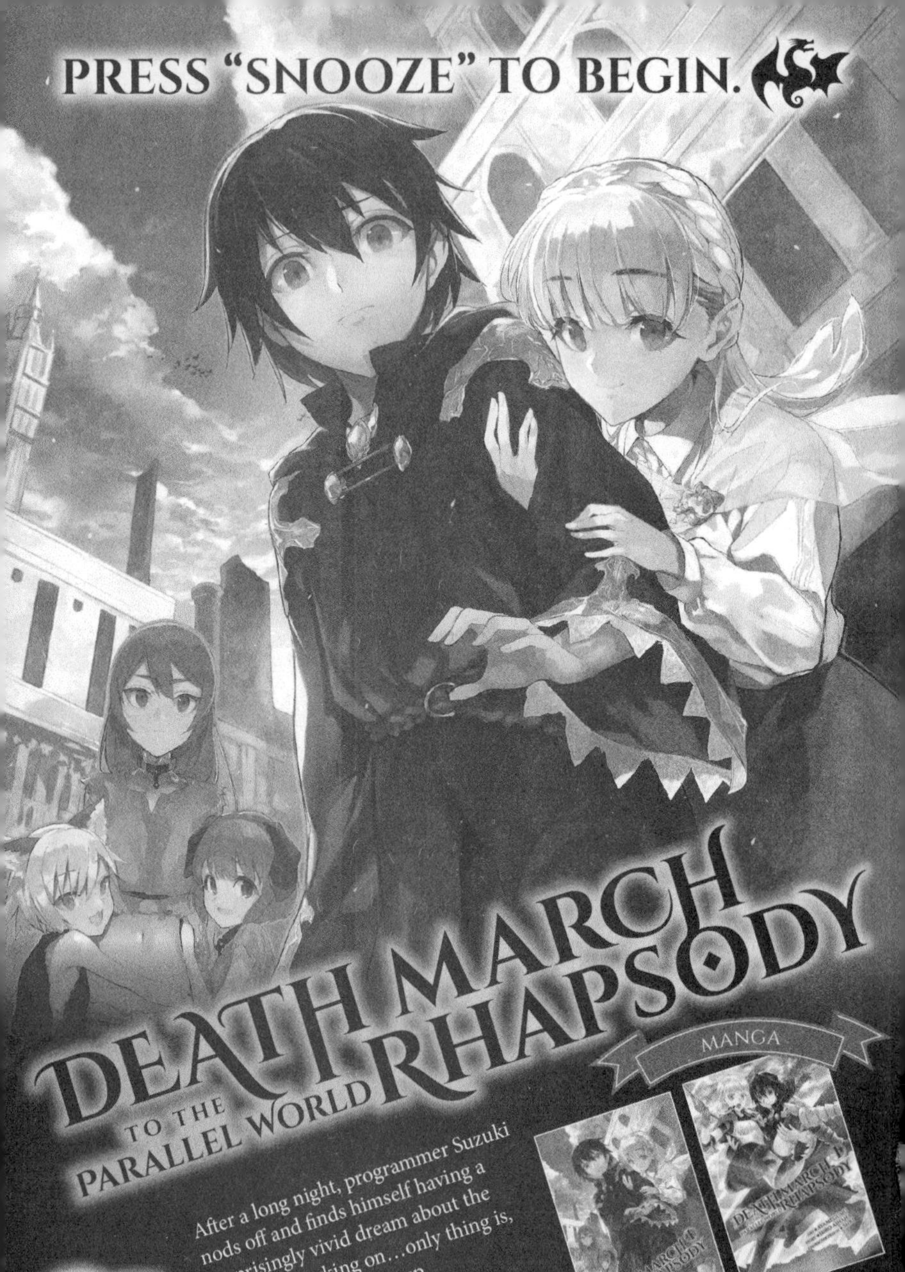
PRESS "SNOOZE" TO BEGIN.
DEATH MARCH TO THE PARALLEL WORLD RHAPSODY
MANGA
LIGHT NOVEL
After a long night, programmer Suzuki nods off and finds himself having a surprisingly vivid dream about the RPG he's working on…only thing is, he can't seem to wake up.
YEN ON

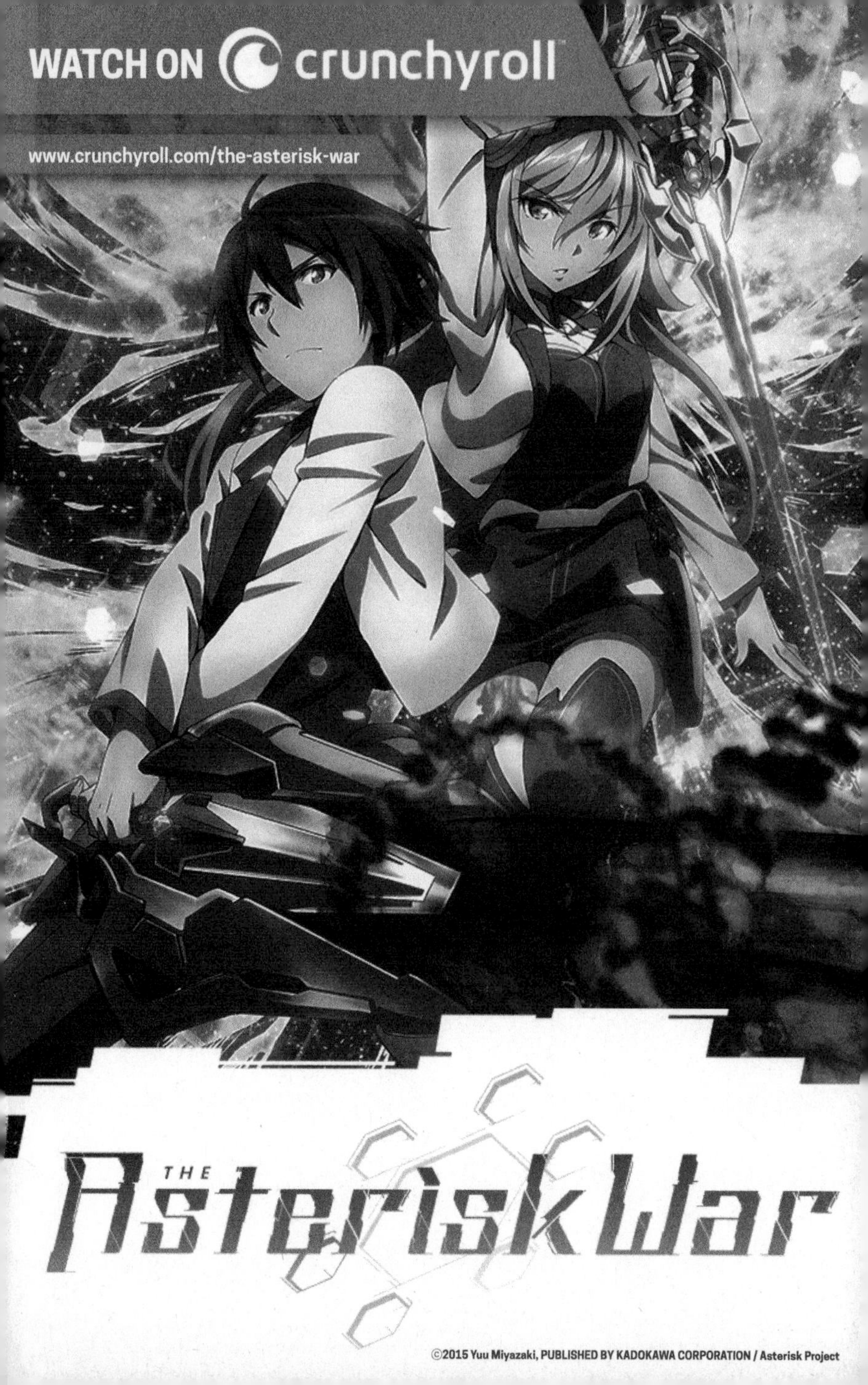

WATCH ON crunchyroll
www.crunchyroll.com/the-asterisk-war
THE Asterisk War
©2015 Yuu Miyazaki, PUBLISHED BY KADOKAWA CORPORATION / Asterisk Project

TRANSLATION NOTES

COMMON HONORIFICS

no honorific: Indicates familiarity or closeness; if used without permission or reason, addressing someone in this manner would constitute an insult.

-san: The Japanese equivalent of Mr./Mrs./Miss. If a situation calls for politeness, this is the fail-safe honorific.

-sama: Conveys great respect; may also indicate that the social status of the speaker is lower than that of the addressee.

-kun: Used most often when referring to boys, this indicates affection or familiarity. Occasionally used by older men among their peers, but it may also be used by anyone referring to a person of lower standing.

-chan: An affectionate honorific indicating familiarity used mostly in reference to girls; also used in reference to cute persons or animals of either gender.

-senpai: A suffix used to address upperclassmen or more experienced coworkers.

-sensei: A respectful term for teachers, artists, or high-level professionals.

Onii-chan, *Nii-san*, etc.: Terms used for older brothers/older brother figures.

Onee-chan, *Nee-san*, etc.: Terms used for older sisters/older sister figures.

Page 39

-shi: A polite and impersonal honorific used in formal speech or writing, often when the speaker/writer has not met the person in question.

THE ASTERISK WAR

04

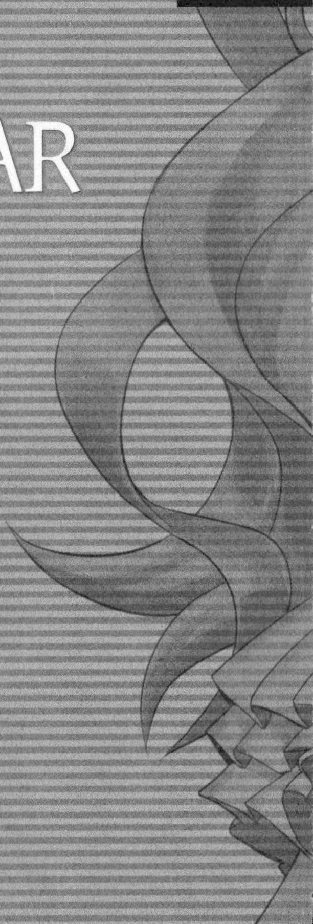

ART: **Ningen**
ORIGINAL STORY: **Yuu Miyazaki**
CHARACTER DESIGN: **okiura**

THE ASTERISK WAR

CHARACTERS

Ayato Amagiri

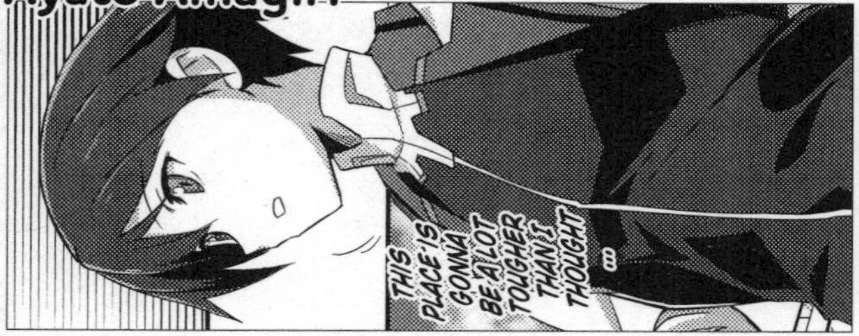
THIS PLACE IS GONNA BE A LOT TOUGHER THAN I THOUGHT...

Transferred into Seidoukan Academy High School on a special scholarship. A skilled swordsman who has been training since he was small in his family's Amagiri Shinmei Sword Style, but the enormous amount of prana he possesses has been sealed away.

Saya Sasamiya

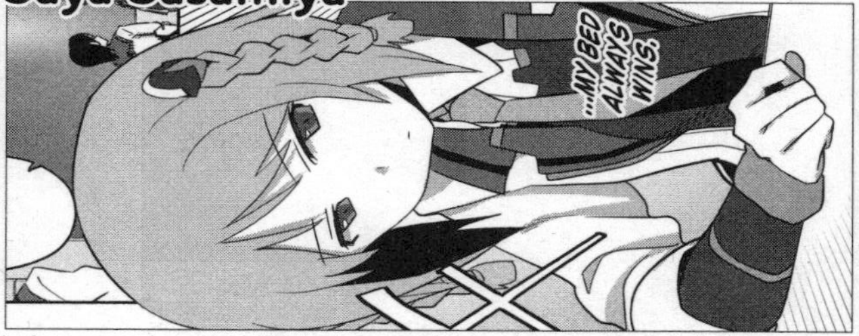
...MY BED ALWAYS WINS.

In the same grade as Ayato. They've known each other since they were small. Always sleepy due to bad circulation. At the request of her father, a scientist in meteoric engineering, she came to Asterisk to advertise the gun he invented. A firm believer that bigger is better when it comes to firearms and an expert in the subject.

Julis-Alexia von Riessfeld

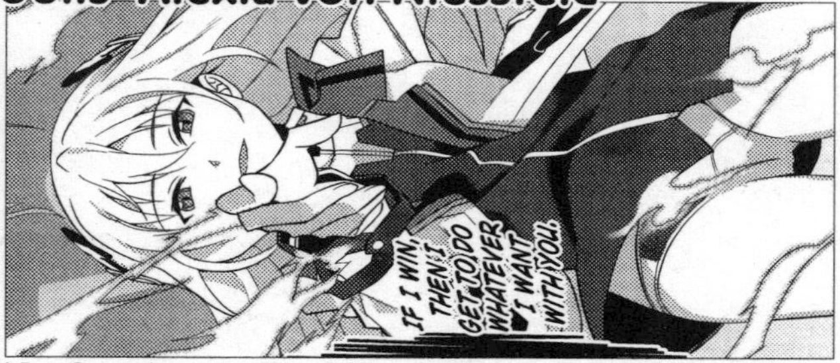
IF I WIN, THEN I GET TO DO WHATEVER I WANT WITH YOU.

A Page One student, ranked fifth at Seidoukan Academy, and a powerful fighter bearing the epithet "Glühen Rose—Witch of the Resplendent Flames." Proud and short-tempered but also conscientious and kind.

Claudia Enfield

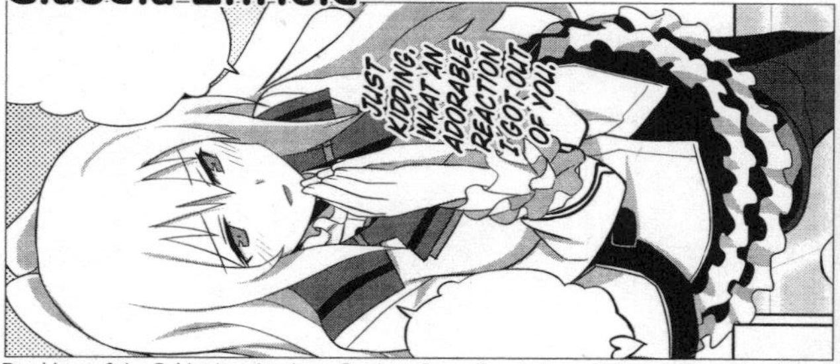
JUST KIDDING. WHAT AN ADORABLE REACTION I GOT OUT OF YOU.

President of the Seidoukan Academy Student Council and also ranked as a Page One. Always smiling, gentle, and polite—but describes herself as blackhearted.

THE WORLD OF ASTERISK

Rikka: the Academy City on the Water

A city that floats on the surface of the North Kanto crater lake, surrounded by six schools. Its hexagonal shape earned it the nickname Asterisk.

Seidoukan Academy

The school our main characters attend, ranked fifth in Asterisk. Seidoukan used to dominate in all three Festa events but has recently been in a slump. A campus culture that emphasizes students' independence attracts many Dantes and Stregas as students.

Queenvale Academy for Young Ladies

The only all-girls' school, Queenvale is consistently ranked last, and the matriculation requirement of "good looks" makes it an odd sort of academy. Students' beauty is on a level with top-class idols, and despite the rankings, they have plenty of fans, even from other schools.

St. Gallardworth Academy

One of the top-ranking schools ever since its founding, Gallardworth also boasts the most overall victories in Asterisk. The rigid culture there values discipline and loyalty above all else, and in principle, even duels are forbidden. Students are on poor terms with Le Wolfe.

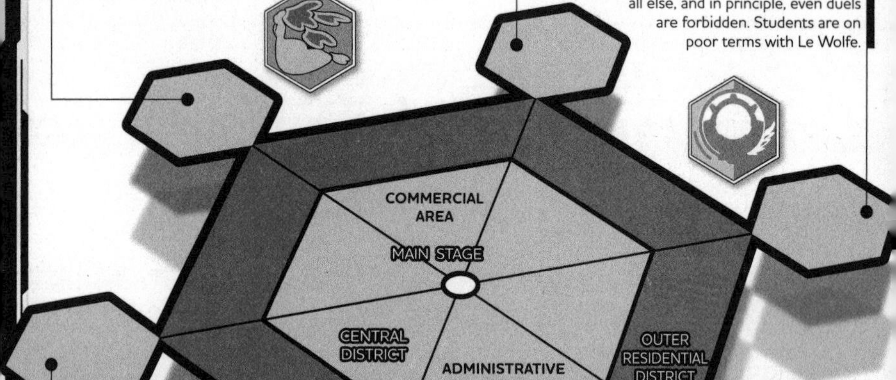
COMMERCIAL AREA
MAIN STAGE
CENTRAL DISTRICT
ADMINISTRATIVE AREA
OUTER RESIDENTIAL DISTRICT

Jie Long Seventh Institute

The largest of the six schools and the only school that has never once fallen to last place in the overall rankings. Bureaucracy clashes with a laissez-faire attitude, making the school culture rather chaotic. The atmosphere has strong Far Eastern leanings, and students boast their own martial art technique known as Star Xianshu.

Le Wolfe Black Institute

Ferociously strong when it comes to one-on-one battles, Le Wolfe has a tremendously belligerent culture, to the point of encouraging duels with students from other schools. The place is practically lawless, and more than a few students end up in mercenary or criminal activity. Whenever there's commotion in the city, Le Wolfe students are likely to be involved.

Allekant Académie

Specializing in meteoric engineering, Allekant is the only one of the six schools with an actual research department. Students' technological expertise shows in the quality of their Lux weapons, which far surpass those of the other schools. With a culture driven by results, they have rapidly progressed to the rank of second place in the last several years.

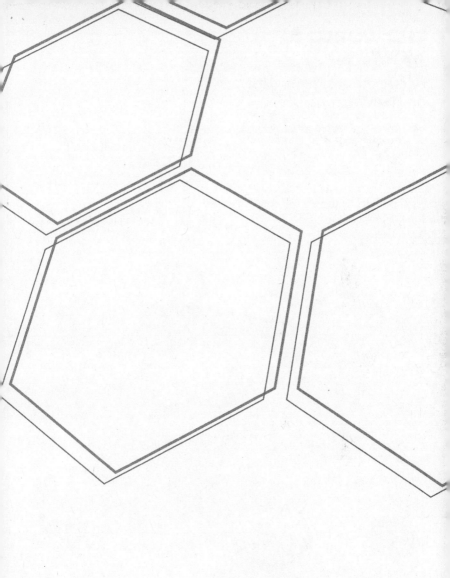

THE
ASTERISK WAR

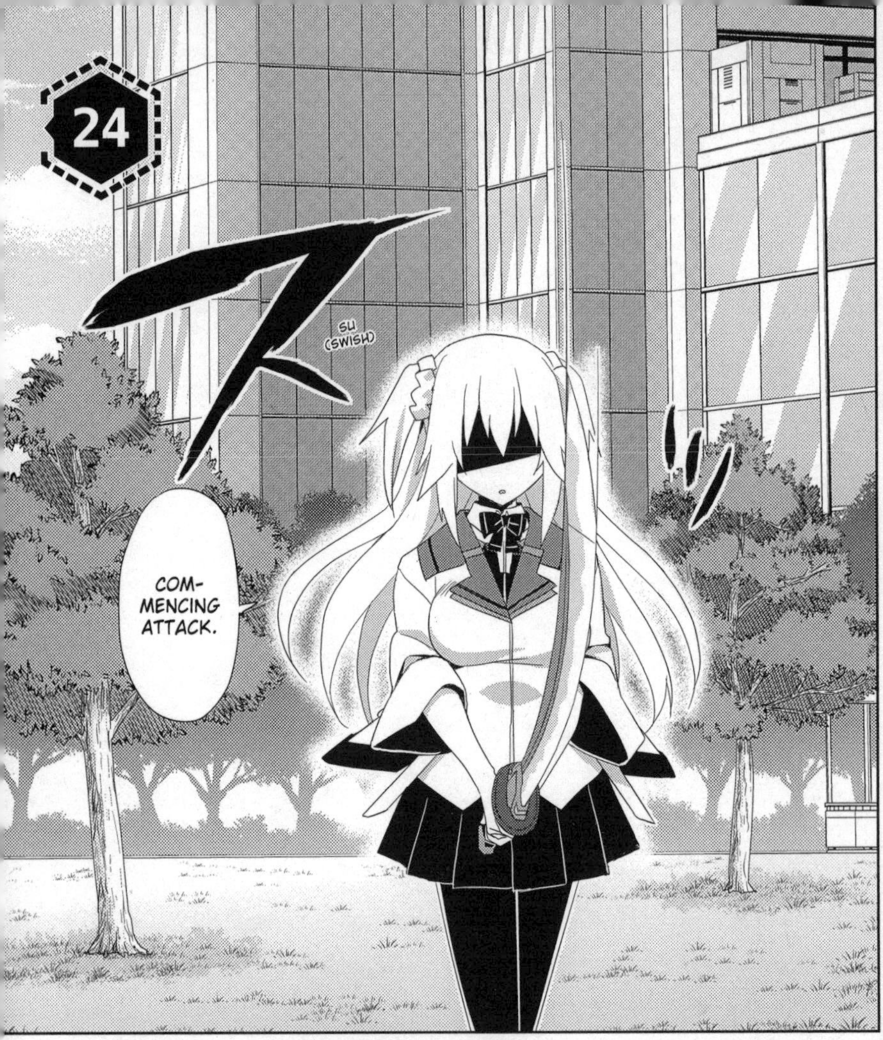
24
SU (SWISH)
COM-MENCING ATTACK.
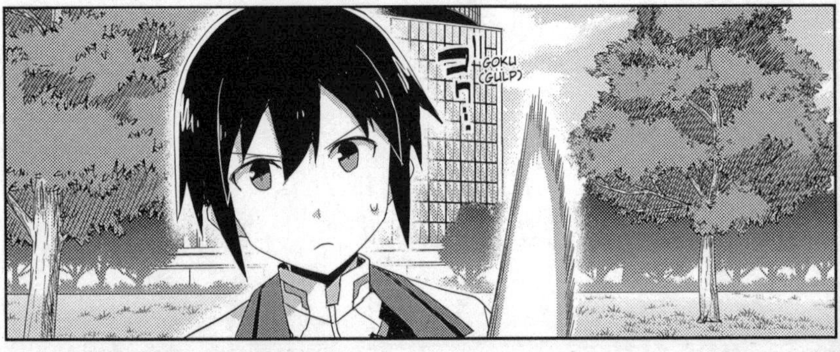
GOKU (GULP)

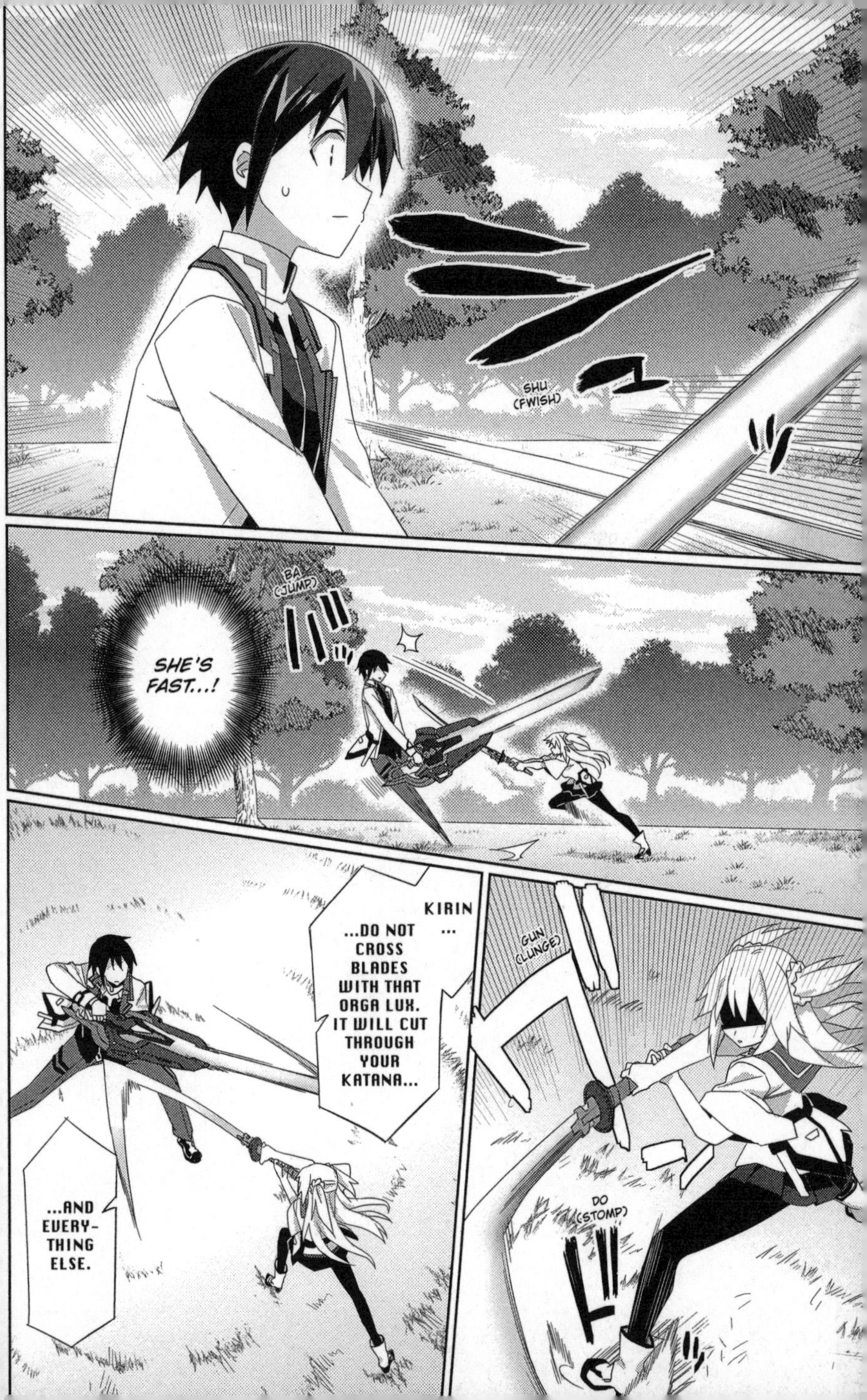
SHU (FWISH)
BA (JUMP)
SHE'S FAST...!
GUN (LUNGE)
DO (STOMP)
KIRIN ...
...DO NOT CROSS BLADES WITH THAT ORGA LUX. IT WILL CUT THROUGH YOUR KATANA...
...AND EVERY-THING ELSE.

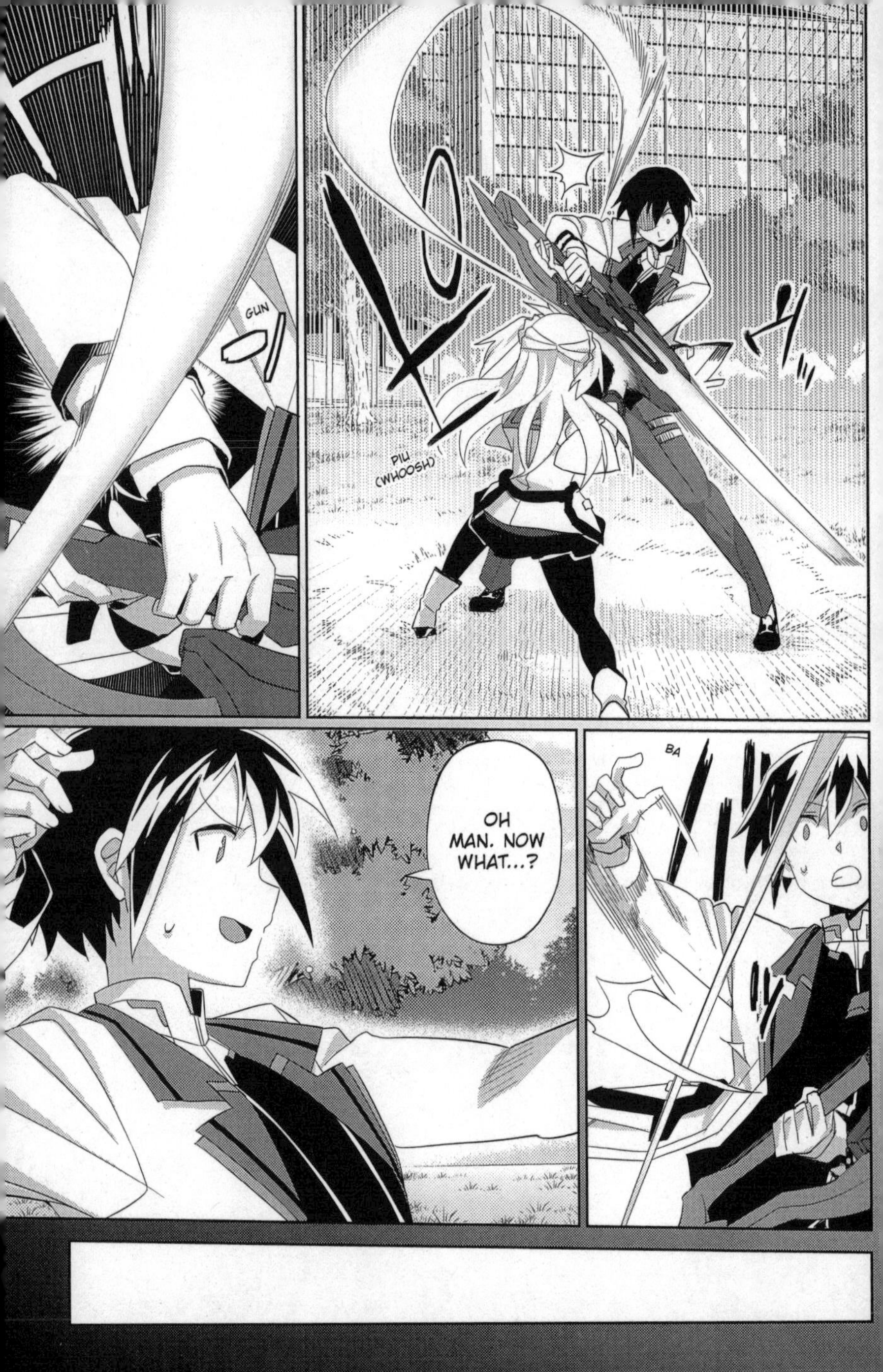
PIU
(WHOOSH)
GUN
BA
OH MAN. NOW WHAT...?

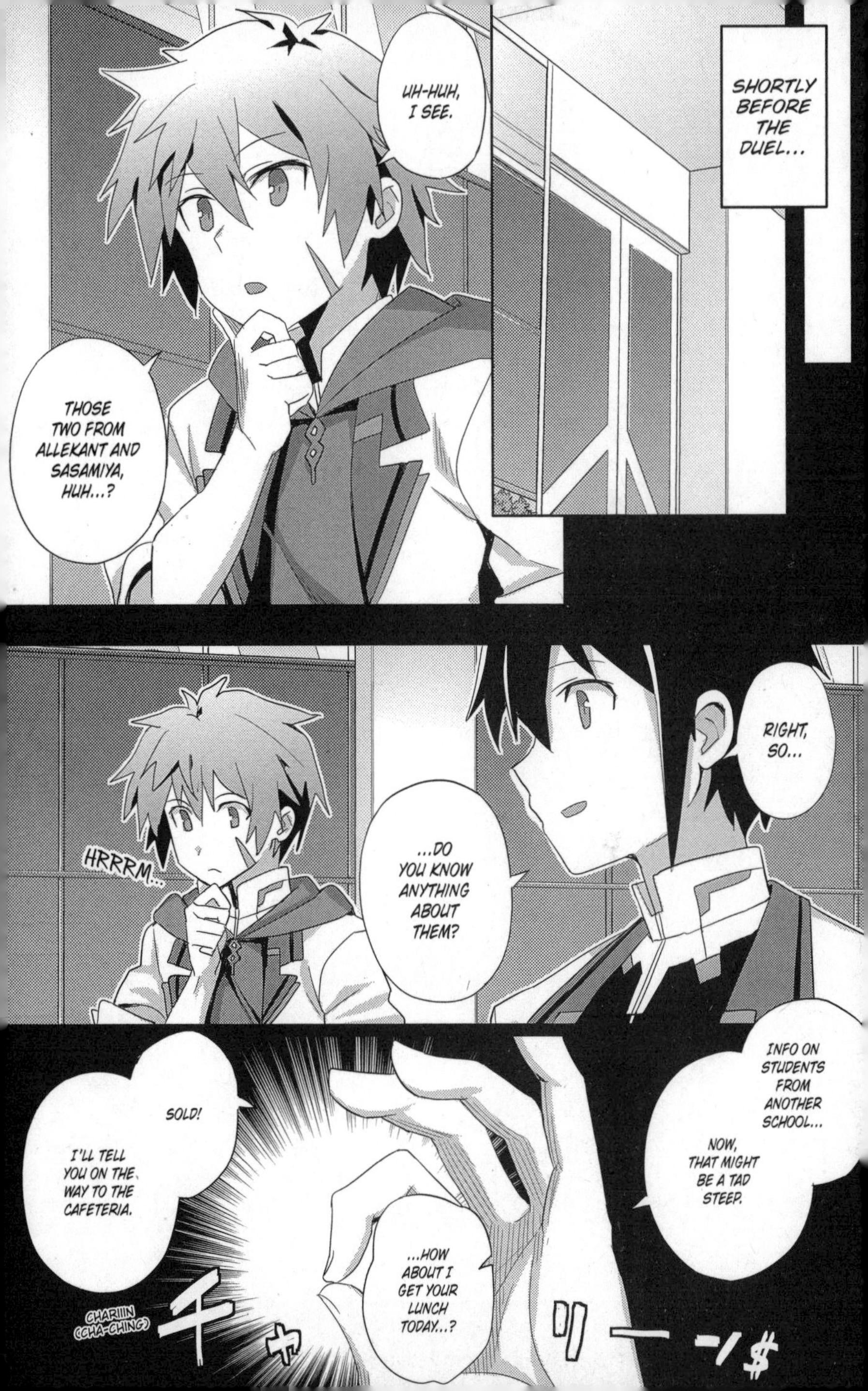
SHORTLY BEFORE THE DUEL...
UH-HUH, I SEE.
THOSE TWO FROM ALLEKANT AND SASAMIYA, HUH...?
RIGHT, SO...
...DO YOU KNOW ANYTHING ABOUT THEM?
HRRRM...
INFO ON STUDENTS FROM ANOTHER SCHOOL...
NOW, THAT MIGHT BE A TAD STEEP.
...HOW ABOUT I GET YOUR LUNCH TODAY...?
SOLD!
I'LL TELL YOU ON THE WAY TO THE CAFETERIA.
CHARIIN (CHA-CHING)

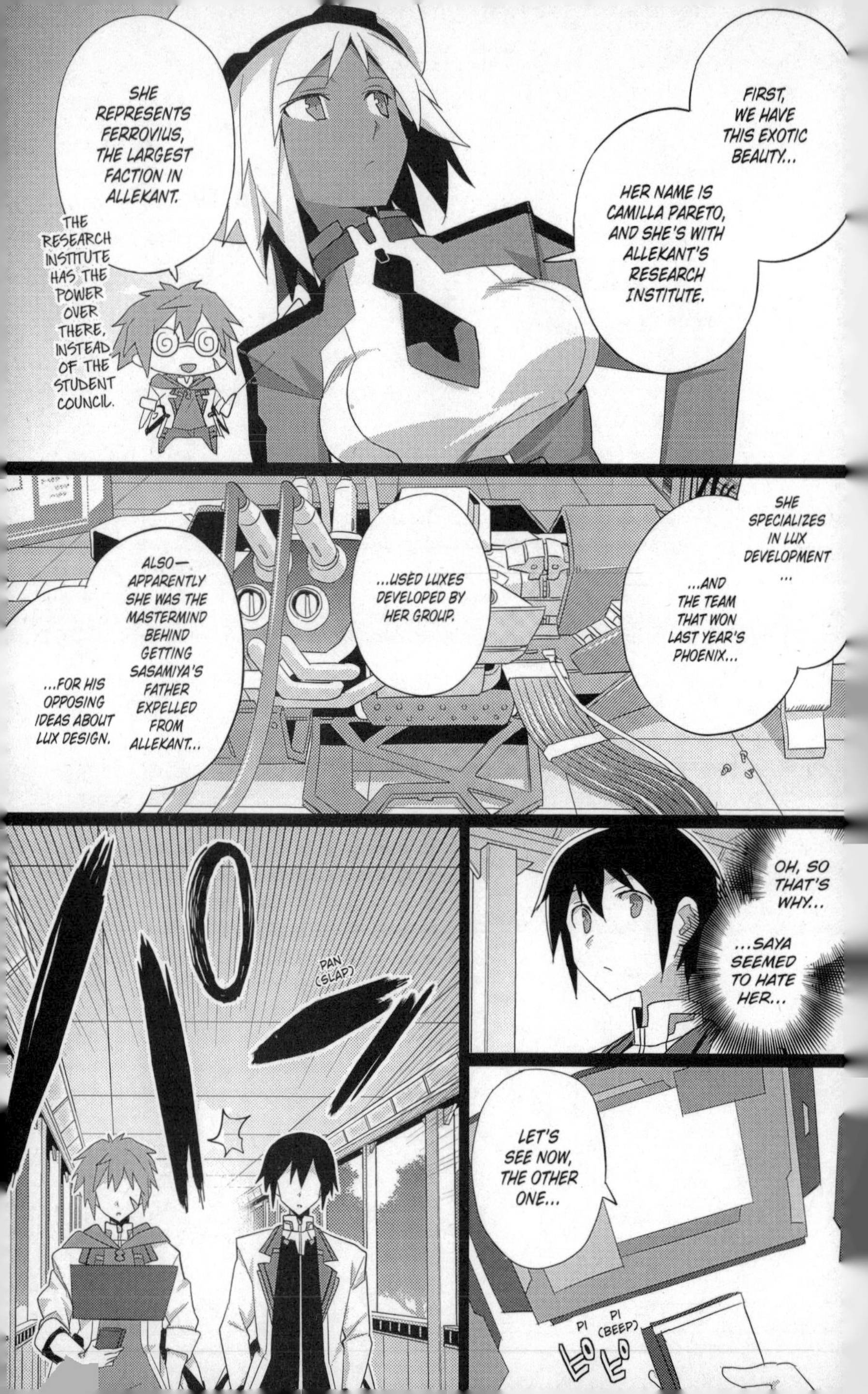
FIRST, WE HAVE THIS EXOTIC BEAUTY...
HER NAME IS CAMILLA PARETO, AND SHE'S WITH ALLEKANT'S RESEARCH INSTITUTE.
SHE REPRESENTS FERROVIUS, THE LARGEST FACTION IN ALLEKANT.
THE RESEARCH INSTITUTE HAS THE POWER OVER THERE, INSTEAD OF THE STUDENT COUNCIL.
SHE SPECIALIZES IN LUX DEVELOPMENT ...
...AND THE TEAM THAT WON LAST YEAR'S PHOENIX...
...USED LUXES DEVELOPED BY HER GROUP.
ALSO— APPARENTLY SHE WAS THE MASTERMIND BEHIND GETTING SASAMIYA'S FATHER EXPELLED FROM ALLEKANT...
...FOR HIS OPPOSING IDEAS ABOUT LUX DESIGN.
OH, SO THAT'S WHY...
...SAYA SEEMED TO HATE HER...
LET'S SEE NOW, THE OTHER ONE...
PI PI (BEEP)
PAN (SLAP)

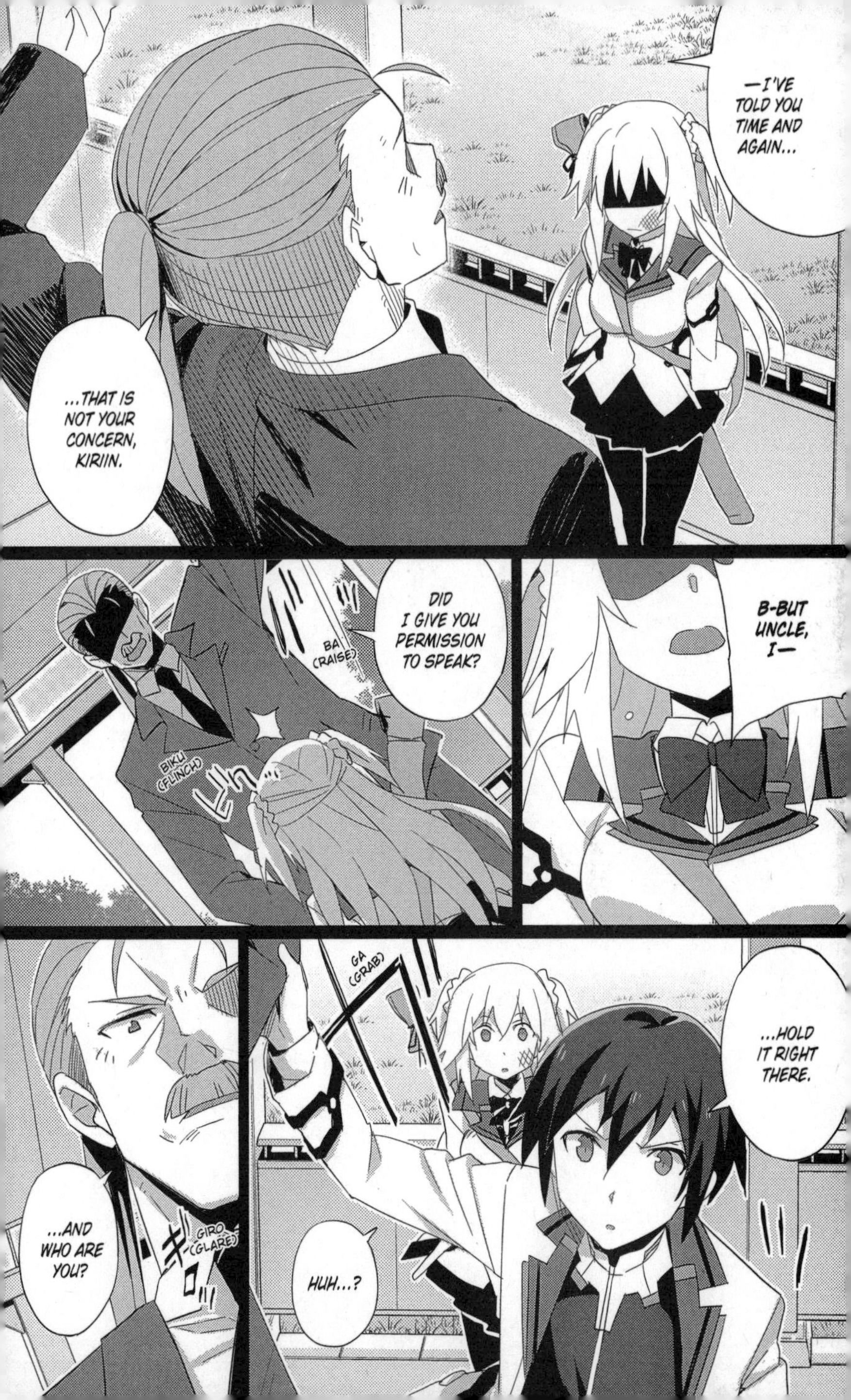
—I'VE TOLD YOU TIME AND AGAIN...
...THAT IS NOT YOUR CONCERN, KIRIIN.
B-BUT UNCLE, I—
BA (RAISE)
DID I GIVE YOU PERMISSION TO SPEAK?
BIKU (FLINCH)
...HOLD IT RIGHT THERE.
GA (GRAB)
HUH...?
GIRO (GLARE)
...AND WHO ARE YOU?

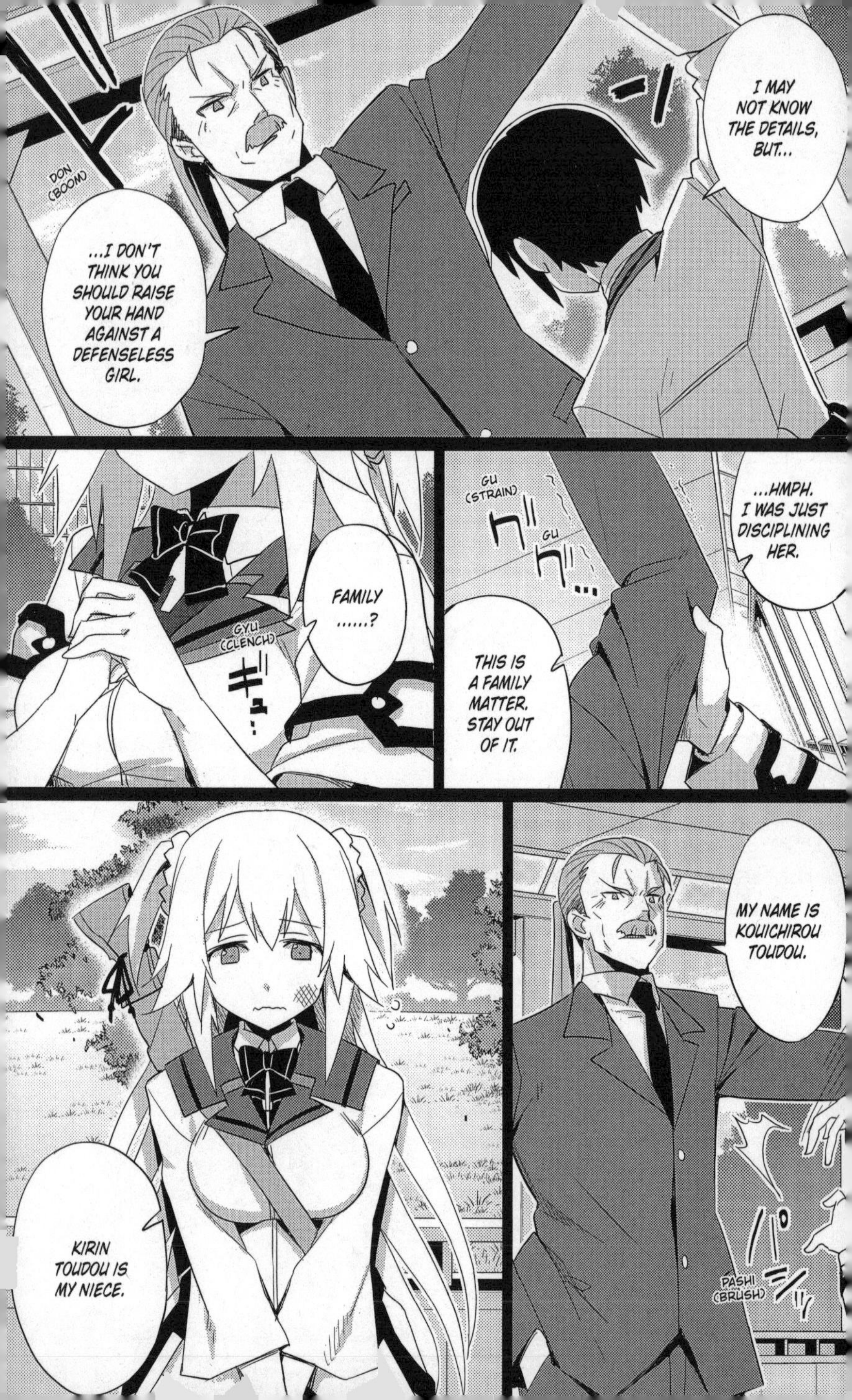
I MAY NOT KNOW THE DETAILS, BUT...
DON (BOOM)
...I DON'T THINK YOU SHOULD RAISE YOUR HAND AGAINST A DEFENSELESS GIRL.
...HMPH. I WAS JUST DISCIPLINING HER.
GU (STRAIN)
GU
THIS IS A FAMILY MATTER. STAY OUT OF IT.
FAMILY ......?
GYU (CLENCH)
MY NAME IS KOUICHIROU TOUDOU.
PASHI (BRUSH)
KIRIN TOUDOU IS MY NIECE.

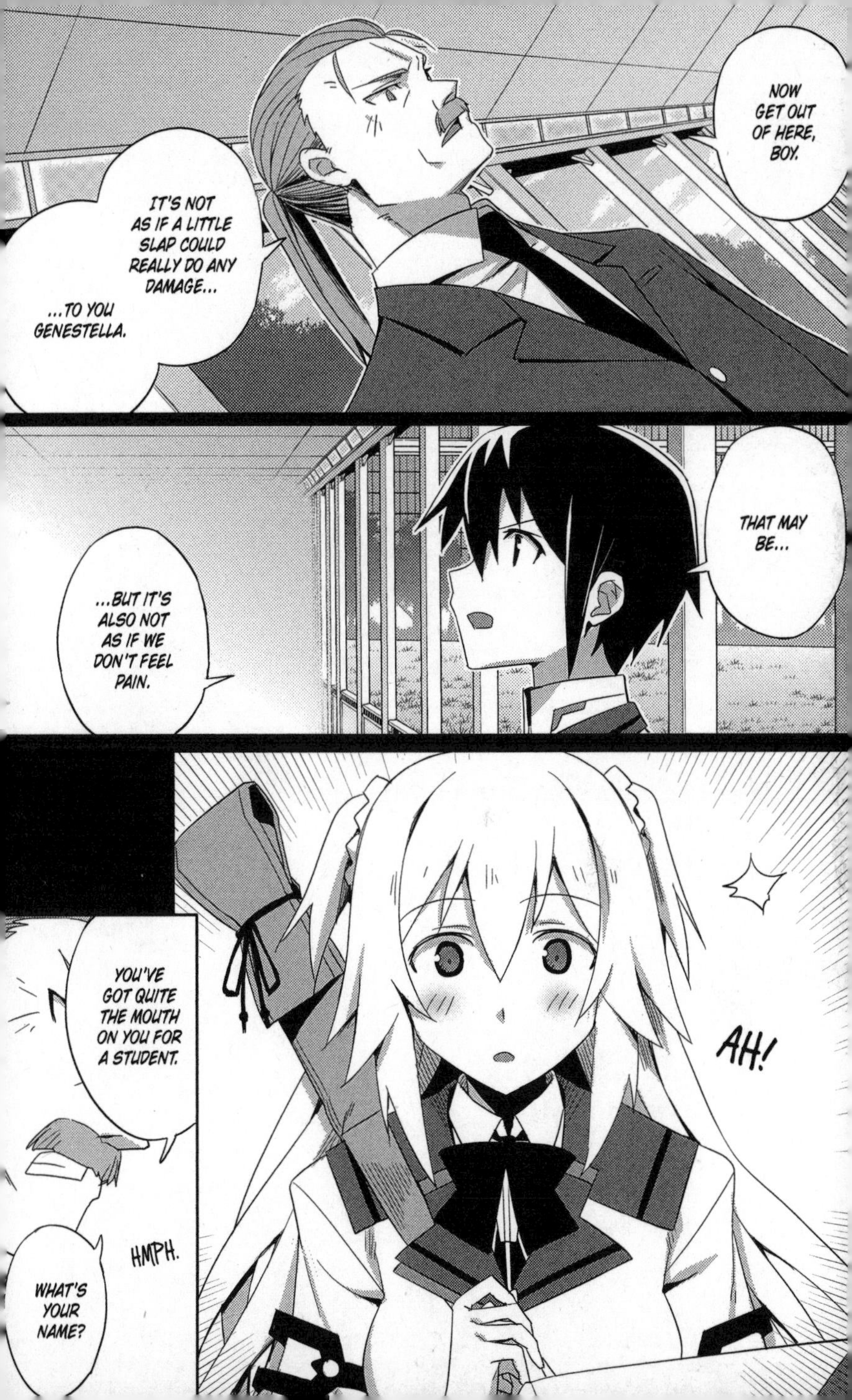
NOW GET OUT OF HERE, BOY.
IT'S NOT AS IF A LITTLE SLAP COULD REALLY DO ANY DAMAGE...
...TO YOU GENESTELLA.
THAT MAY BE...
...BUT IT'S ALSO NOT AS IF WE DON'T FEEL PAIN.
AH!
YOU'VE GOT QUITE THE MOUTH ON YOU FOR A STUDENT.
HMPH.
WHAT'S YOUR NAME?

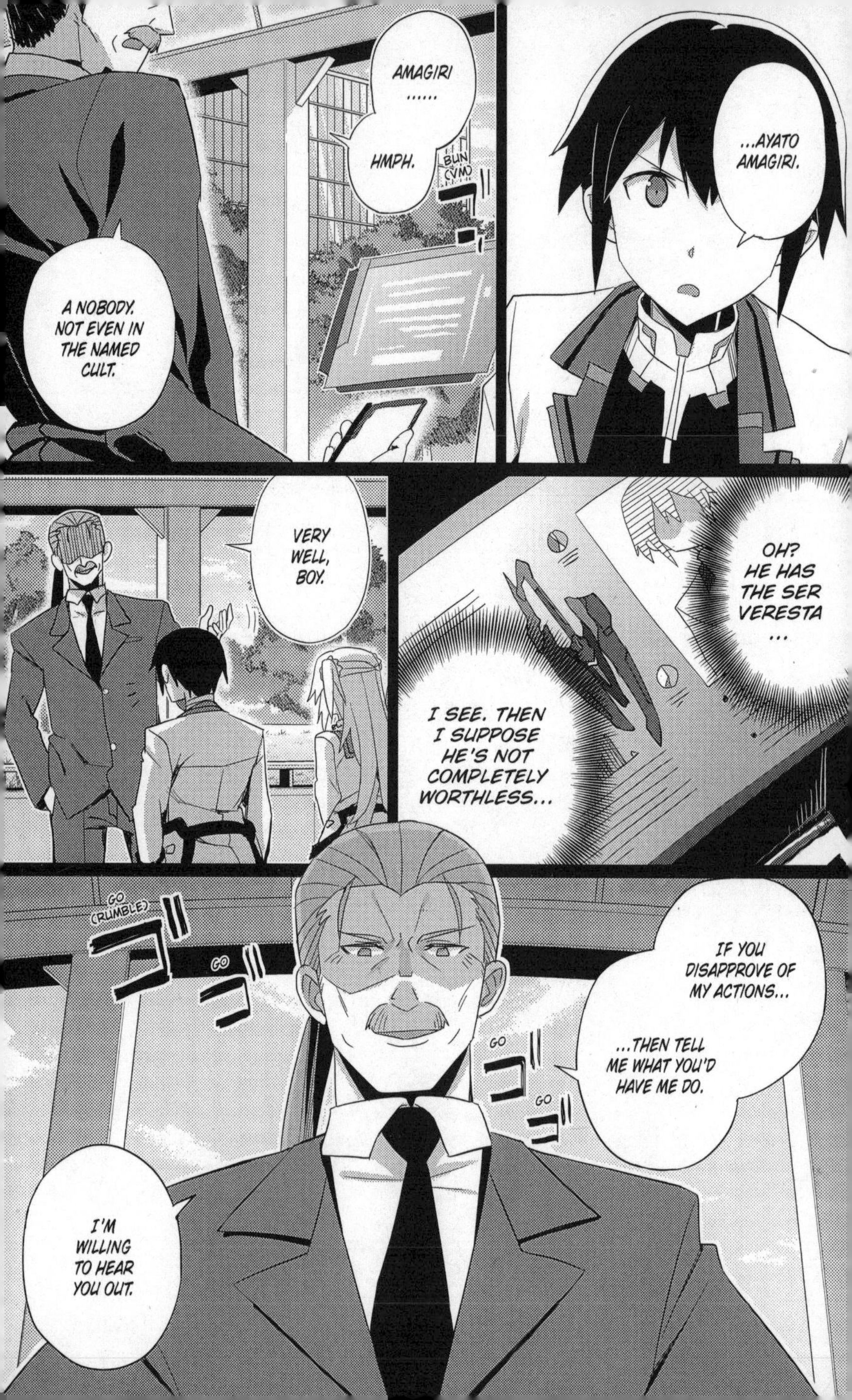
...AYATO AMAGIRI.
AMAGIRI ......
HMPH.
BUN (VM)
A NOBODY. NOT EVEN IN THE NAMED CULT.
OH? HE HAS THE SER VERESTA ...
I SEE. THEN I SUPPOSE HE'S NOT COMPLETELY WORTHLESS...
VERY WELL, BOY.
IF YOU DISAPPROVE OF MY ACTIONS...
...THEN TELL ME WHAT YOU'D HAVE ME DO.
GO
GO
GO (RUMBLE)
GO
I'M WILLING TO HEAR YOU OUT.

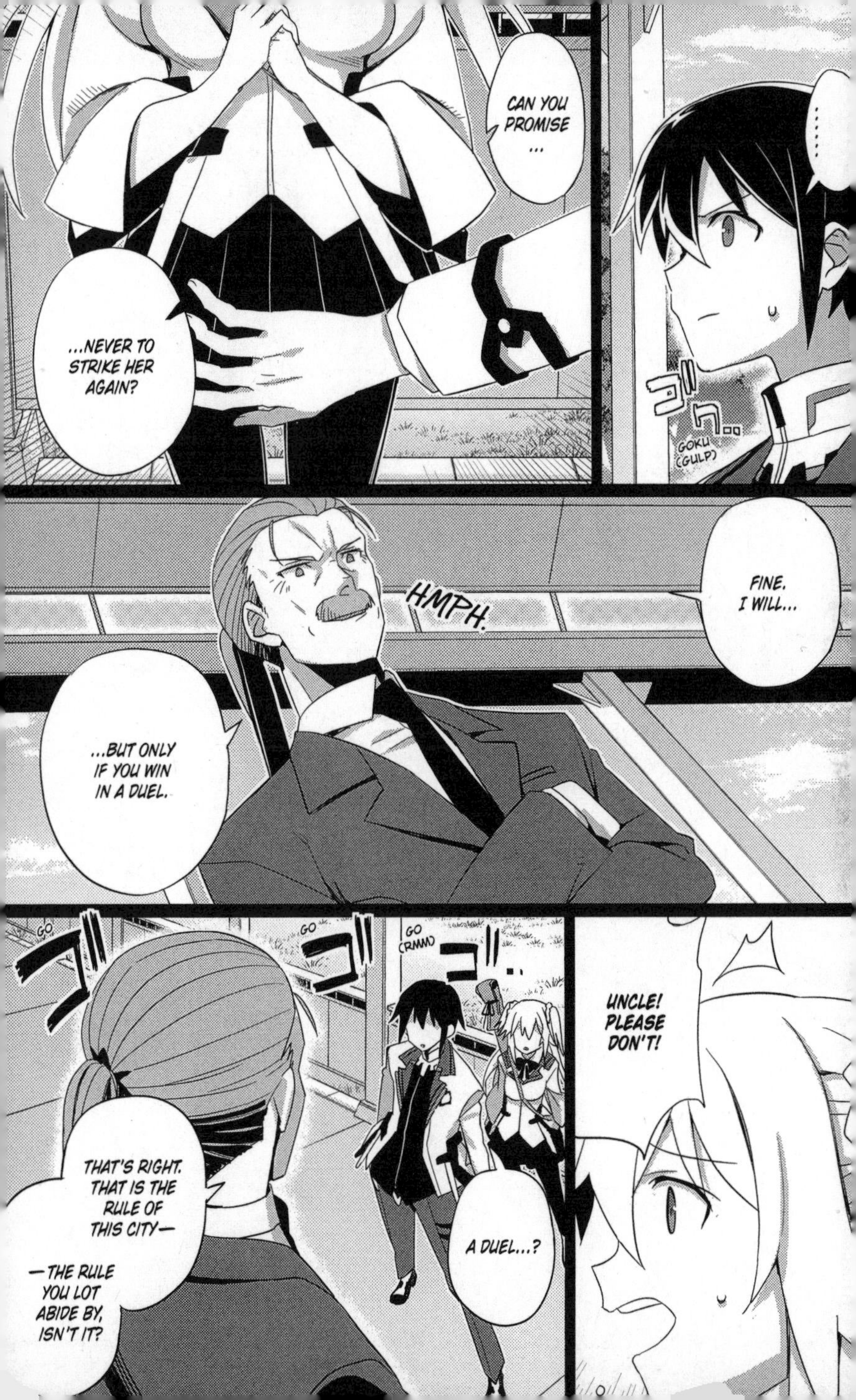
......
GOKU (GULP)
CAN YOU PROMISE ...
...NEVER TO STRIKE HER AGAIN?
FINE. I WILL...
HMPH.
...BUT ONLY IF YOU WIN IN A DUEL.
UNCLE! PLEASE DON'T!
GO (RMM)
A DUEL...?
GO
GO
THAT'S RIGHT. THAT IS THE RULE OF THIS CITY—
—THE RULE YOU LOT ABIDE BY, ISN'T IT?

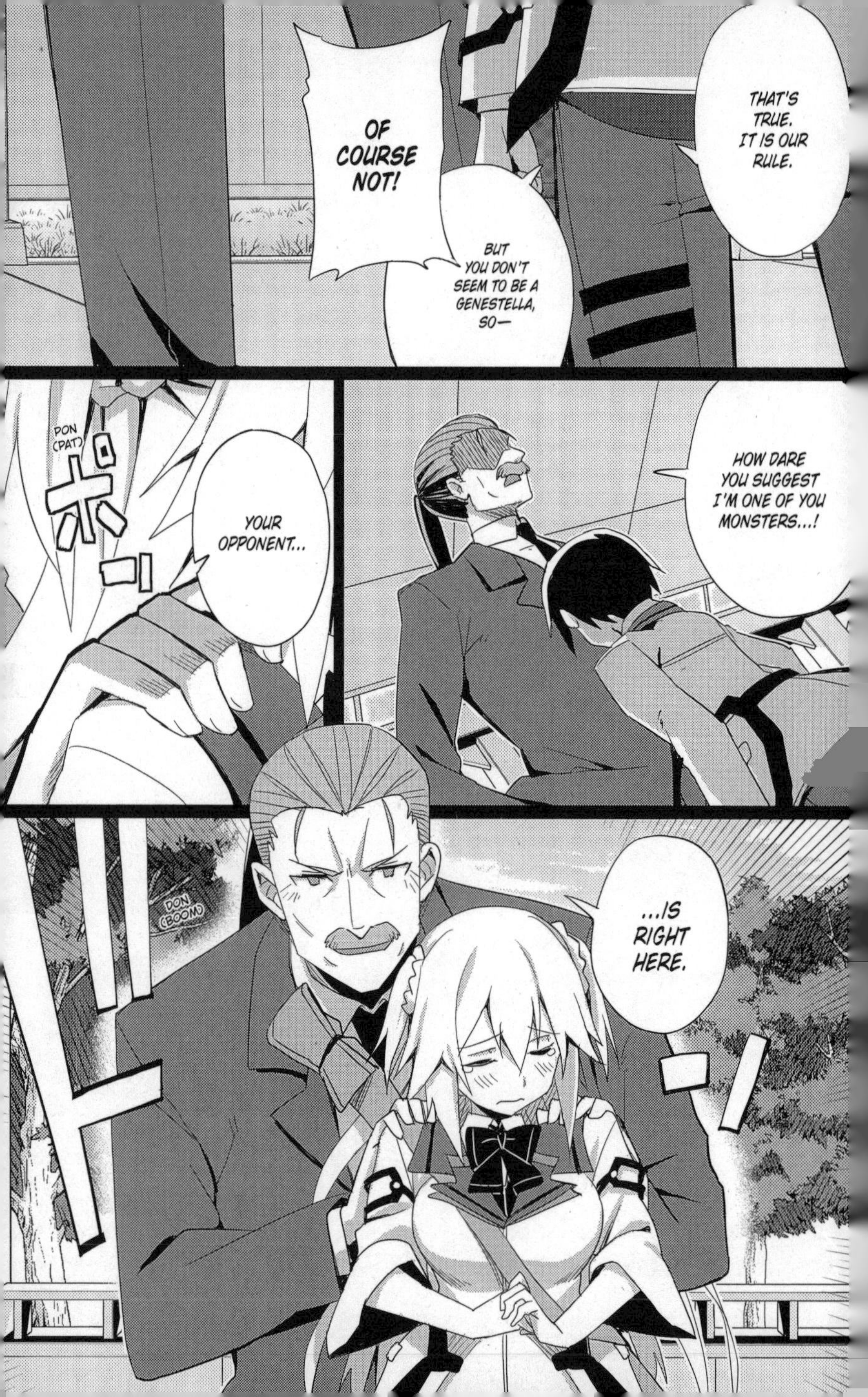
THAT'S TRUE. IT IS OUR RULE.
BUT YOU DON'T SEEM TO BE A GENESTELLA, SO—
OF COURSE NOT!
HOW DARE YOU SUGGEST I'M ONE OF YOU MONSTERS...!
YOUR OPPONENT...
PON (PAT)
...IS RIGHT HERE.
DON (BOOM)

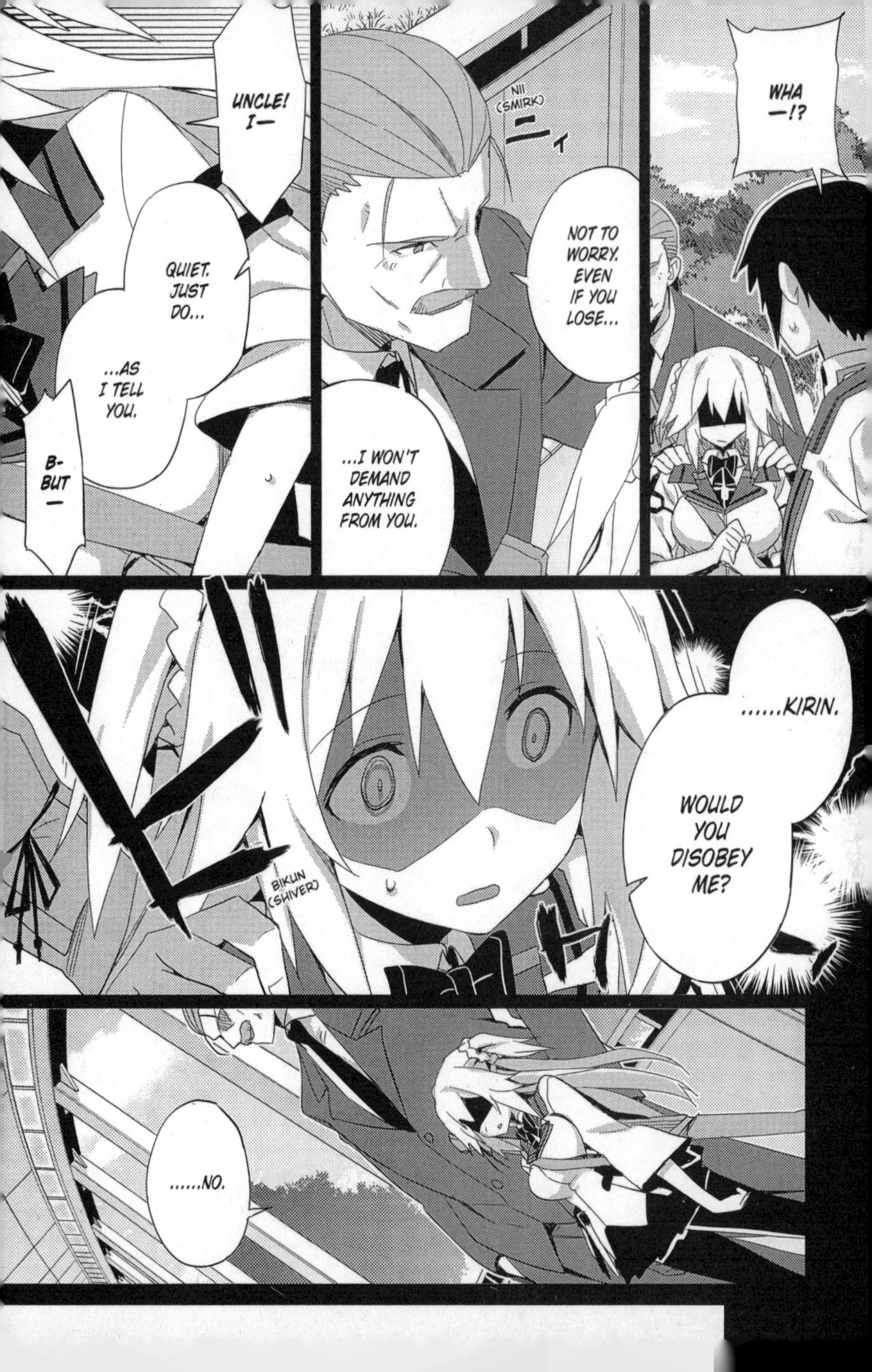
WHA—!?
NII (SMIRK)
NOT TO WORRY. EVEN IF YOU LOSE...
...I WON'T DEMAND ANYTHING FROM YOU.
UNCLE! I—
QUIET. JUST DO...
...AS I TELL YOU.
B-BUT—
......KIRIN.
WOULD YOU DISOBEY ME?
BIKUN (SHIVER)
......NO.

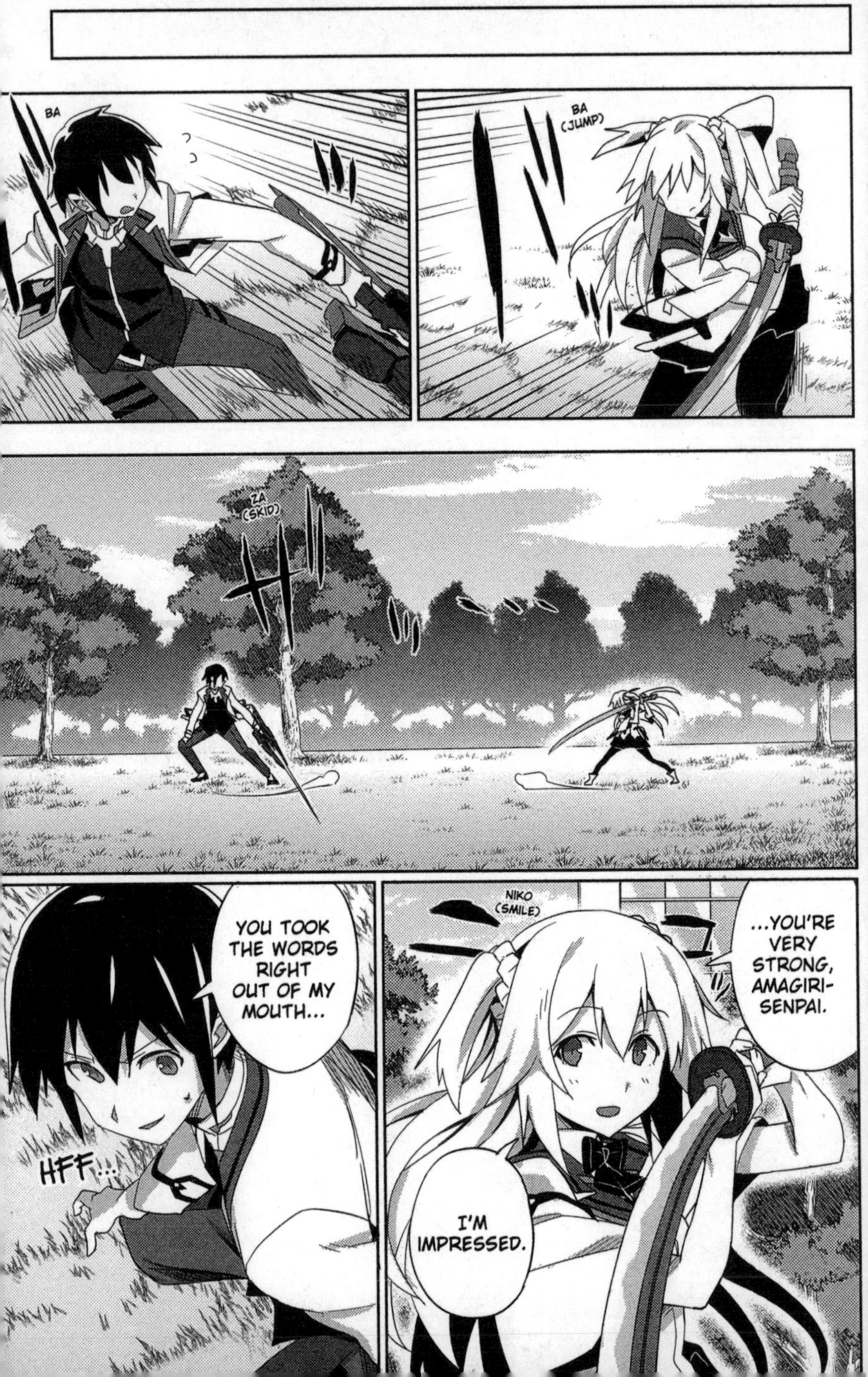
BA (JUMP)
BA
ZA (SKID)
NIKO (SMILE)
...YOU'RE VERY STRONG, AMAGIRI-SENPAI.
I'M IMPRESSED.
YOU TOOK THE WORDS RIGHT OUT OF MY MOUTH...
HFF...

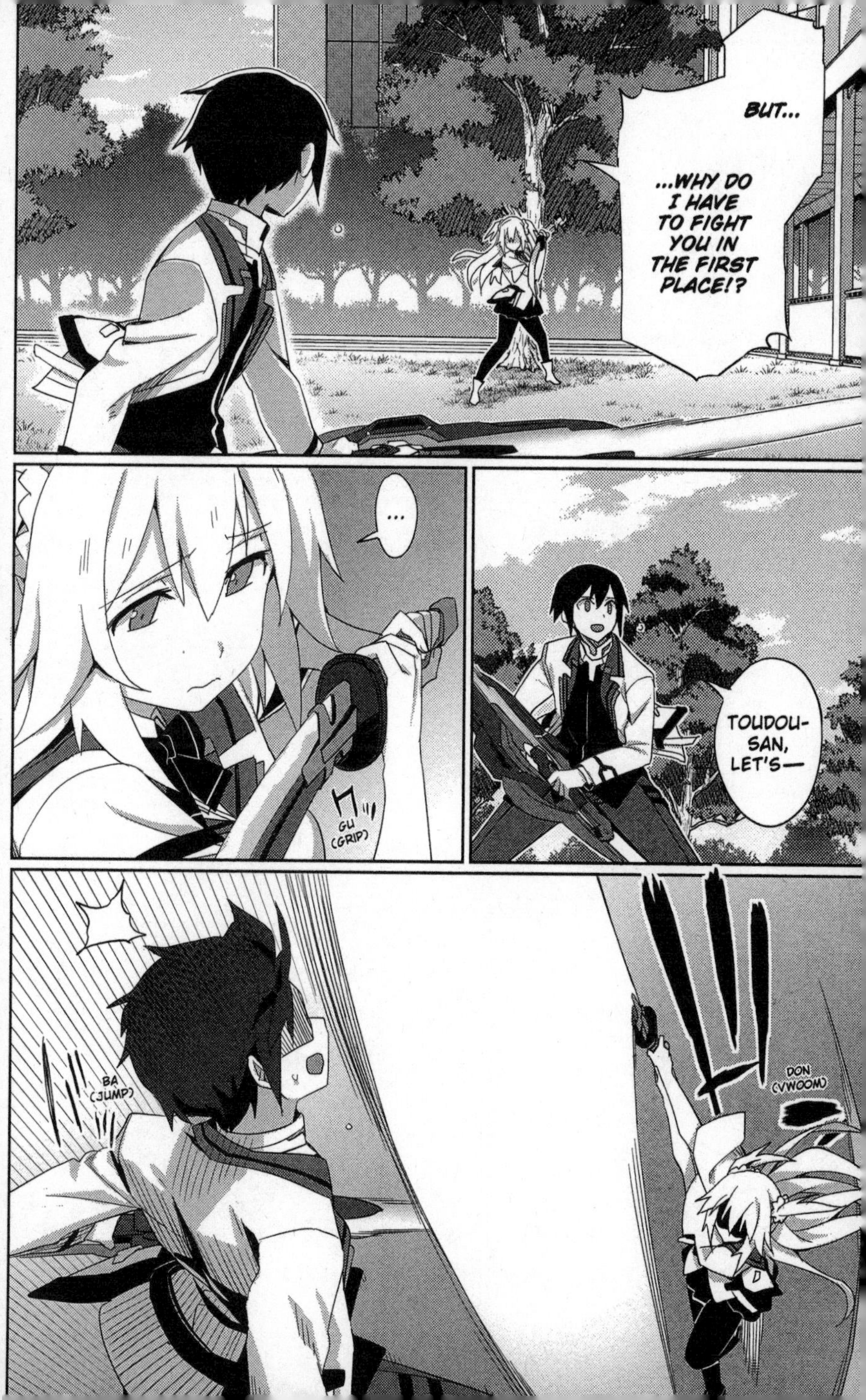
BUT...
...WHY DO I HAVE TO FIGHT YOU IN THE FIRST PLACE!?
TOUDOU-SAN, LET'S—
...
GU (GRIP)
DON (VWOOM)
BA (JUMP)

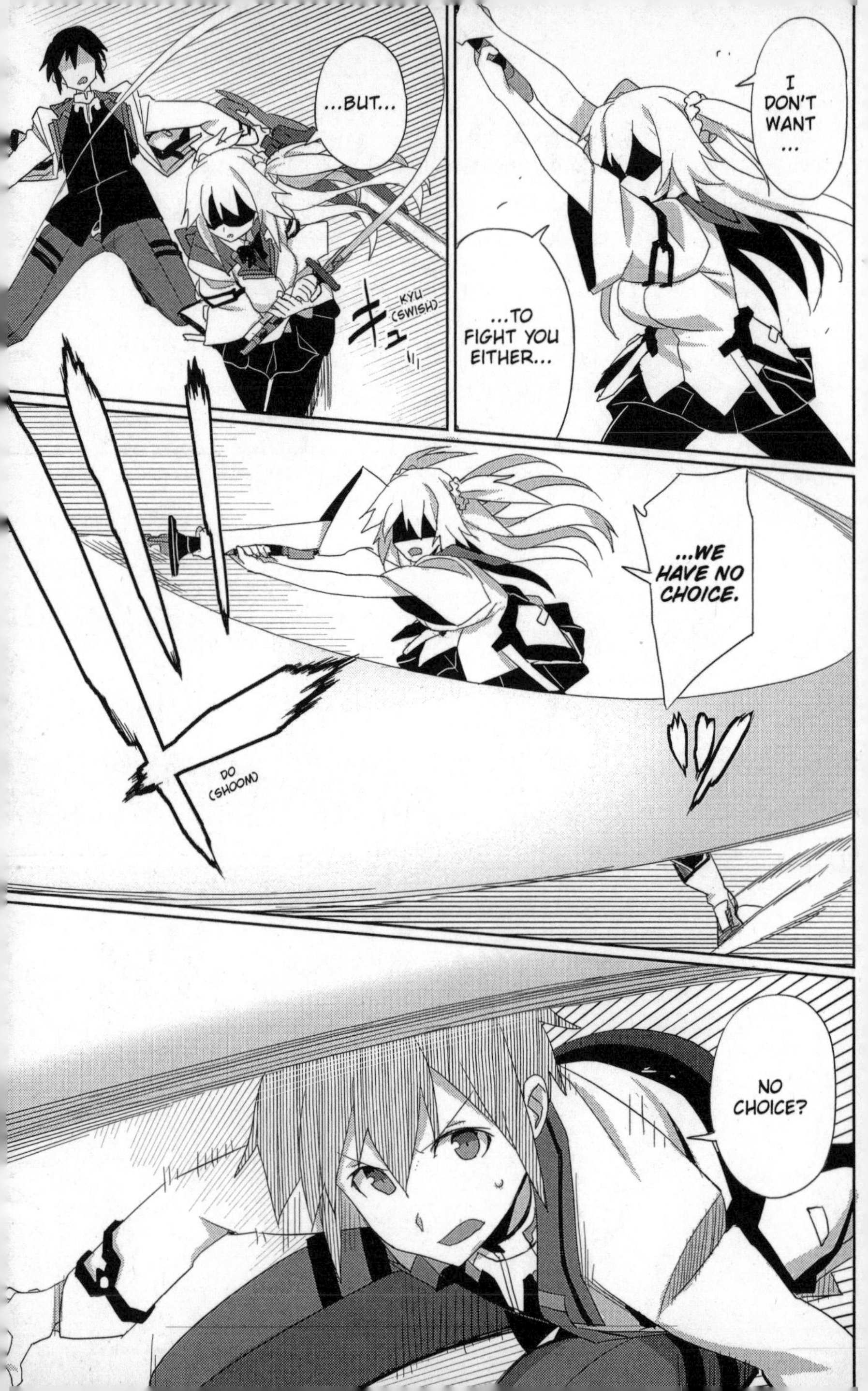
I DON'T WANT ...
...TO FIGHT YOU EITHER...
...BUT...
KYU (SWISH)
...WE HAVE NO CHOICE.
DO (SHOOM)
NO CHOICE?

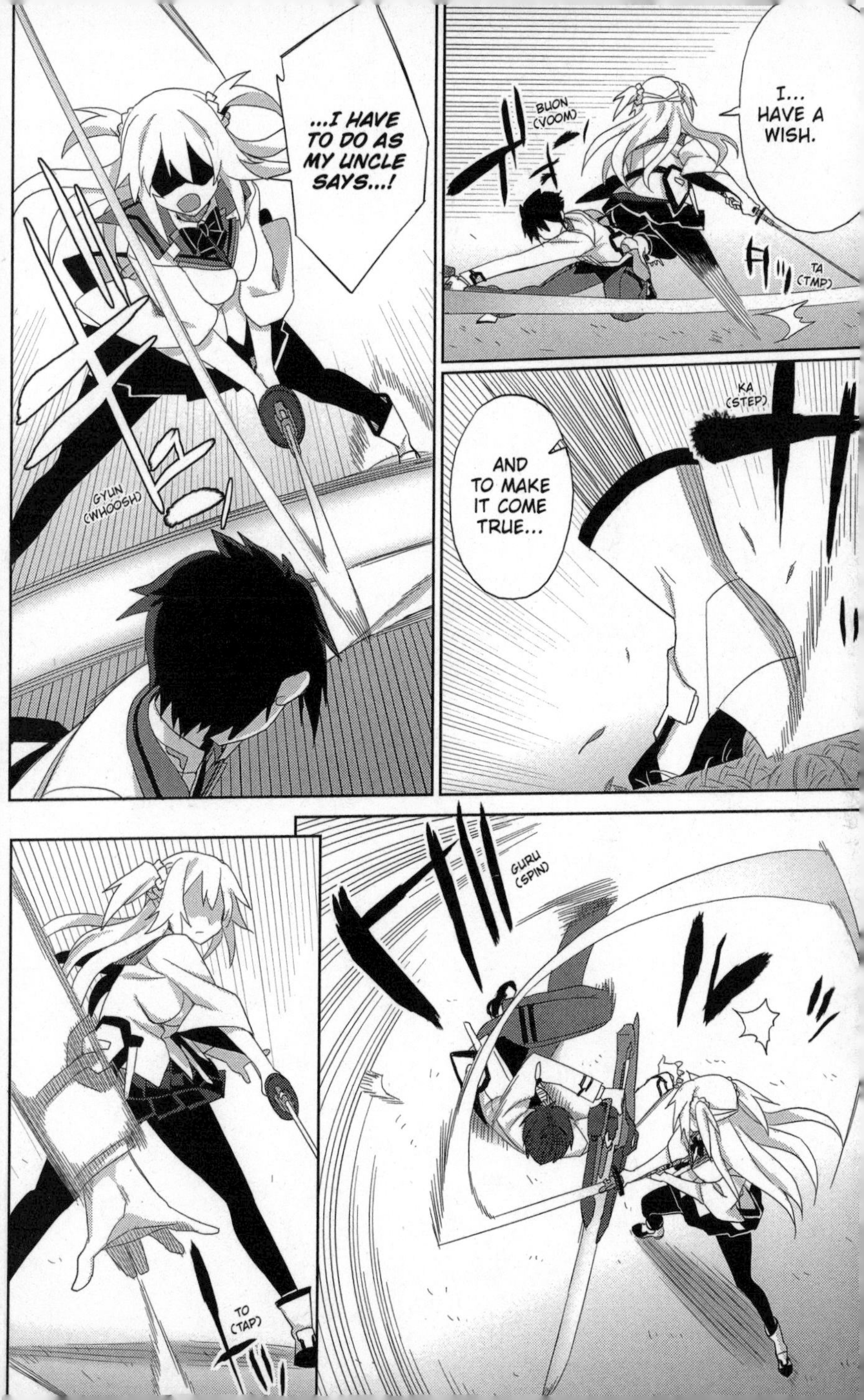
I... HAVE A WISH.
BUON (VOOM)
TA (TMP)
KA (STEP)
AND TO MAKE IT COME TRUE...
...I HAVE TO DO AS MY UNCLE SAYS...!
GYUN (WHOOSH)
GURU (SPIN)
TO (TAP)

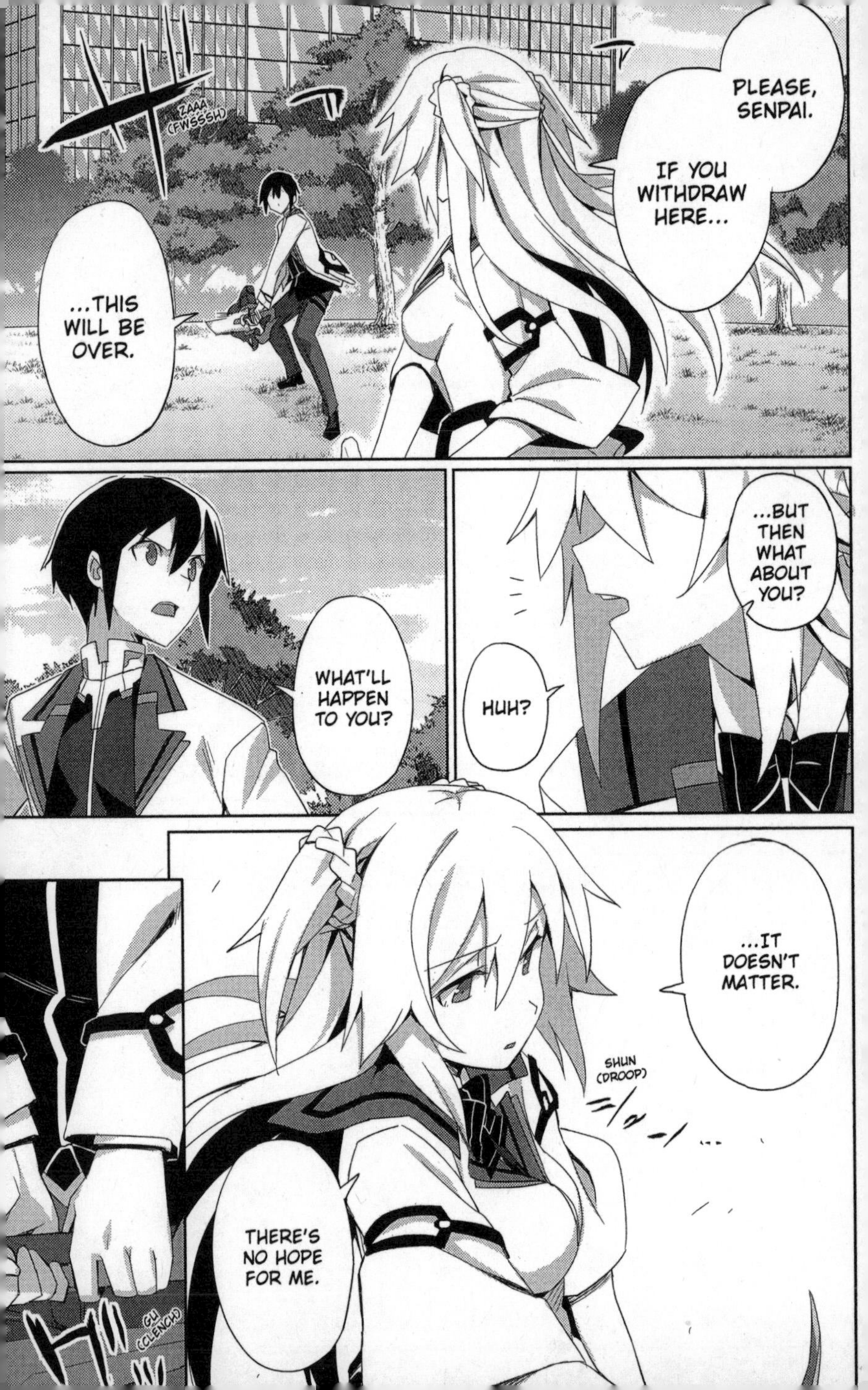
PLEASE, SENPAI.
IF YOU WITHDRAW HERE...
ZAAA (FWSSSH)
...THIS WILL BE OVER.
...BUT THEN WHAT ABOUT YOU?
HUH?
WHAT'LL HAPPEN TO YOU?
...IT DOESN'T MATTER.
SHUN (DROOP)
THERE'S NO HOPE FOR ME.
GU (CLENCH)

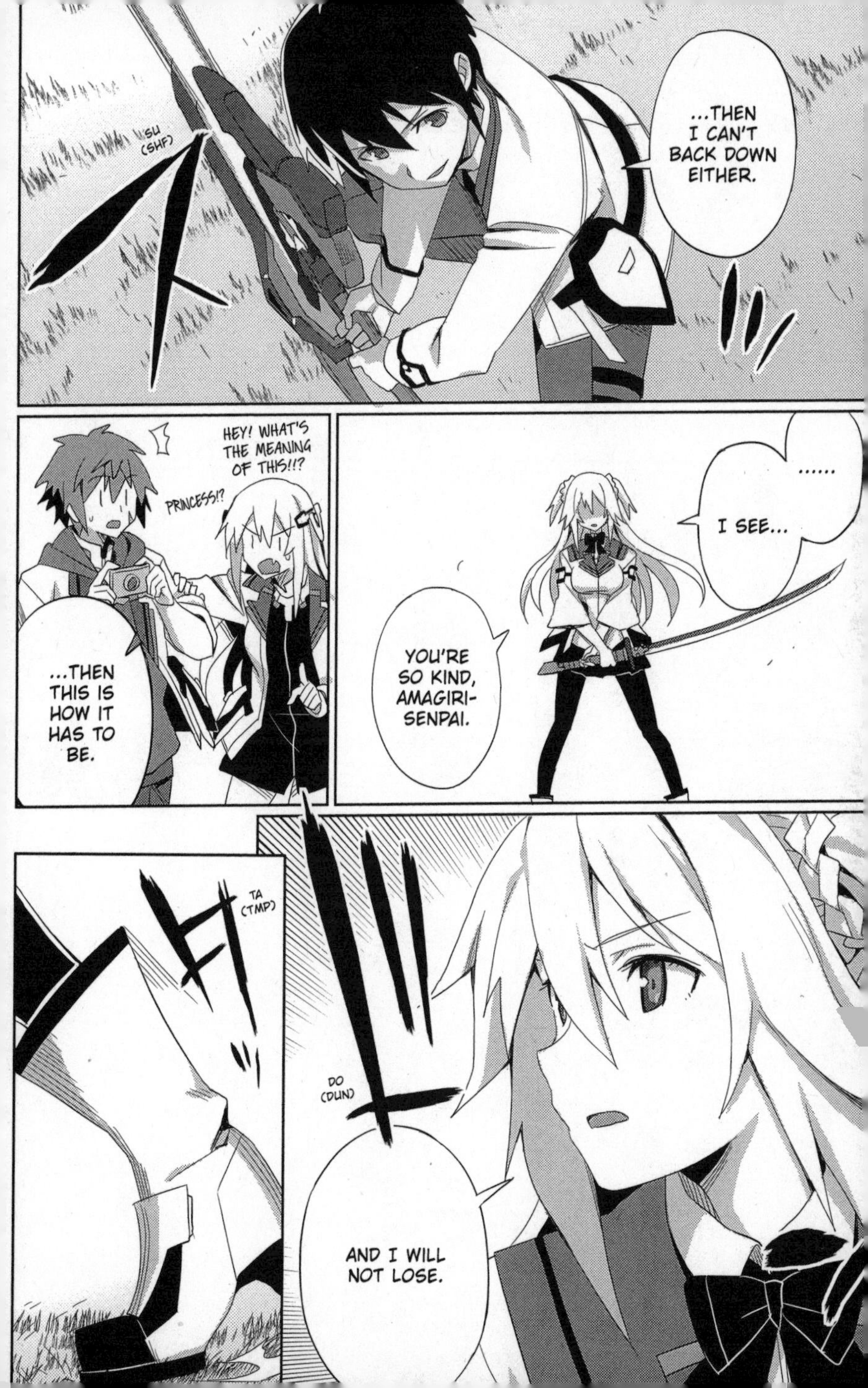
SU (SHF)
...THEN I CAN'T BACK DOWN EITHER.
......
I SEE...
YOU'RE SO KIND, AMAGIRI-SENPAI.
HEY! WHAT'S THE MEANING OF THIS!!?
PRINCESS!?
...THEN THIS IS HOW IT HAS TO BE.
DO (DUN)
AND I WILL NOT LOSE.
TA (TMP)

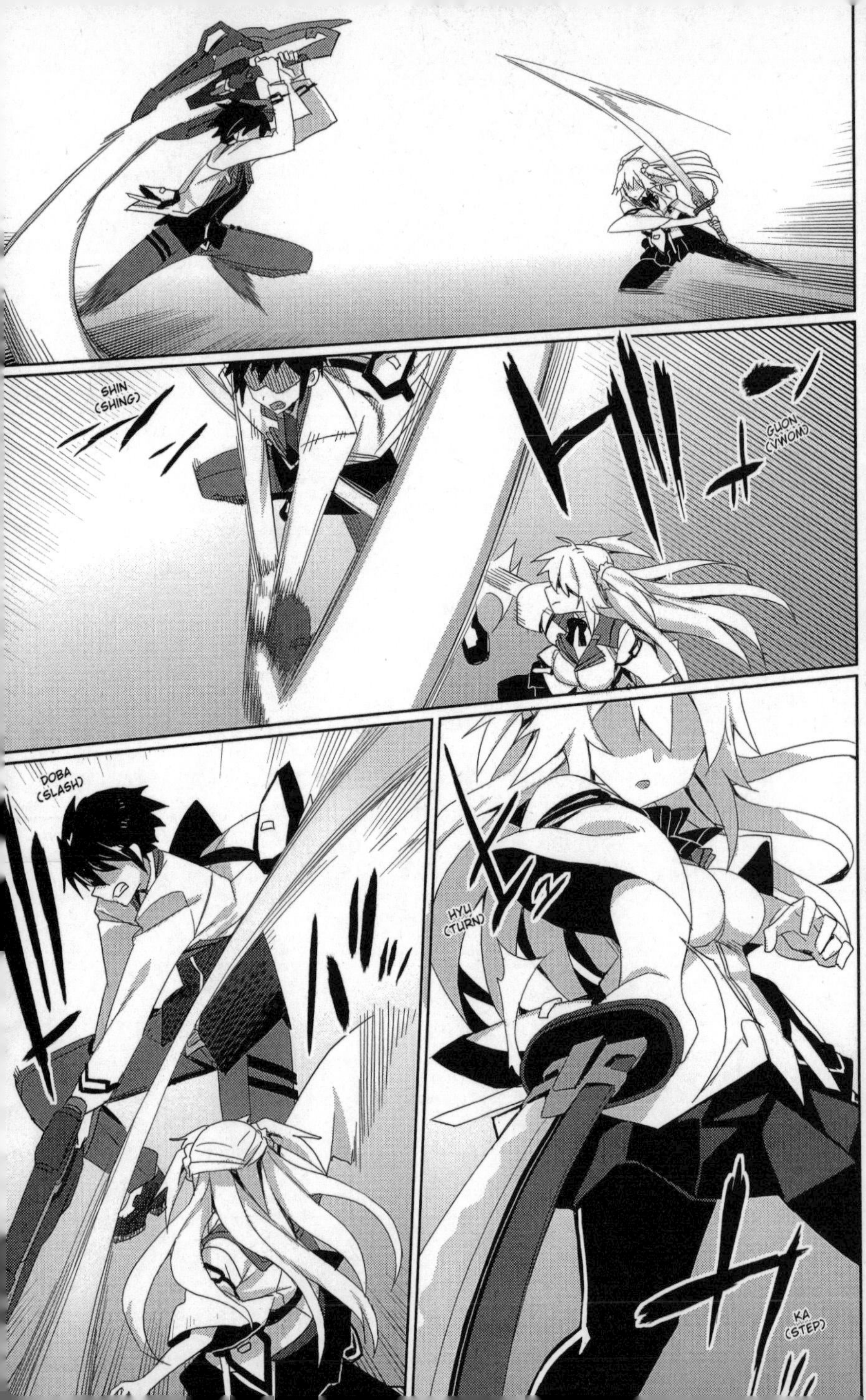
GUON (VWOM)
SHIN (SHING)
HYU (TURN)
KA (STEP)
DOBA (SLASH)

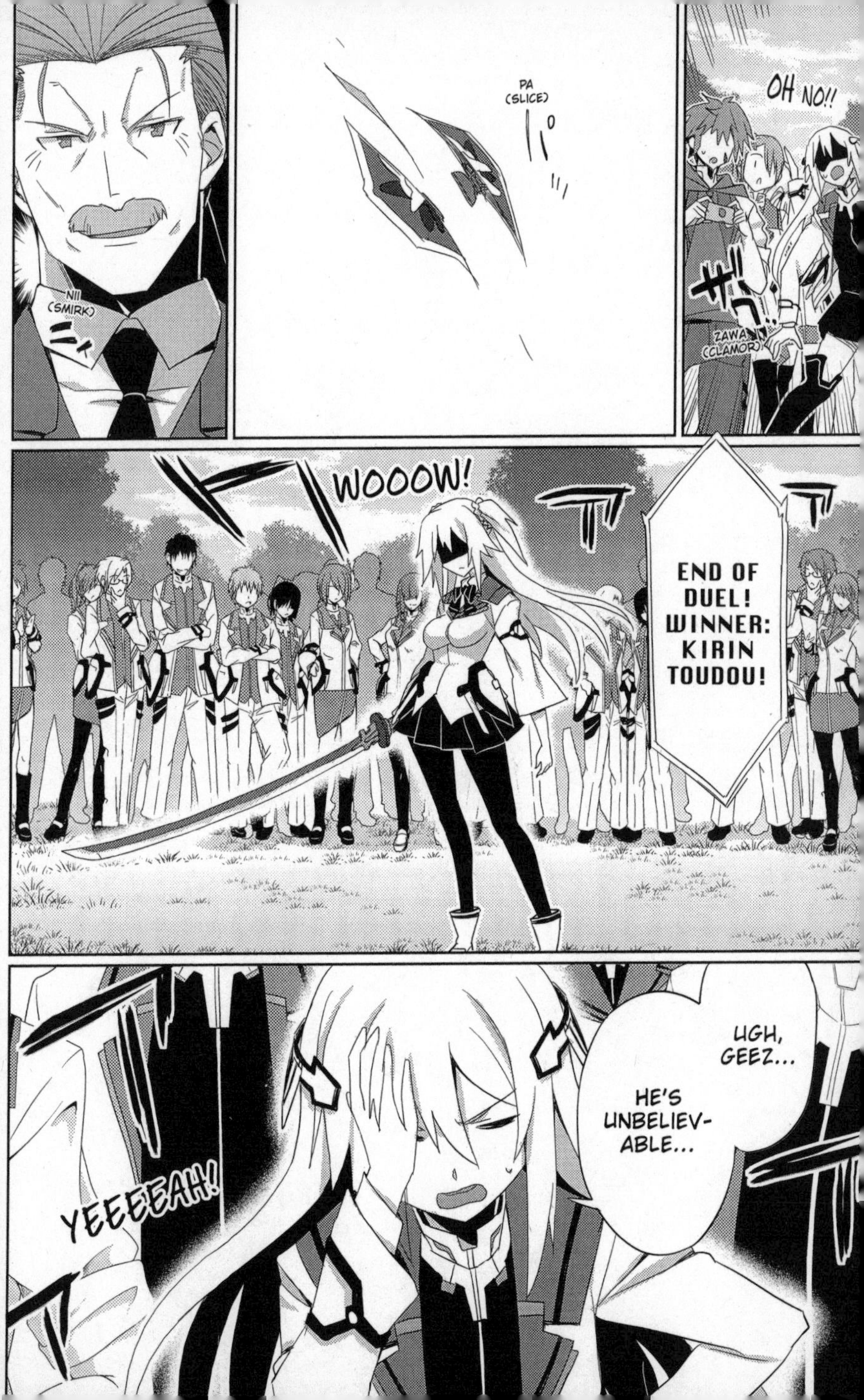
OH NO!!
ZAWA (CLAMOR)
PA (SLICE)
NII (SMIRK)
END OF DUEL! WINNER: KIRIN TOUDOU!
WOOOW!
UGH, GEEZ...
HE'S UNBELIEV-ABLE...
YEEEEAH!

THE ASTERISK WAR

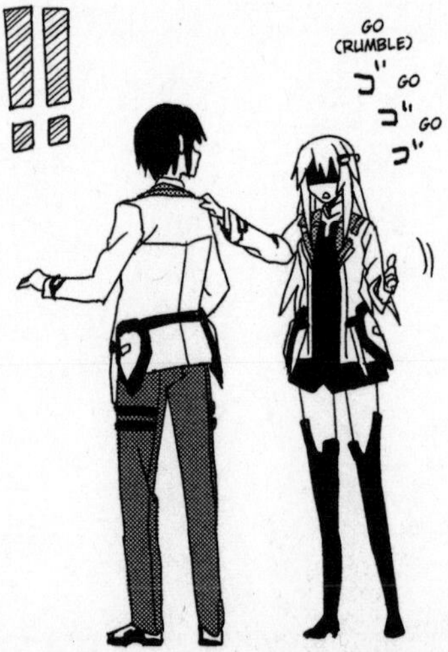
!!
GO (RUMBLE)
ゴ GO
ゴ GO
ゴ

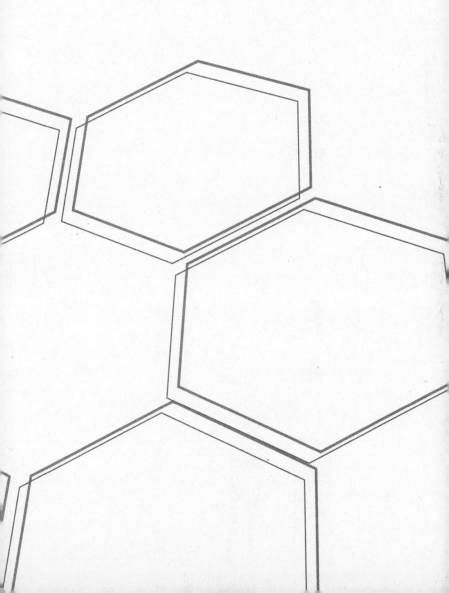

THE
ASTERISK WAR

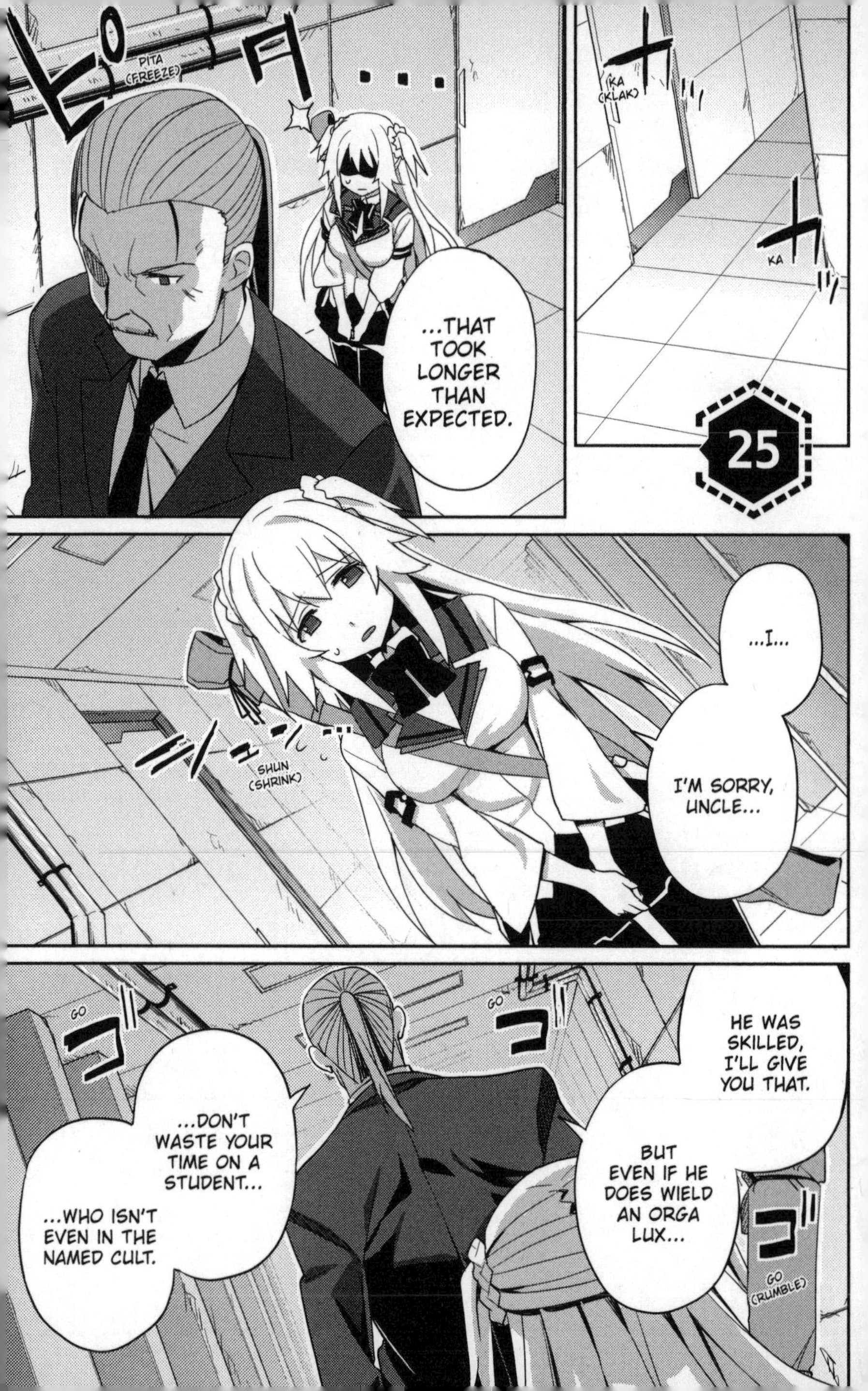

KA (KLAK)
KA
25
PITA (FREEZE)
...THAT TOOK LONGER THAN EXPECTED.
...I...
I'M SORRY, UNCLE...
SHUN (SHRINK)
HE WAS SKILLED, I'LL GIVE YOU THAT.
BUT EVEN IF HE DOES WIELD AN ORGA LUX...
GO (RUMBLE)
GO
...DON'T WASTE YOUR TIME ON A STUDENT...
...WHO ISN'T EVEN IN THE NAMED CULT.
GO

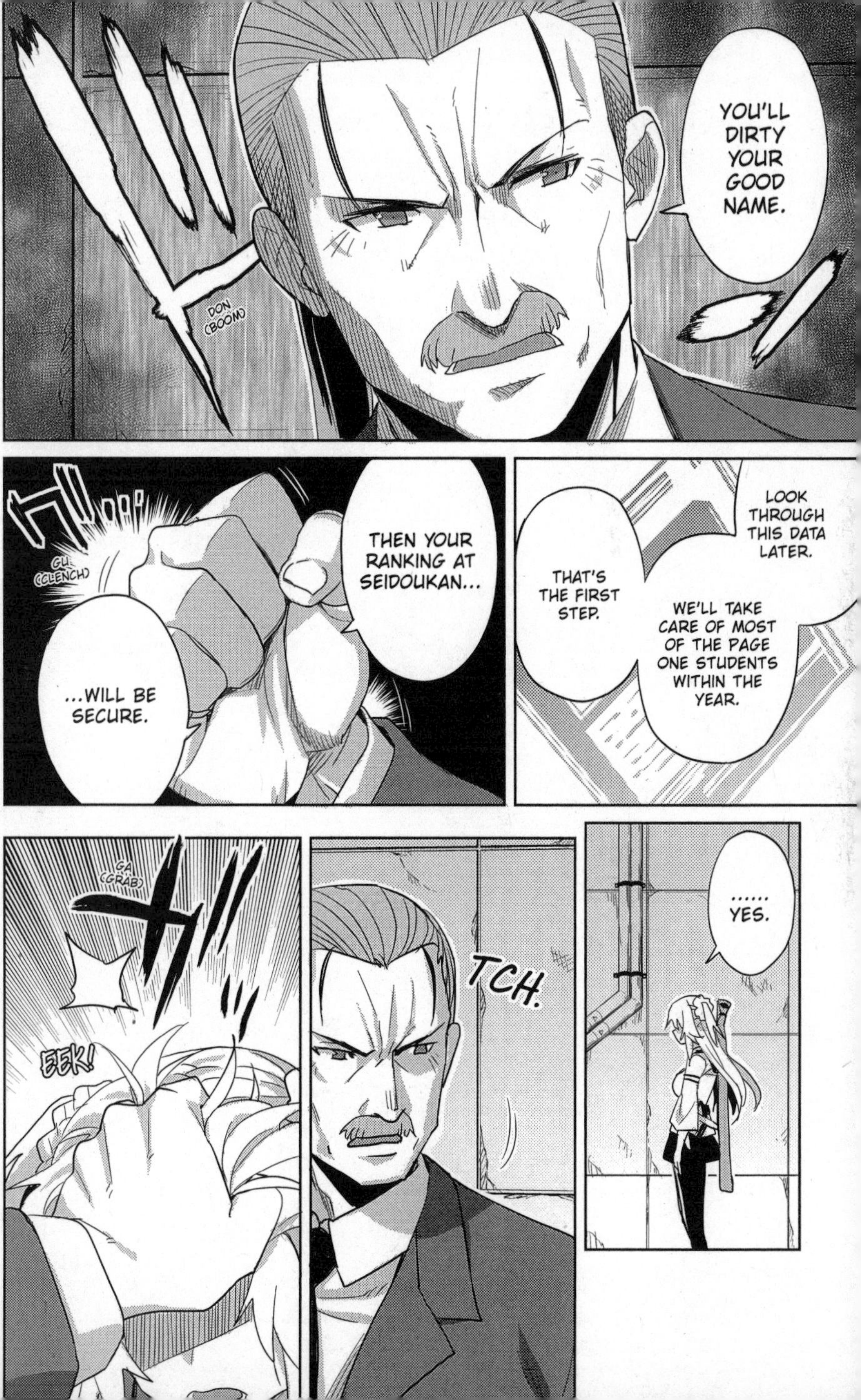
YOU'LL DIRTY YOUR GOOD NAME.
DON (BOOM)
LOOK THROUGH THIS DATA LATER.
WE'LL TAKE CARE OF MOST OF THE PAGE ONE STUDENTS WITHIN THE YEAR.
THAT'S THE FIRST STEP.
GU (CLENCH)
THEN YOUR RANKING AT SEIDOUKAN...
...WILL BE SECURE.
......YES.
TCH.
GA (GRAB)
EEK!

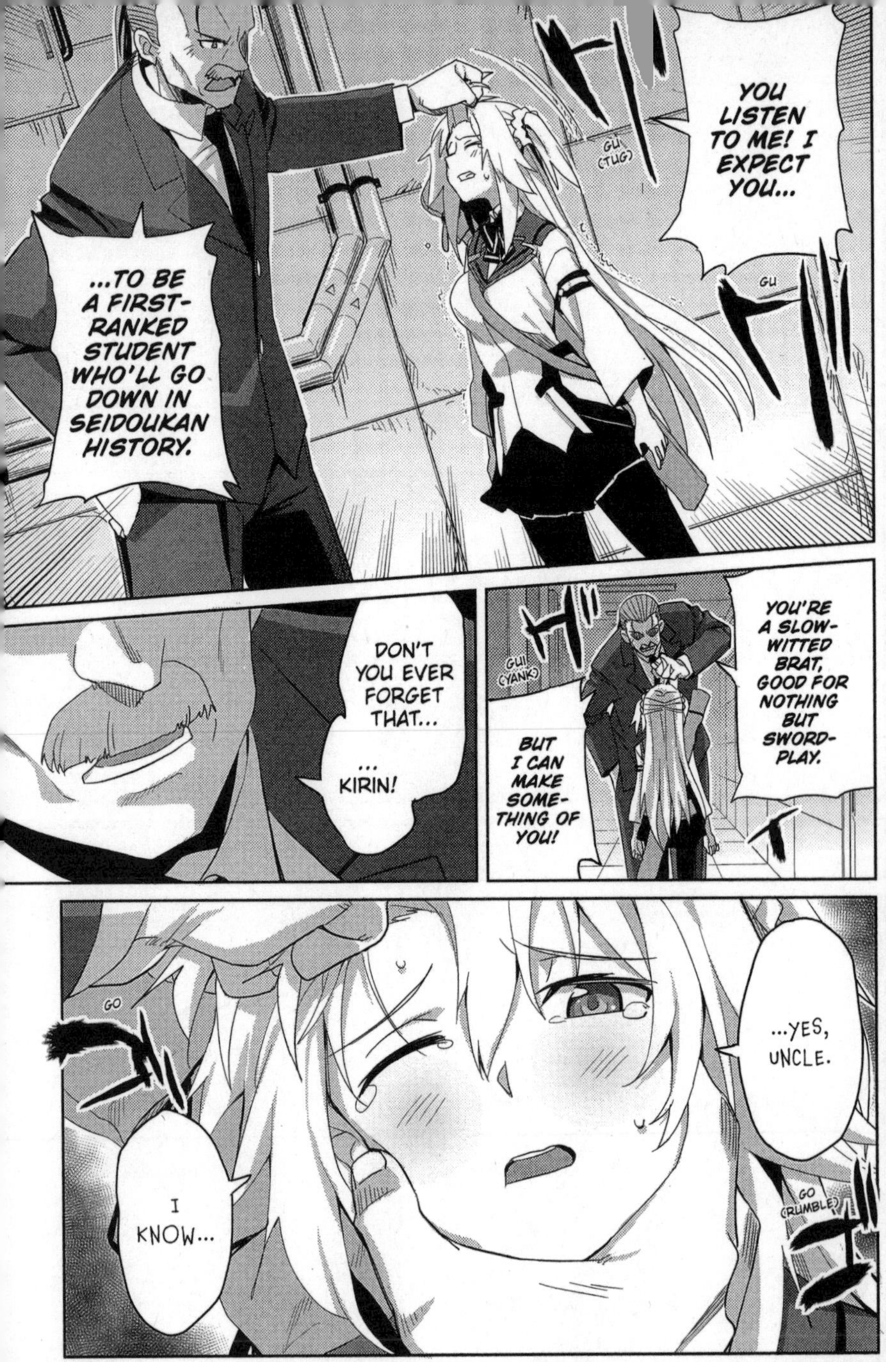
YOU LISTEN TO ME! I EXPECT YOU...
GU (TUG)
GU
...TO BE A FIRST-RANKED STUDENT WHO'LL GO DOWN IN SEIDOUKAN HISTORY.
YOU'RE A SLOW-WITTED BRAT, GOOD FOR NOTHING BUT SWORD-PLAY.
GUI (YANK)
BUT I CAN MAKE SOME-THING OF YOU!
DON'T YOU EVER FORGET THAT...
...KIRIN!
...YES, UNCLE.
GO (RUMBLE)
GO
I KNOW...

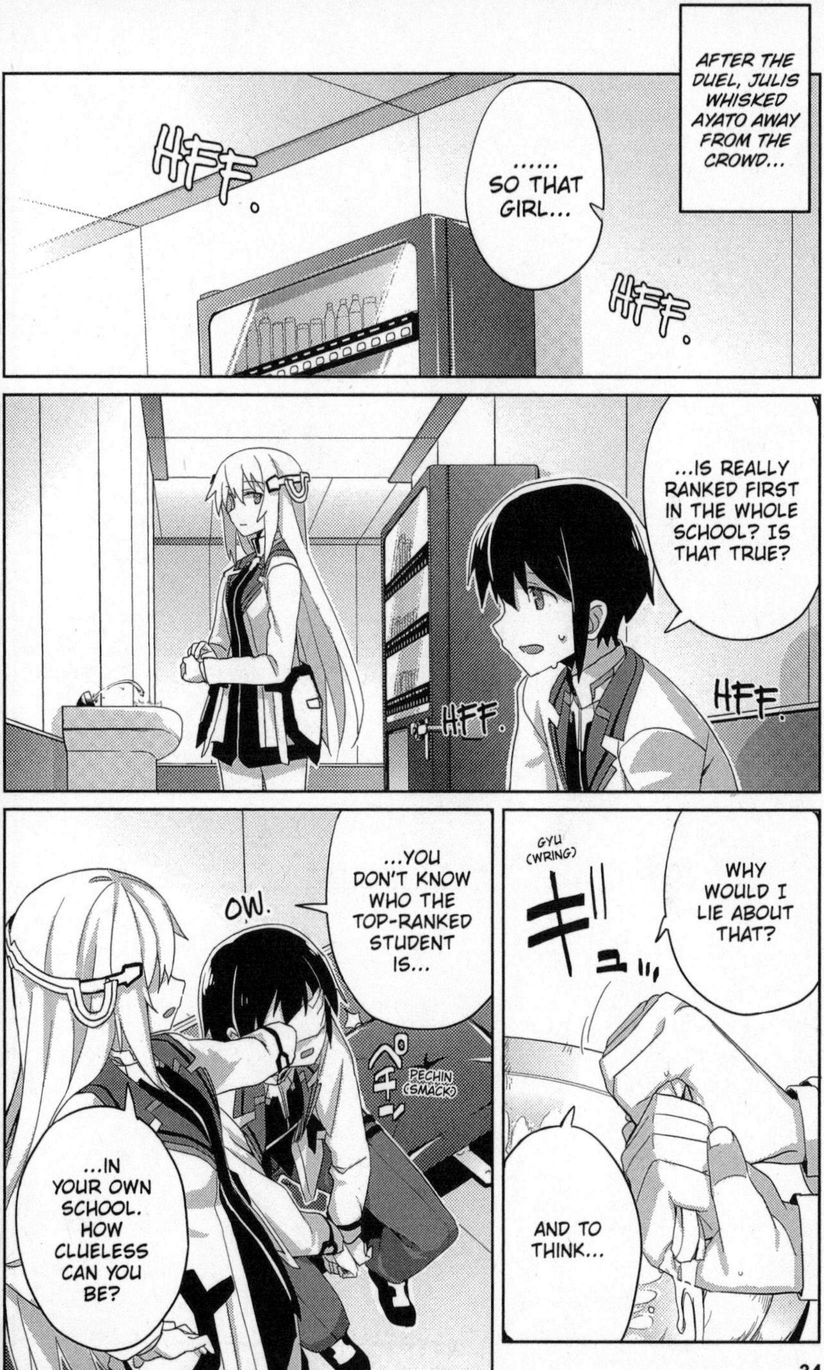
AFTER THE DUEL, JULIS WHISKED AYATO AWAY FROM THE CROWD...
HFF.
...... SO THAT GIRL...
HFF.
...IS REALLY RANKED FIRST IN THE WHOLE SCHOOL? IS THAT TRUE?
HFF.
HFF.
GYU (WRING)
WHY WOULD I LIE ABOUT THAT?
AND TO THINK...
...YOU DON'T KNOW WHO THE TOP-RANKED STUDENT IS...
OW.
PECHIN (SMACK)
...IN YOUR OWN SCHOOL. HOW CLUELESS CAN YOU BE?

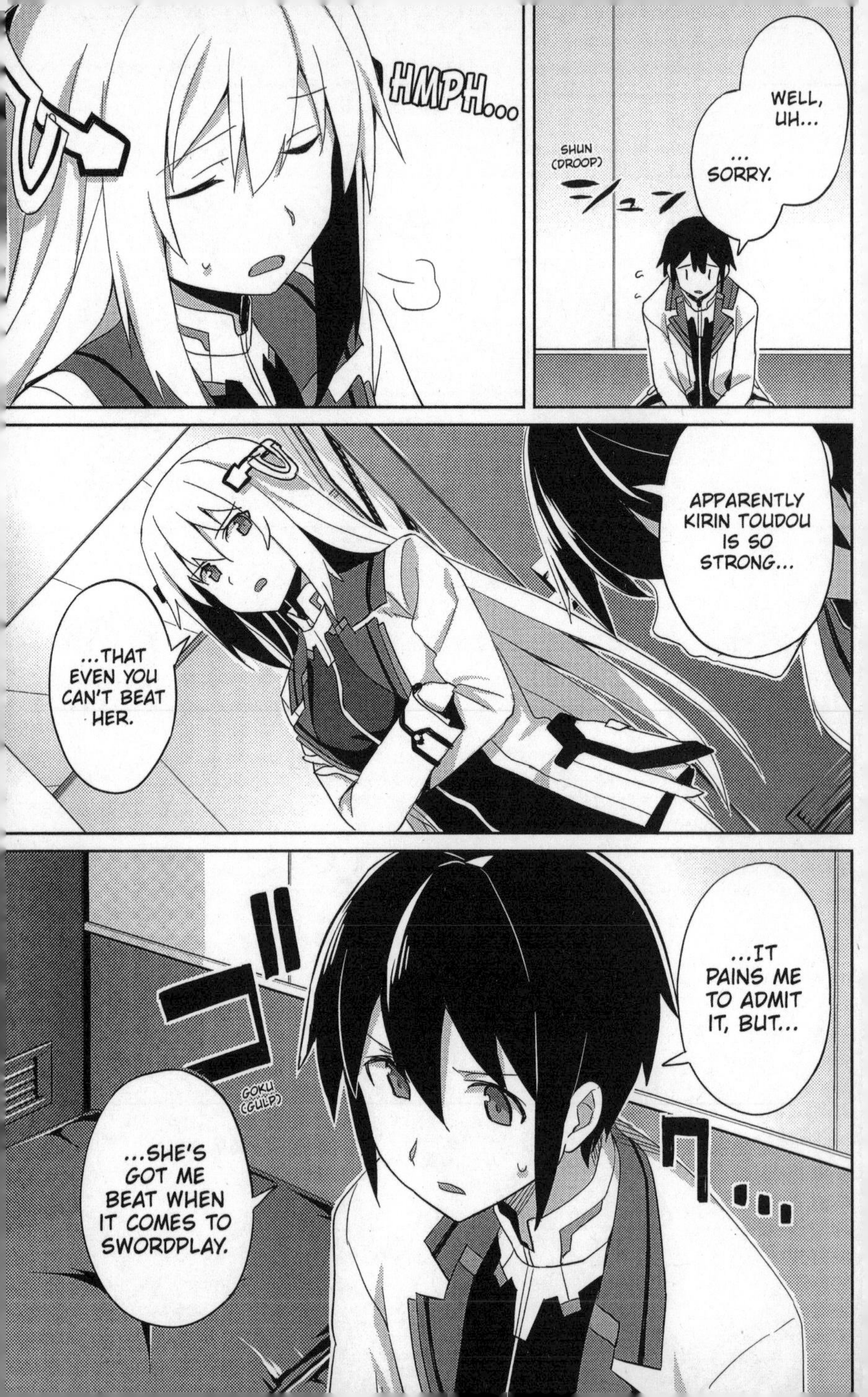
WELL, UH... ... SORRY.
SHUN (DROOP)
HMPH...
APPARENTLY KIRIN TOUDOU IS SO STRONG...
...THAT EVEN YOU CAN'T BEAT HER.
...IT PAINS ME TO ADMIT IT, BUT...
GOKU (GULP)
...SHE'S GOT ME BEAT WHEN IT COMES TO SWORDPLAY.

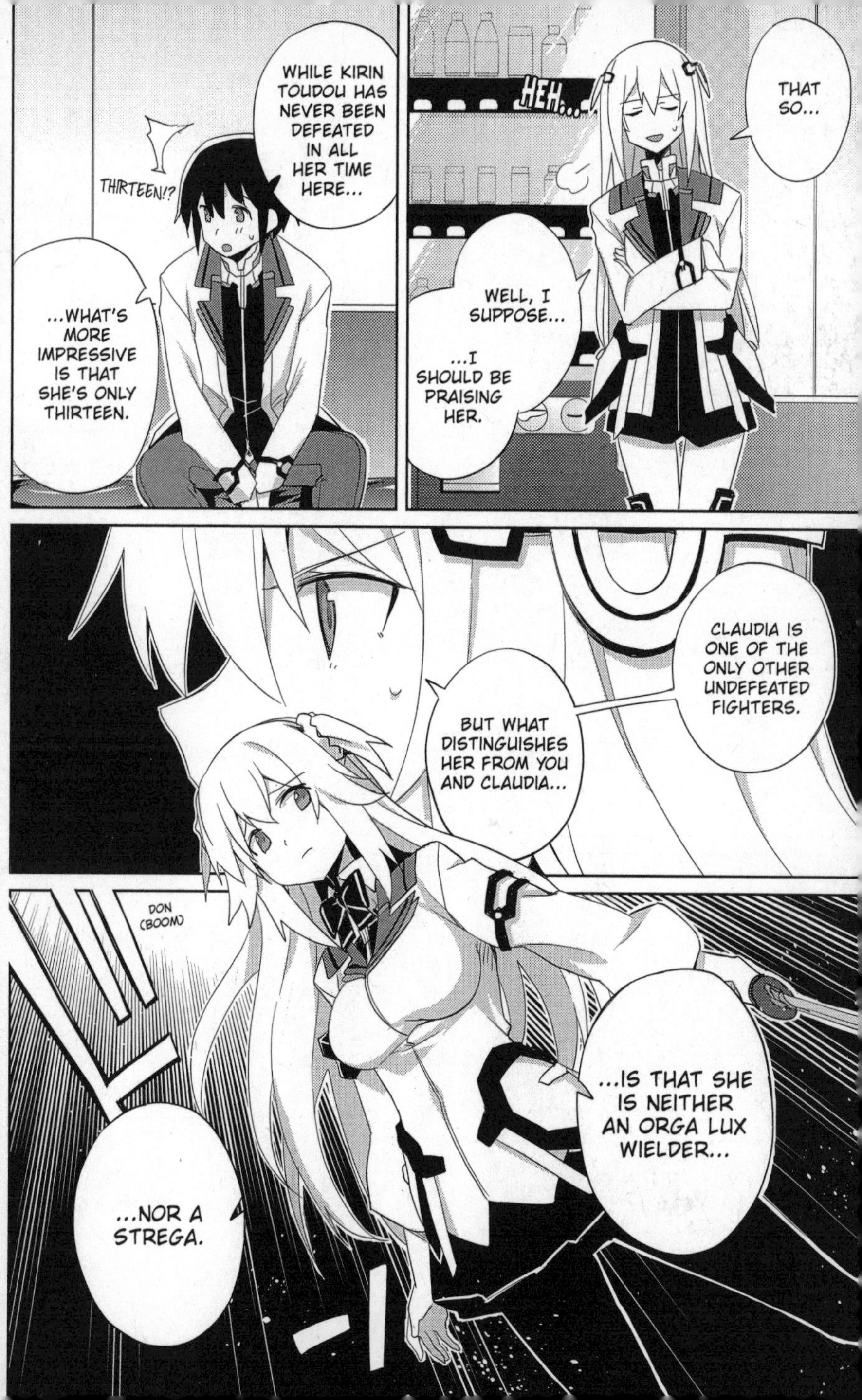
THAT SO...
HEH...
WELL, I SUPPOSE...
...I SHOULD BE PRAISING HER.
WHILE KIRIN TOUDOU HAS NEVER BEEN DEFEATED IN ALL HER TIME HERE...
...WHAT'S MORE IMPRESSIVE IS THAT SHE'S ONLY THIRTEEN.
THIRTEEN!?
CLAUDIA IS ONE OF THE ONLY OTHER UNDEFEATED FIGHTERS.
BUT WHAT DISTINGUISHES HER FROM YOU AND CLAUDIA...
DON (BOOM)
...IS THAT SHE IS NEITHER AN ORGA LUX WIELDER...
...NOR A STREGA.

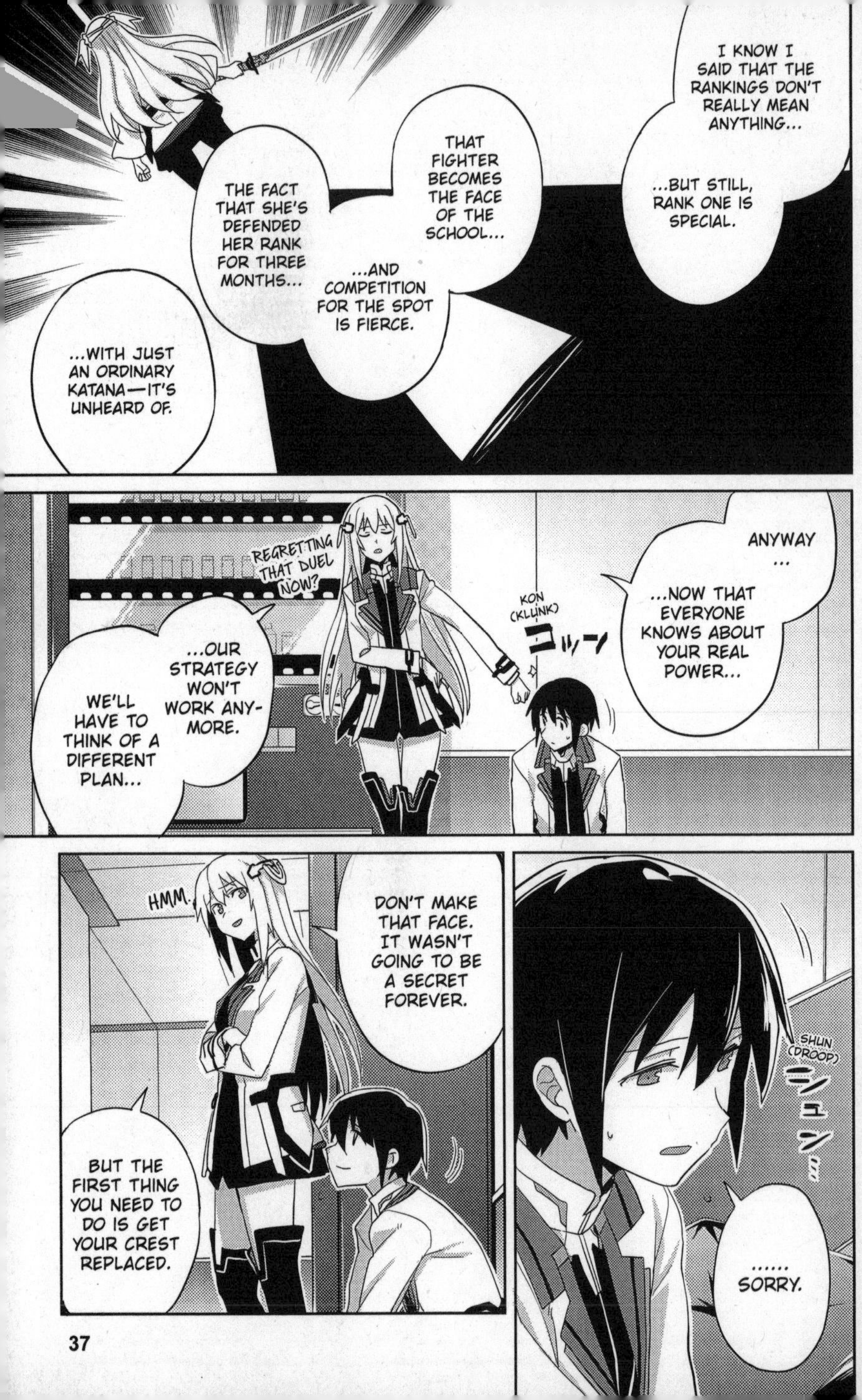
I KNOW I SAID THAT THE RANKINGS DON'T REALLY MEAN ANYTHING...
...BUT STILL, RANK ONE IS SPECIAL.
THAT FIGHTER BECOMES THE FACE OF THE SCHOOL...
...AND COMPETITION FOR THE SPOT IS FIERCE.
THE FACT THAT SHE'S DEFENDED HER RANK FOR THREE MONTHS...
...WITH JUST AN ORDINARY KATANA—IT'S UNHEARD OF.
ANYWAY...
...NOW THAT EVERYONE KNOWS ABOUT YOUR REAL POWER...
KON (KLUNK)
REGRETTING THAT DUEL NOW?
...OUR STRATEGY WON'T WORK ANYMORE.
WE'LL HAVE TO THINK OF A DIFFERENT PLAN...
SHUN (DROOP)
......SORRY.
DON'T MAKE THAT FACE. IT WASN'T GOING TO BE A SECRET FOREVER.
HMM.
BUT THE FIRST THING YOU NEED TO DO IS GET YOUR CREST REPLACED.

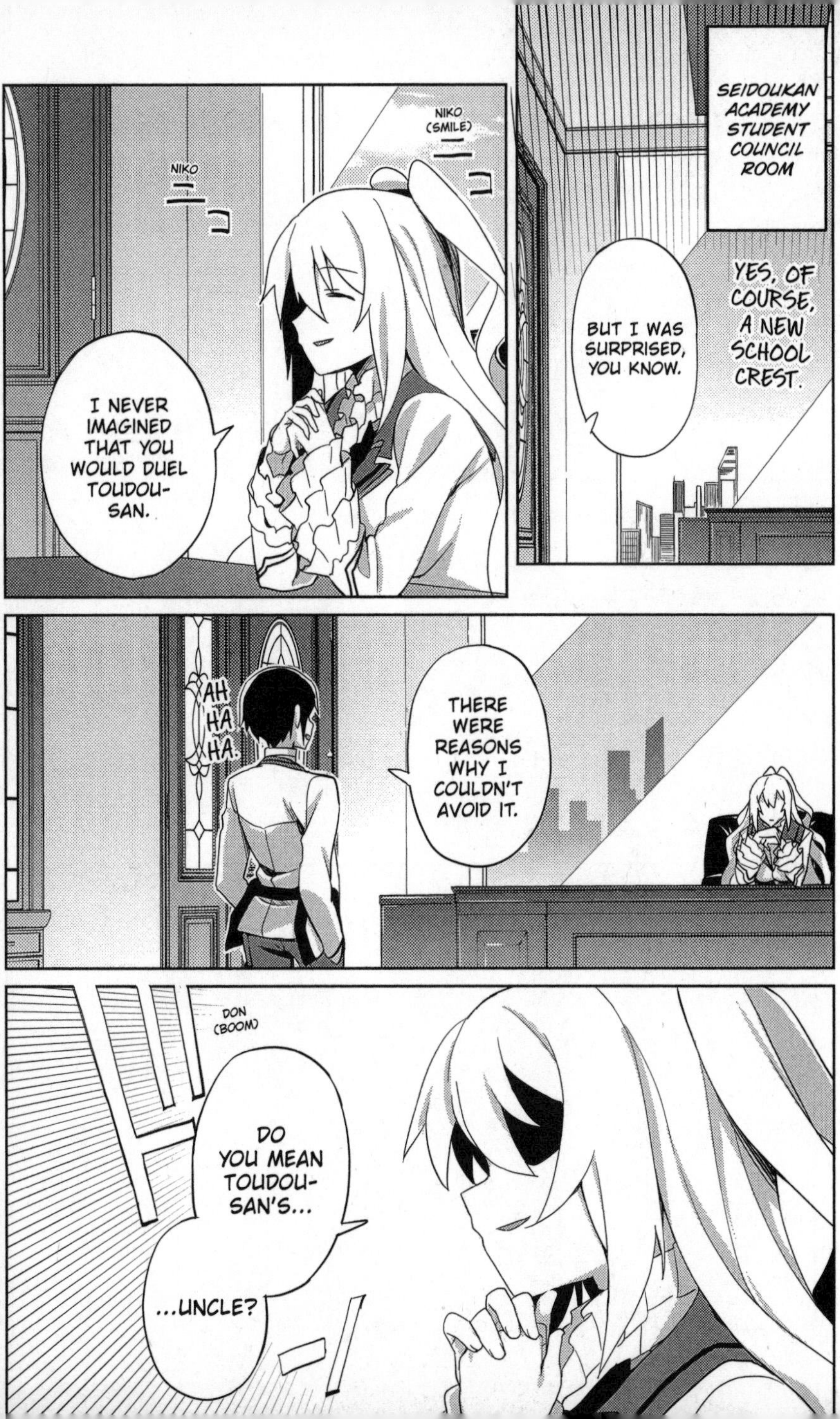
SEIDOUKAN ACADEMY STUDENT COUNCIL ROOM
YES, OF COURSE, A NEW SCHOOL CREST.
BUT I WAS SURPRISED, YOU KNOW.
NIKO (SMILE)
NIKO
I NEVER IMAGINED THAT YOU WOULD DUEL TOUDOU-SAN.
THERE WERE REASONS WHY I COULDN'T AVOID IT.
AH HA HA.
DON (BOOM)
DO YOU MEAN TOUDOU-SAN'S...
...UNCLE?

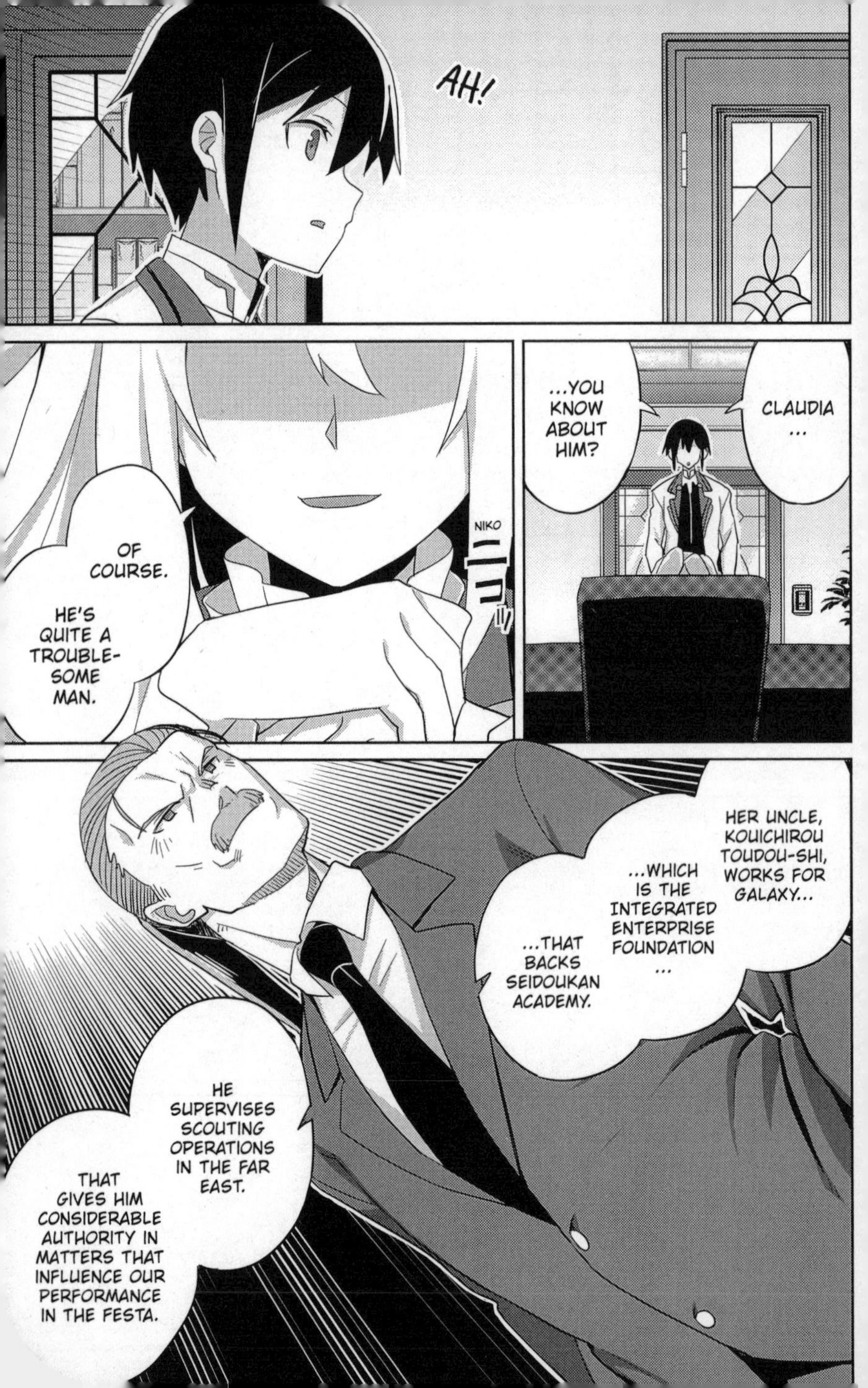
AH!
CLAUDIA...
...YOU KNOW ABOUT HIM?
NIKO
ニコッ
OF COURSE.
HE'S QUITE A TROUBLE-SOME MAN.
HER UNCLE, KOUICHIROU TOUDOU-SHI, WORKS FOR GALAXY...
...WHICH IS THE INTEGRATED ENTERPRISE FOUNDATION...
...THAT BACKS SEIDOUKAN ACADEMY.
HE SUPERVISES SCOUTING OPERATIONS IN THE FAR EAST.
THAT GIVES HIM CONSIDERABLE AUTHORITY IN MATTERS THAT INFLUENCE OUR PERFORMANCE IN THE FESTA.

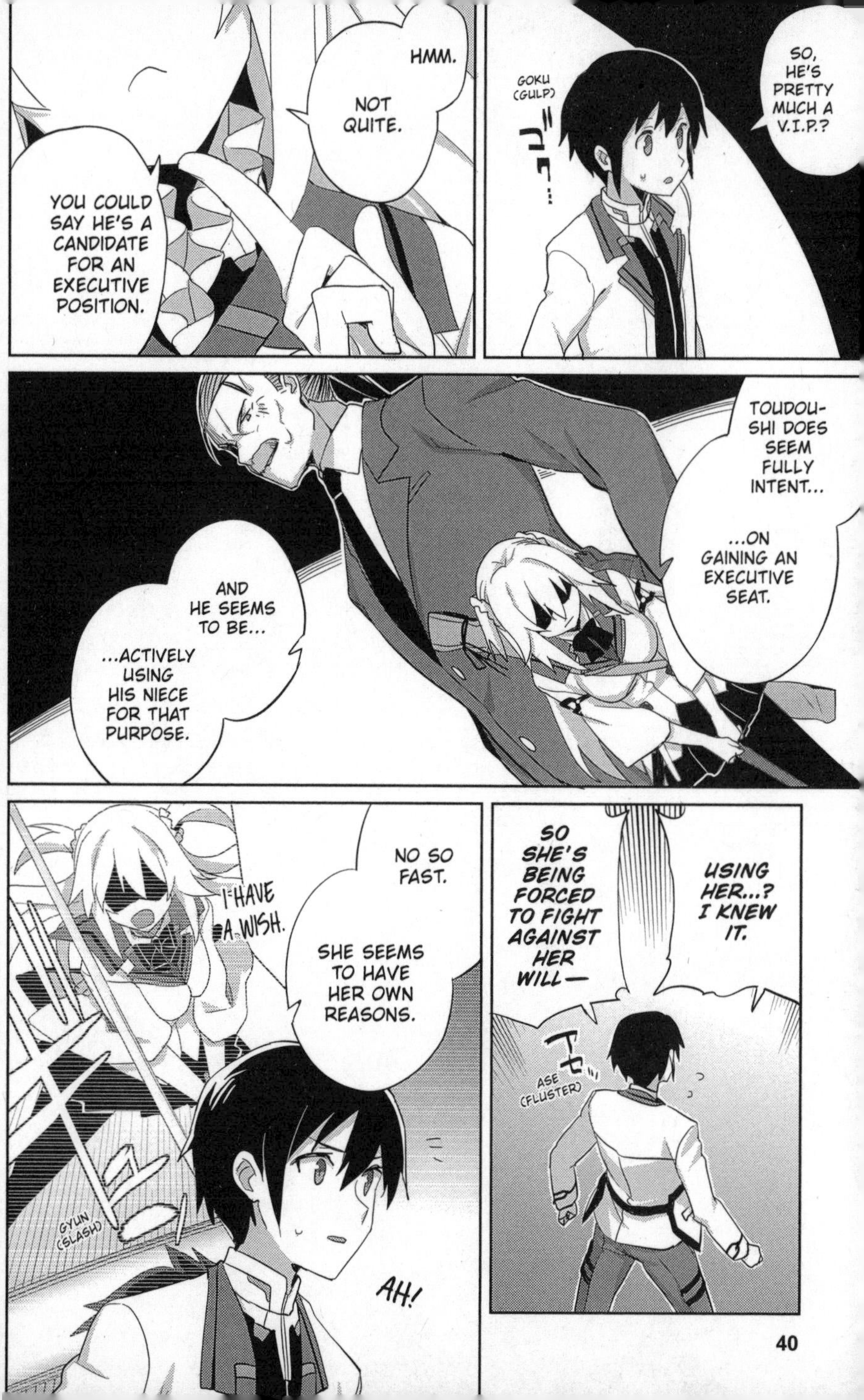
SO, HE'S PRETTY MUCH A V.I.P.?
GOKU (GULP)
HMM.
NOT QUITE.
YOU COULD SAY HE'S A CANDIDATE FOR AN EXECUTIVE POSITION.
TOUDOU-SHI DOES SEEM FULLY INTENT...
...ON GAINING AN EXECUTIVE SEAT.
AND HE SEEMS TO BE...
...ACTIVELY USING HIS NIECE FOR THAT PURPOSE.
USING HER...? I KNEW IT.
SO SHE'S BEING FORCED TO FIGHT AGAINST HER WILL—
ASE (FLUSTER)
NO SO FAST.
SHE SEEMS TO HAVE HER OWN REASONS.
I HAVE A WISH.
GYUN (SLASH)
AH!

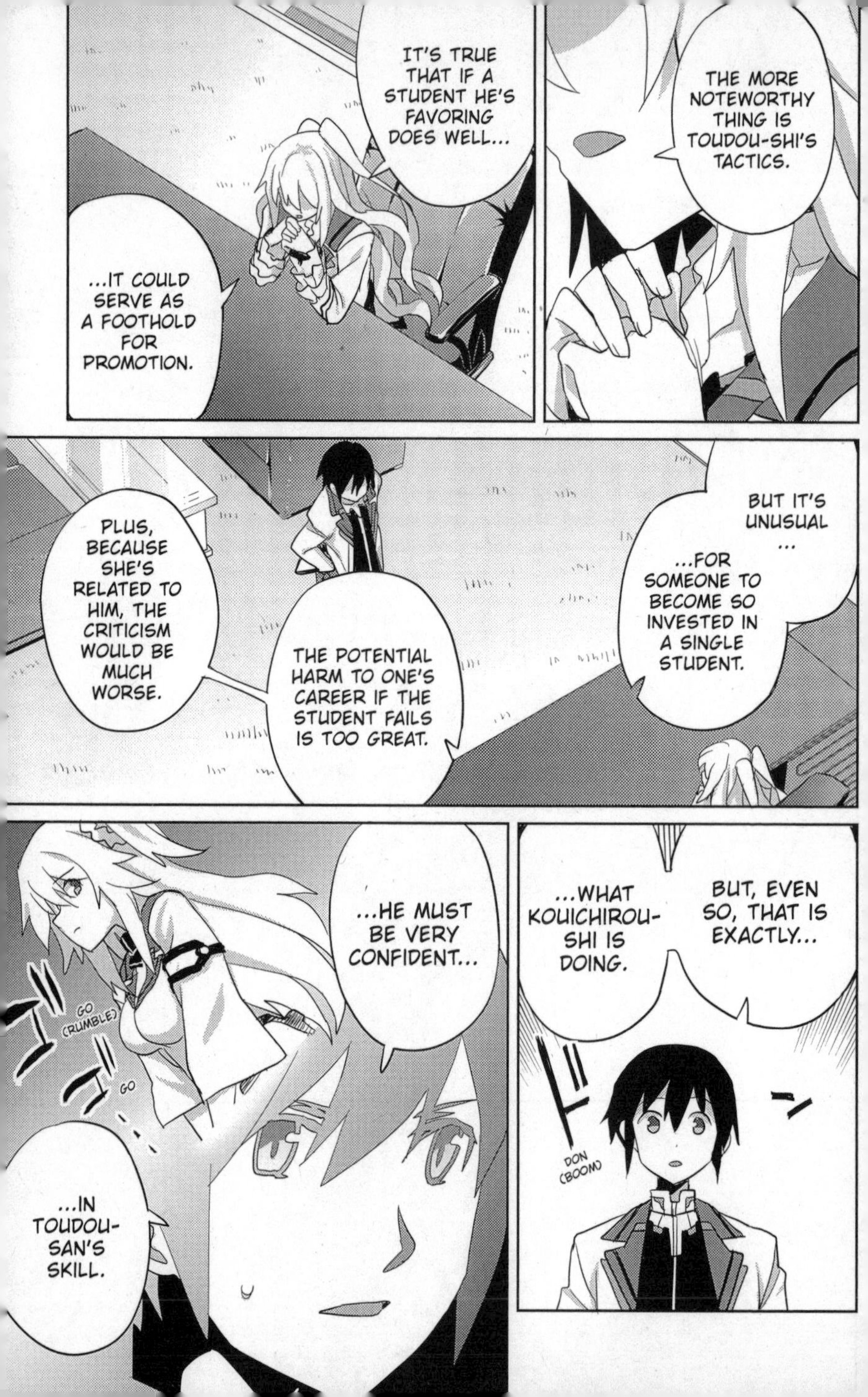
THE MORE NOTEWORTHY THING IS TOUDOU-SHI'S TACTICS.
IT'S TRUE THAT IF A STUDENT HE'S FAVORING DOES WELL...
...IT COULD SERVE AS A FOOTHOLD FOR PROMOTION.
BUT IT'S UNUSUAL ...
...FOR SOMEONE TO BECOME SO INVESTED IN A SINGLE STUDENT.
THE POTENTIAL HARM TO ONE'S CAREER IF THE STUDENT FAILS IS TOO GREAT.
PLUS, BECAUSE SHE'S RELATED TO HIM, THE CRITICISM WOULD BE MUCH WORSE.
BUT, EVEN SO, THAT IS EXACTLY...
...WHAT KOUICHIROU-SHI IS DOING.
DON (BOOM)
...HE MUST BE VERY CONFIDENT...
GO (RUMBLE)
GO
...IN TOUDOU-SAN'S SKILL.

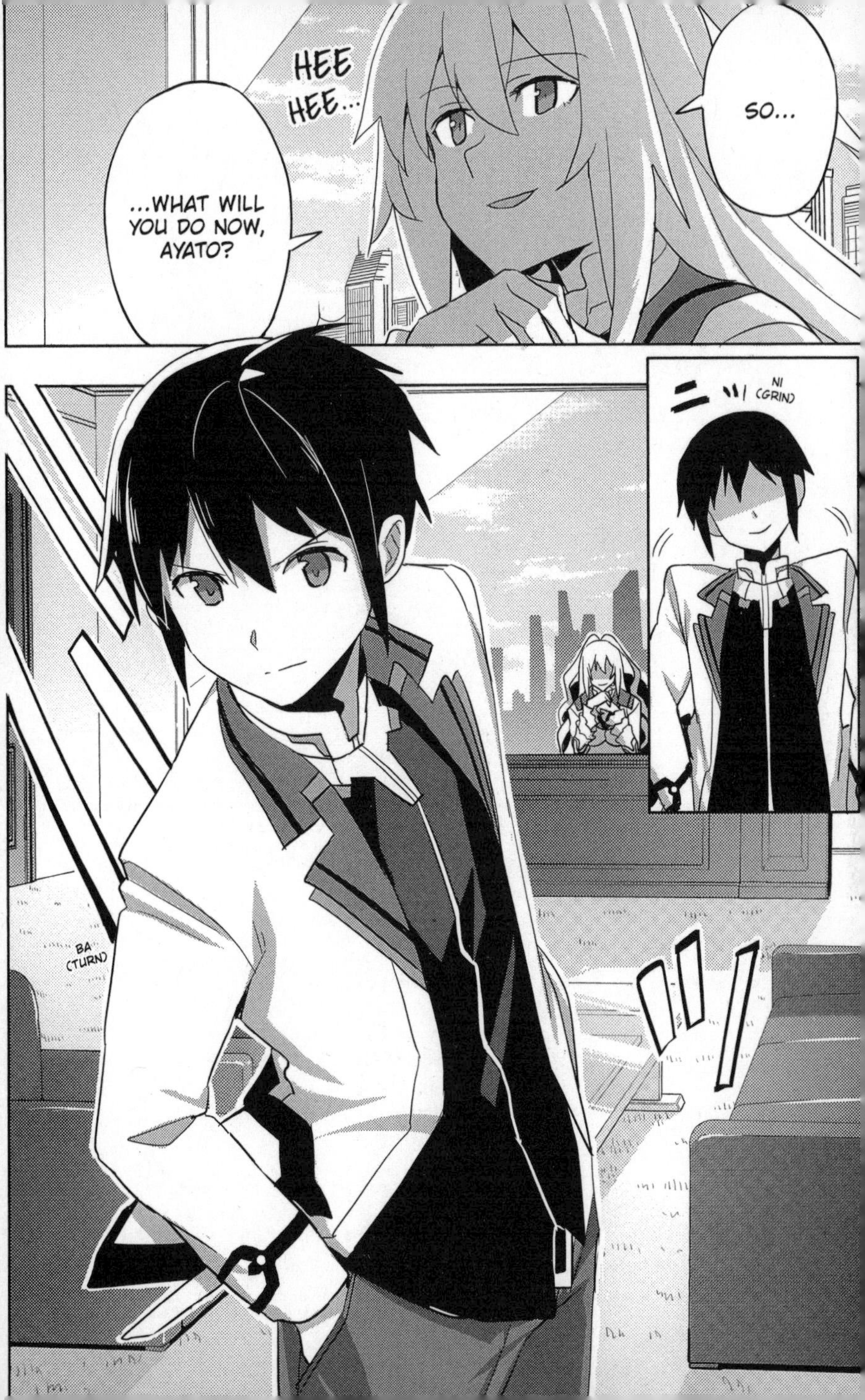
SO...
HEE HEE...
...WHAT WILL YOU DO NOW, AYATO?
NI (GRIN)
BA (TURN)

THE ASTERISK WAR

THAT'S
WHAT I LIKE
ABOUT YOU,
AYATO...

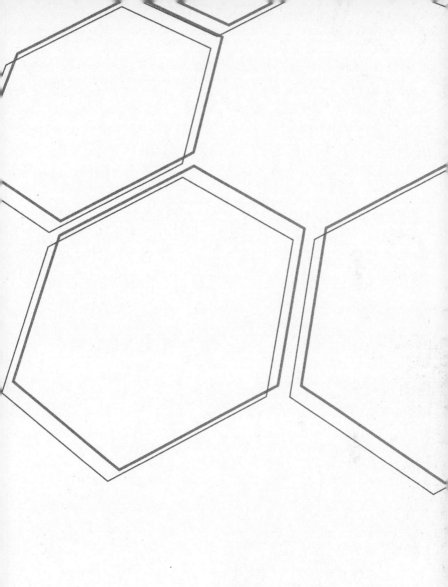

THE
ASTERISK WAR

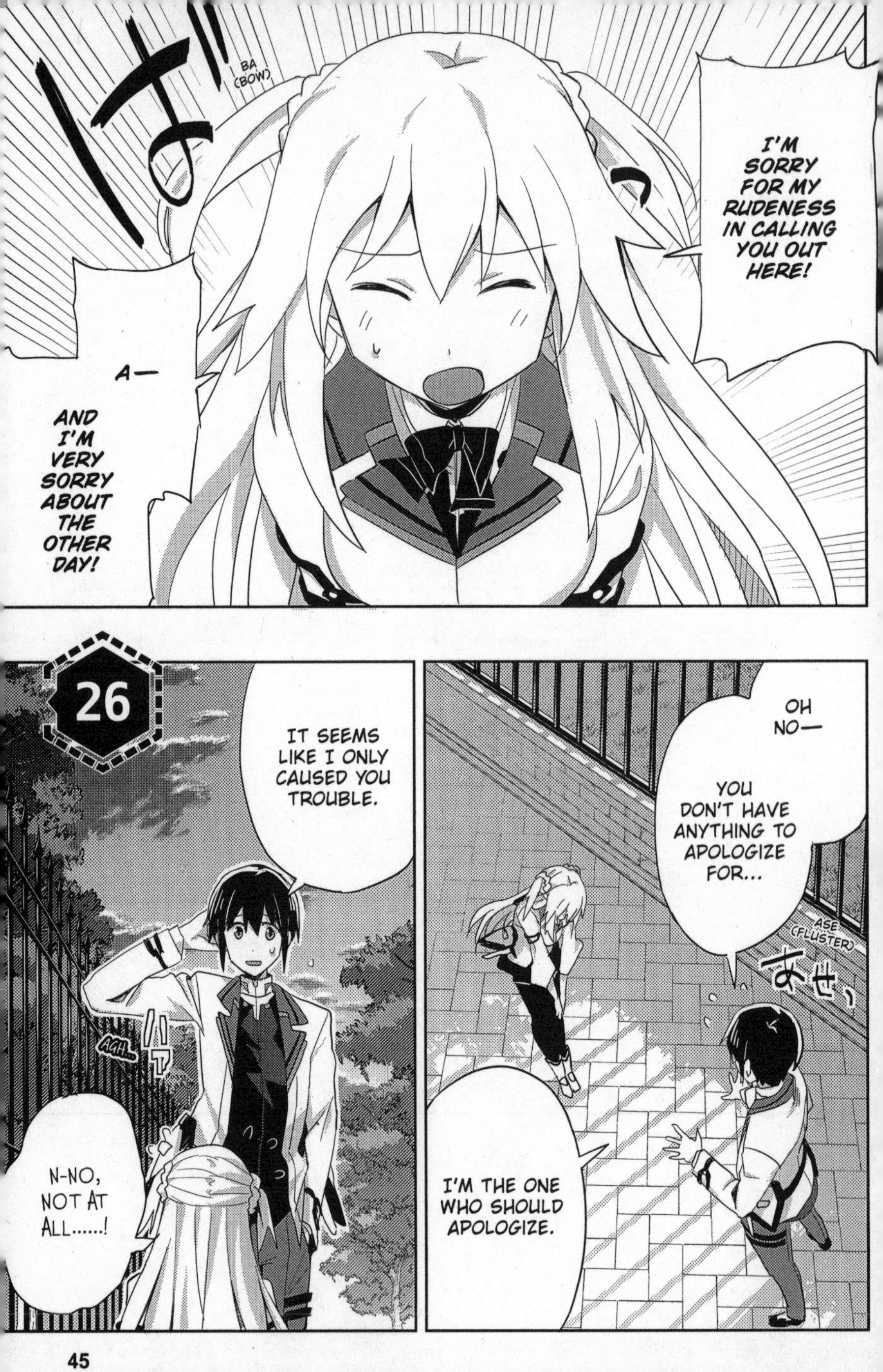
BA (BOW)
I'M SORRY FOR MY RUDENESS IN CALLING YOU OUT HERE!
A—
AND I'M VERY SORRY ABOUT THE OTHER DAY!
OH NO—
YOU DON'T HAVE ANYTHING TO APOLOGIZE FOR...
ASE (FLUSTER)
I'M THE ONE WHO SHOULD APOLOGIZE.
26
IT SEEMS LIKE I ONLY CAUSED YOU TROUBLE.
AGH...
N-NO, NOT AT ALL......!

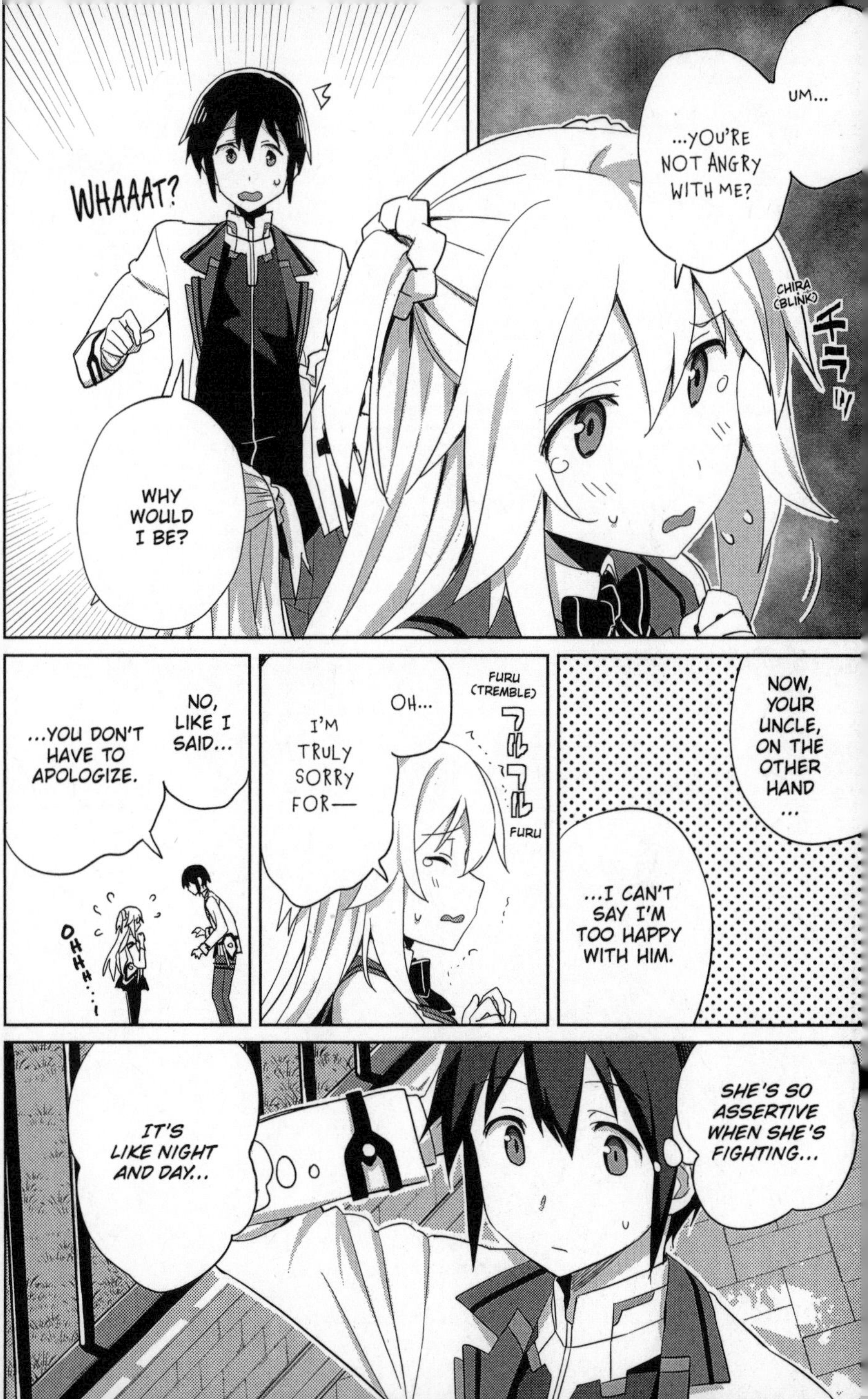

UM...
...YOU'RE NOT ANGRY WITH ME?
CHIRA (BLINK)
チラッ
WHAAAT?
WHY WOULD I BE?
NOW, YOUR UNCLE, ON THE OTHER HAND...
...I CAN'T SAY I'M TOO HAPPY WITH HIM.
FURU (TREMBLE)
フルフル
FURU
OH...
I'M TRULY SORRY FOR—
NO, LIKE I SAID...
...YOU DON'T HAVE TO APOLOGIZE.
OHHH...!
SHE'S SO ASSERTIVE WHEN SHE'S FIGHTING...
IT'S LIKE NIGHT AND DAY...

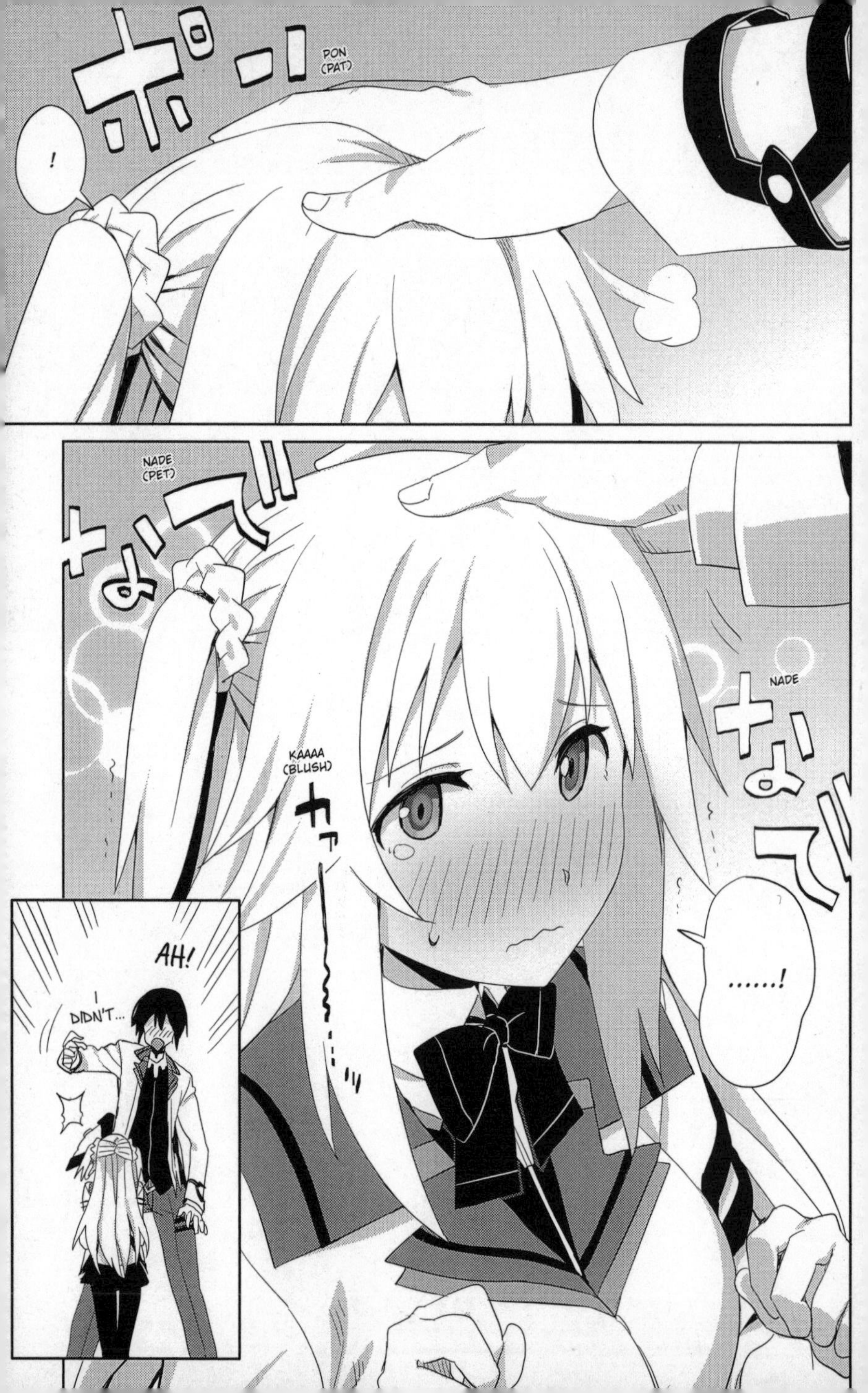
PON (PAT)
!
NADE (PET)
NADE
KAAAA (BLUSH)
......!
AH!
I DIDN'T...

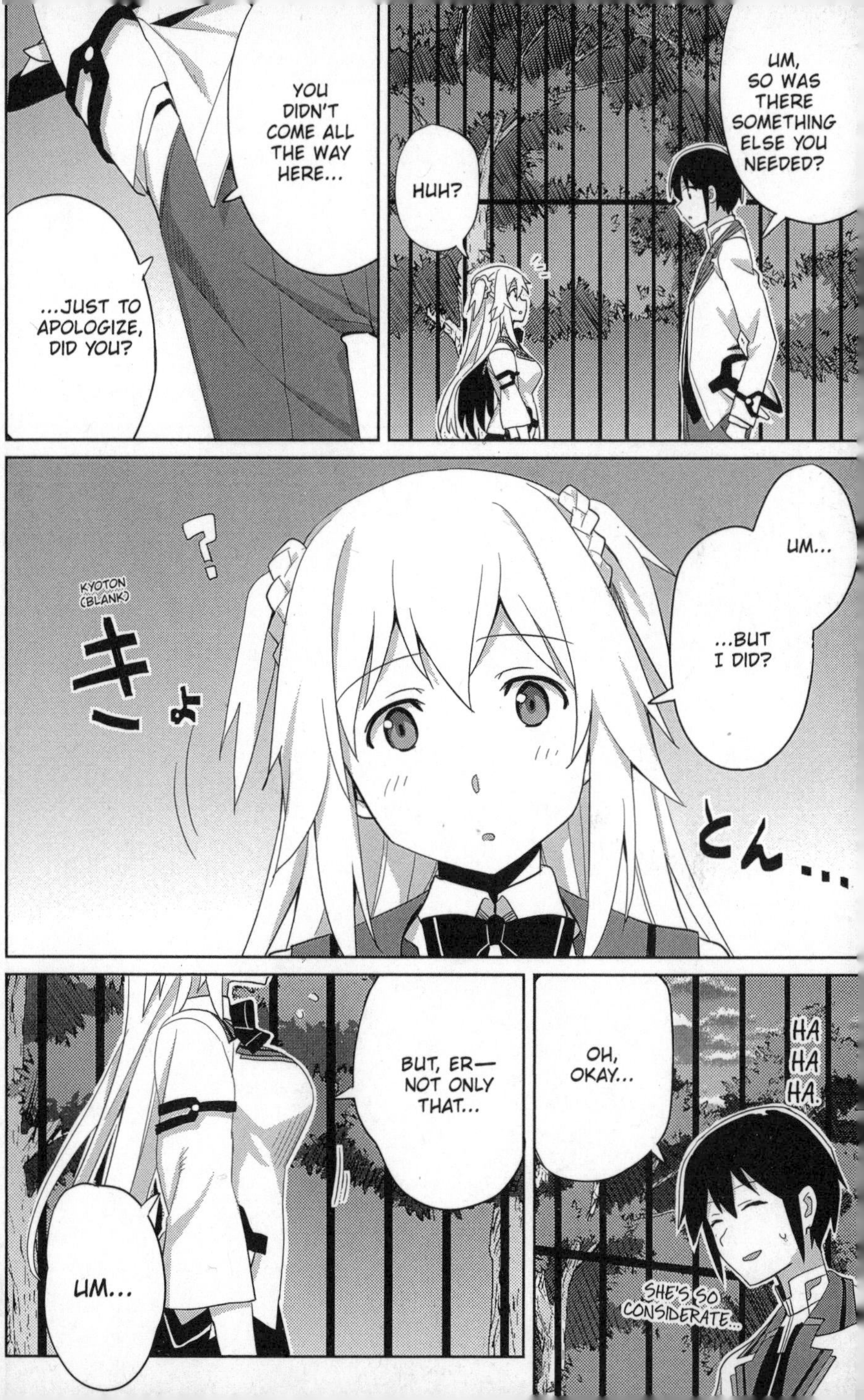
UM, SO WAS THERE SOMETHING ELSE YOU NEEDED?
HUH?
YOU DIDN'T COME ALL THE WAY HERE...
...JUST TO APOLOGIZE, DID YOU?
UM...
...BUT I DID?
とん…
?
KYOTON (BLANK)
キョ
HA HA HA.
OH, OKAY...
SHE'S SO CONSIDERATE...
BUT, ER— NOT ONLY THAT...
UM...

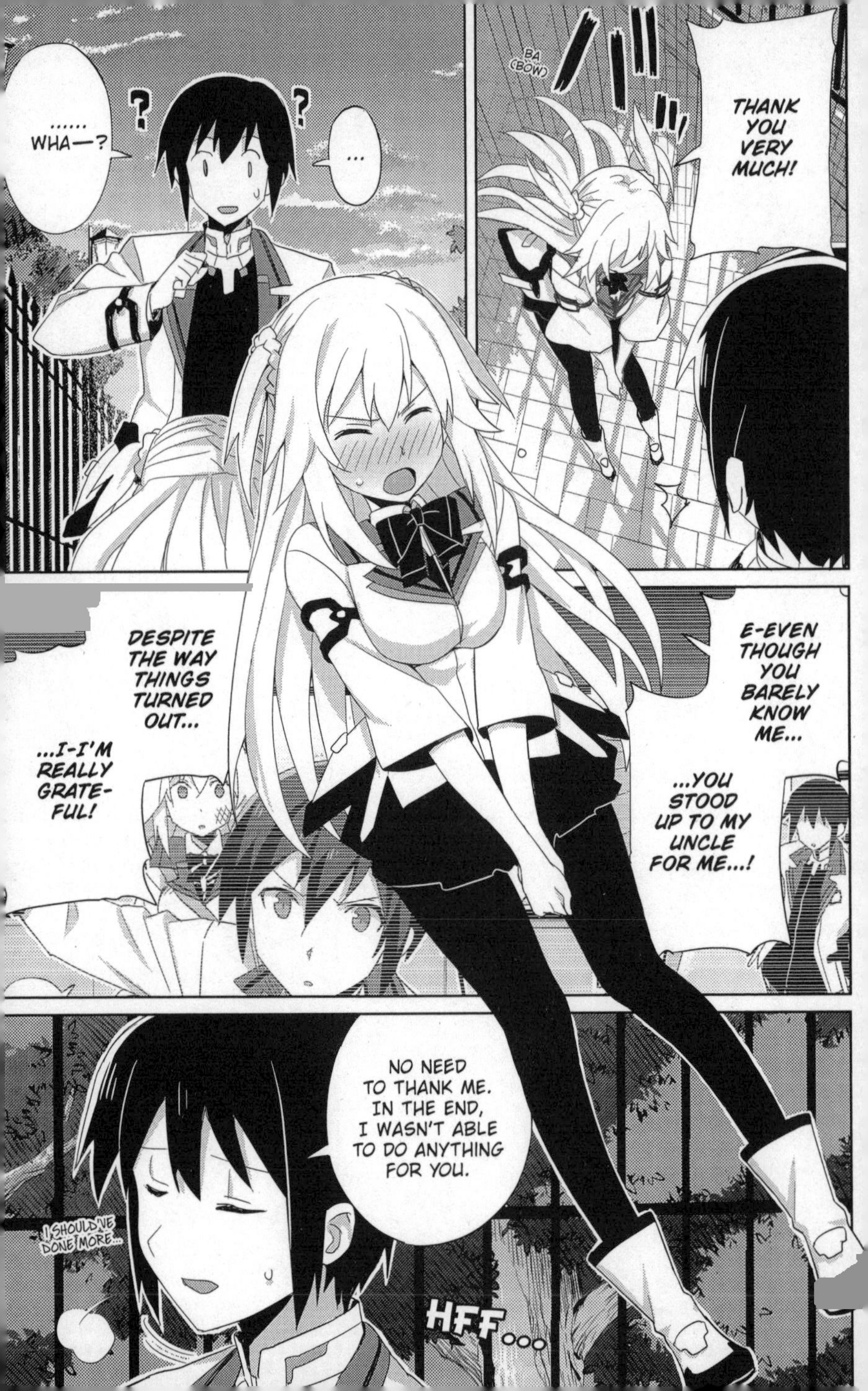
THANK YOU VERY MUCH!
BA (BOW)
...
...... WHA—?
E-EVEN THOUGH YOU BARELY KNOW ME...
...YOU STOOD UP TO MY UNCLE FOR ME...!
DESPITE THE WAY THINGS TURNED OUT...
...I-I'M REALLY GRATE-FUL!
NO NEED TO THANK ME. IN THE END, I WASN'T ABLE TO DO ANYTHING FOR YOU.
I SHOULD'VE DONE MORE...
HFF...

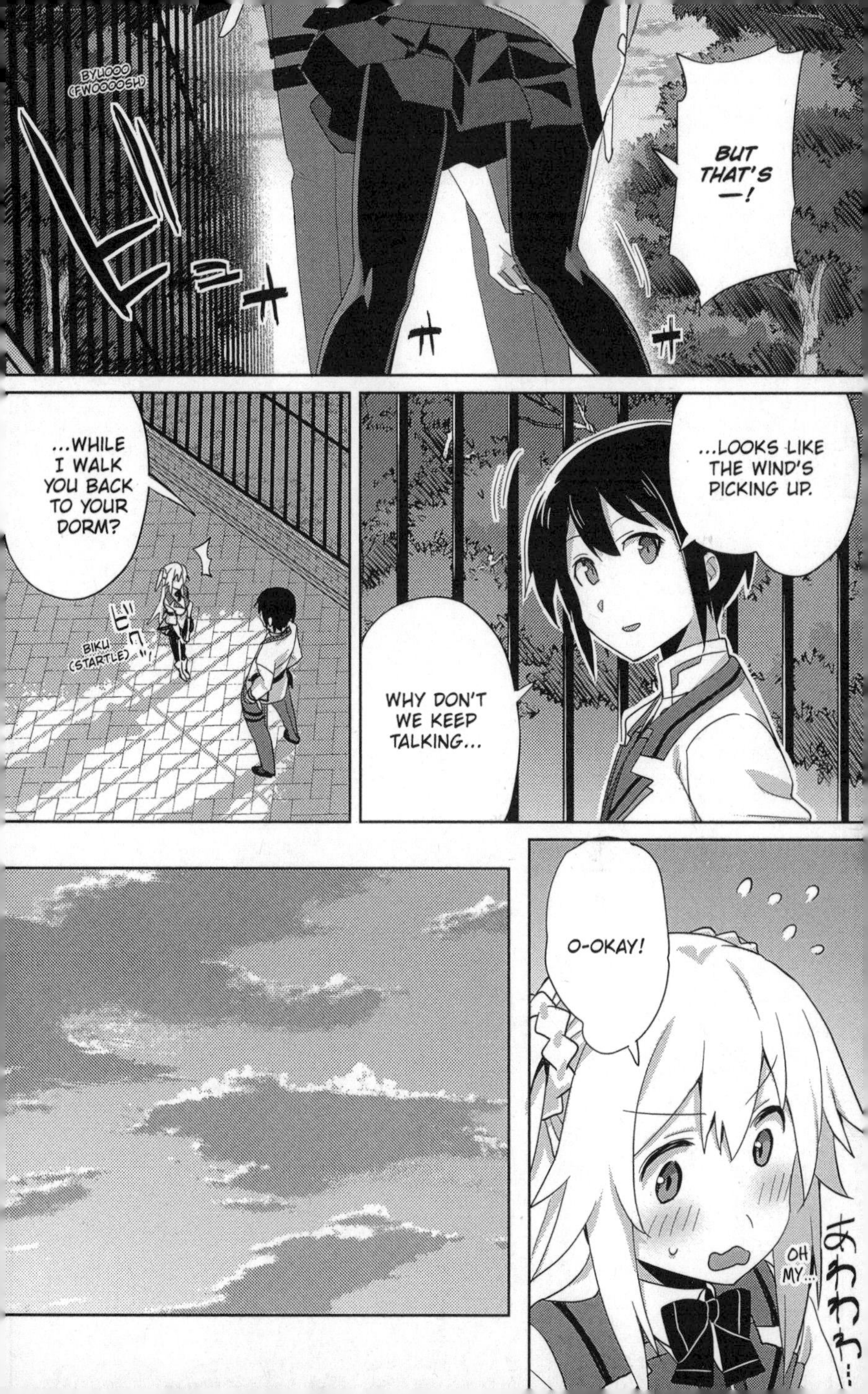
BUT THAT'S —!
BYUOOO (FWOOOOSH)
...LOOKS LIKE THE WIND'S PICKING UP.
WHY DON'T WE KEEP TALKING...
...WHILE I WALK YOU BACK TO YOUR DORM?
BIKU (STARTLE)
O-OKAY!
OH MY...

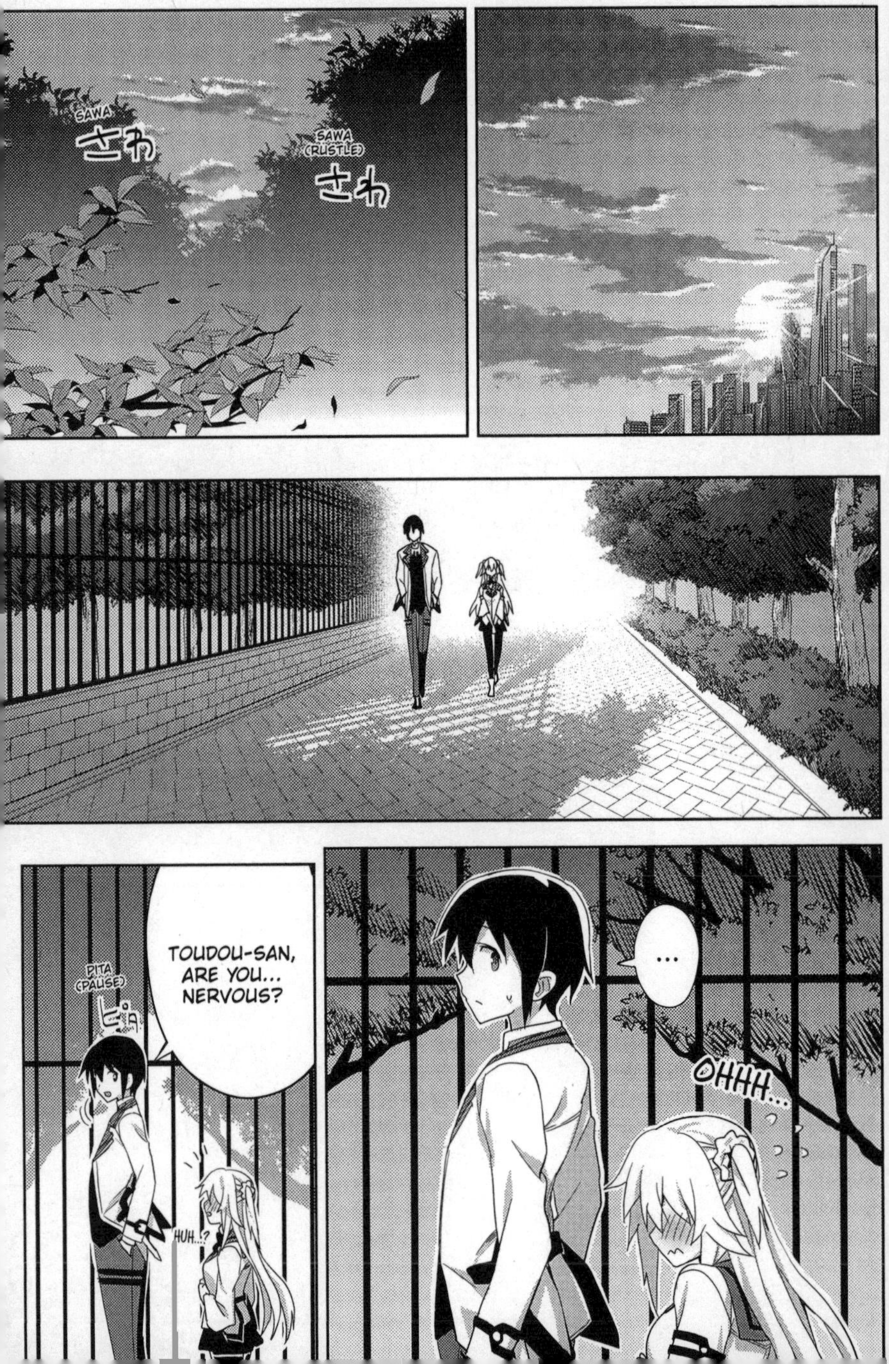
SAWA (RUSTLE)
さわ
SAWA
さわ
...
OHHH...
TOUDOU-SAN, ARE YOU... NERVOUS?
PITA (PAUSE)
ピタ
HUH...?

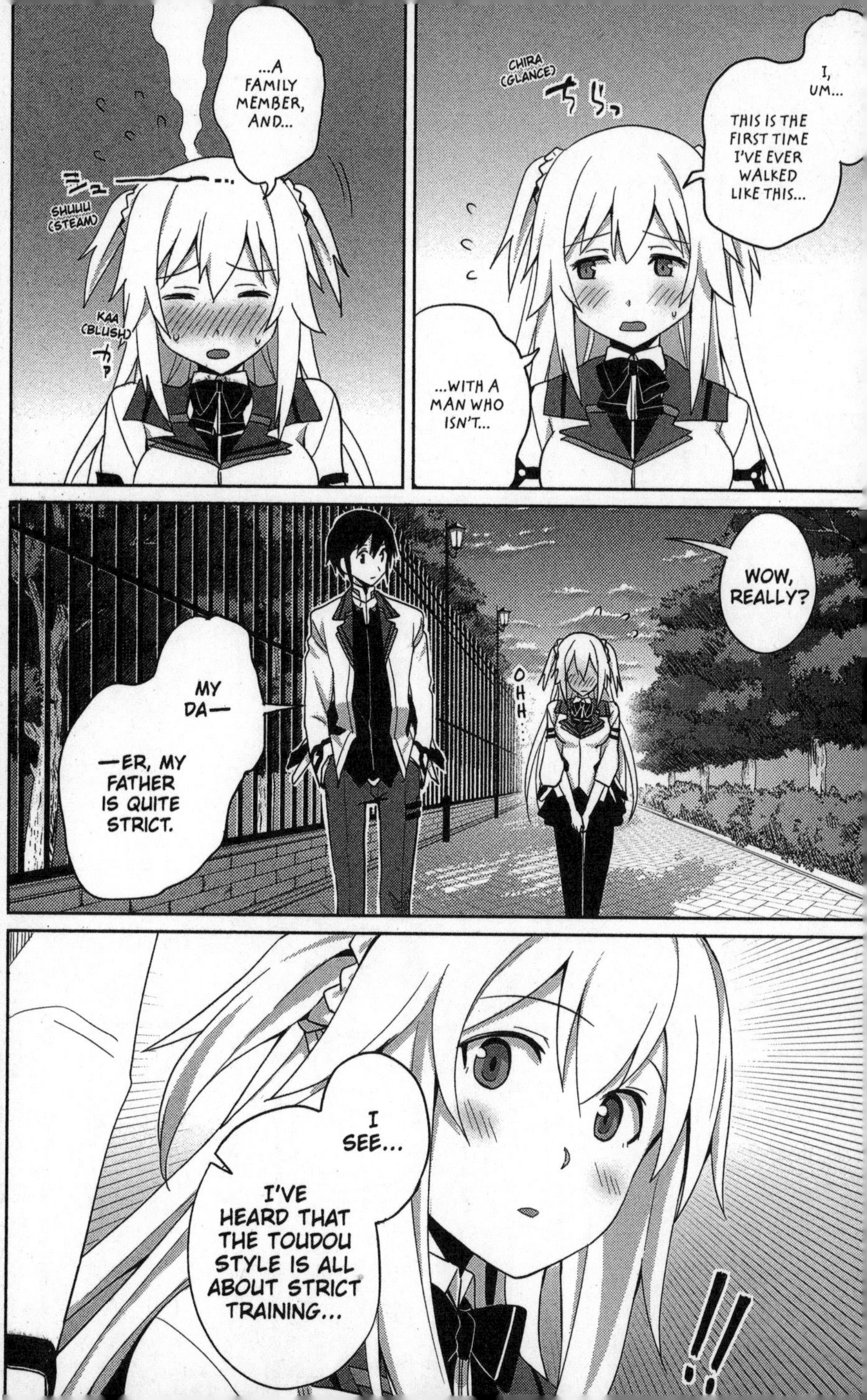
CHIRA (GLANCE)
ちらっ
I, UM...
THIS IS THE FIRST TIME I'VE EVER WALKED LIKE THIS...
...WITH A MAN WHO ISN'T...
...A FAMILY MEMBER, AND...
SHUUU (STEAM)
KAA (BLUSH)
WOW, REALLY?
OHH
MY DA—
—ER, MY FATHER IS QUITE STRICT.
I SEE...
I'VE HEARD THAT THE TOUDOU STYLE IS ALL ABOUT STRICT TRAINING...
!!

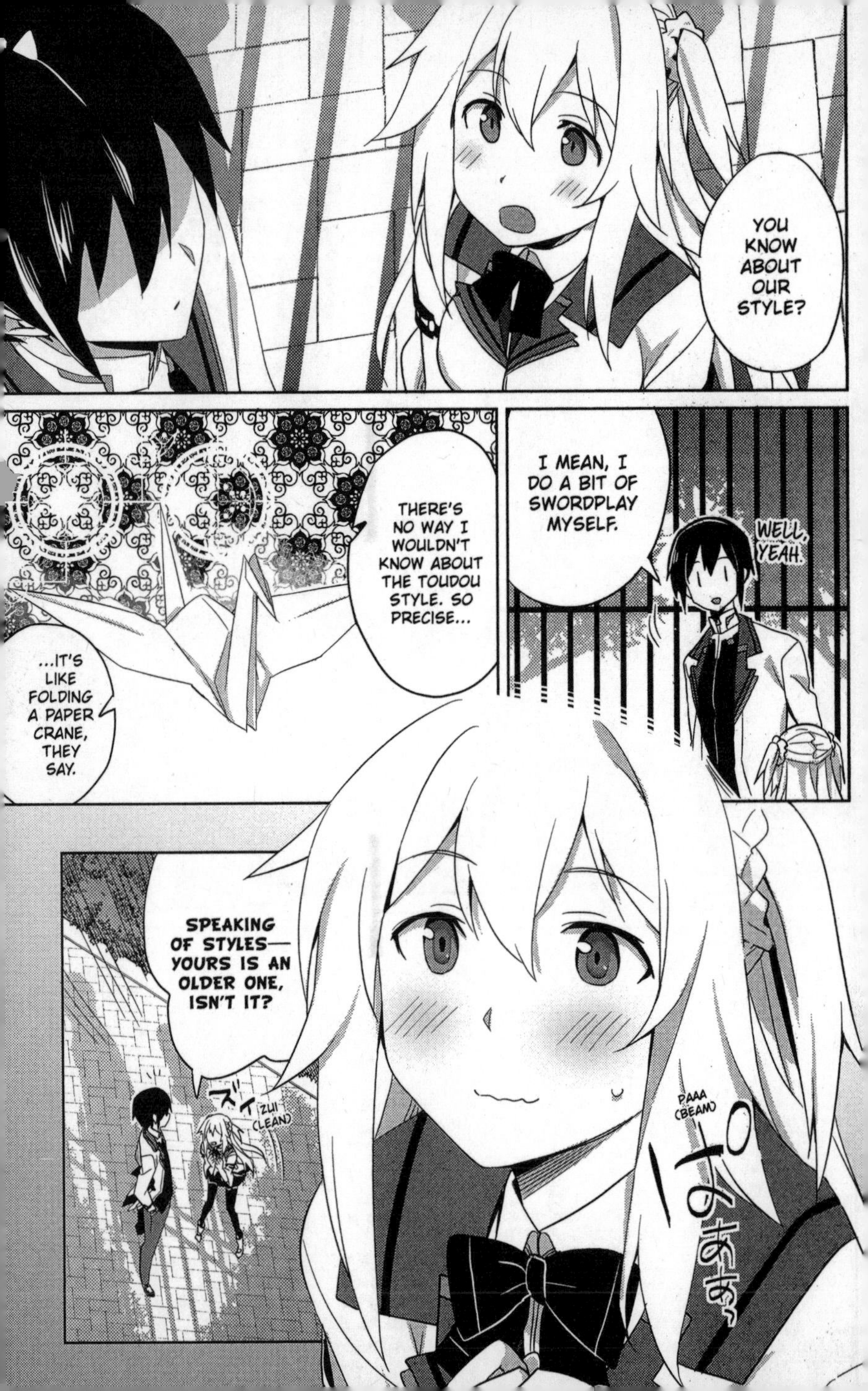
YOU KNOW ABOUT OUR STYLE?
I MEAN, I DO A BIT OF SWORDPLAY MYSELF.
WELL, YEAH.
THERE'S NO WAY I WOULDN'T KNOW ABOUT THE TOUDOU STYLE. SO PRECISE...
...IT'S LIKE FOLDING A PAPER CRANE, THEY SAY.
PAAA (BEAM)
SPEAKING OF STYLES— YOURS IS AN OLDER ONE, ISN'T IT?
ZUI (LEAN)

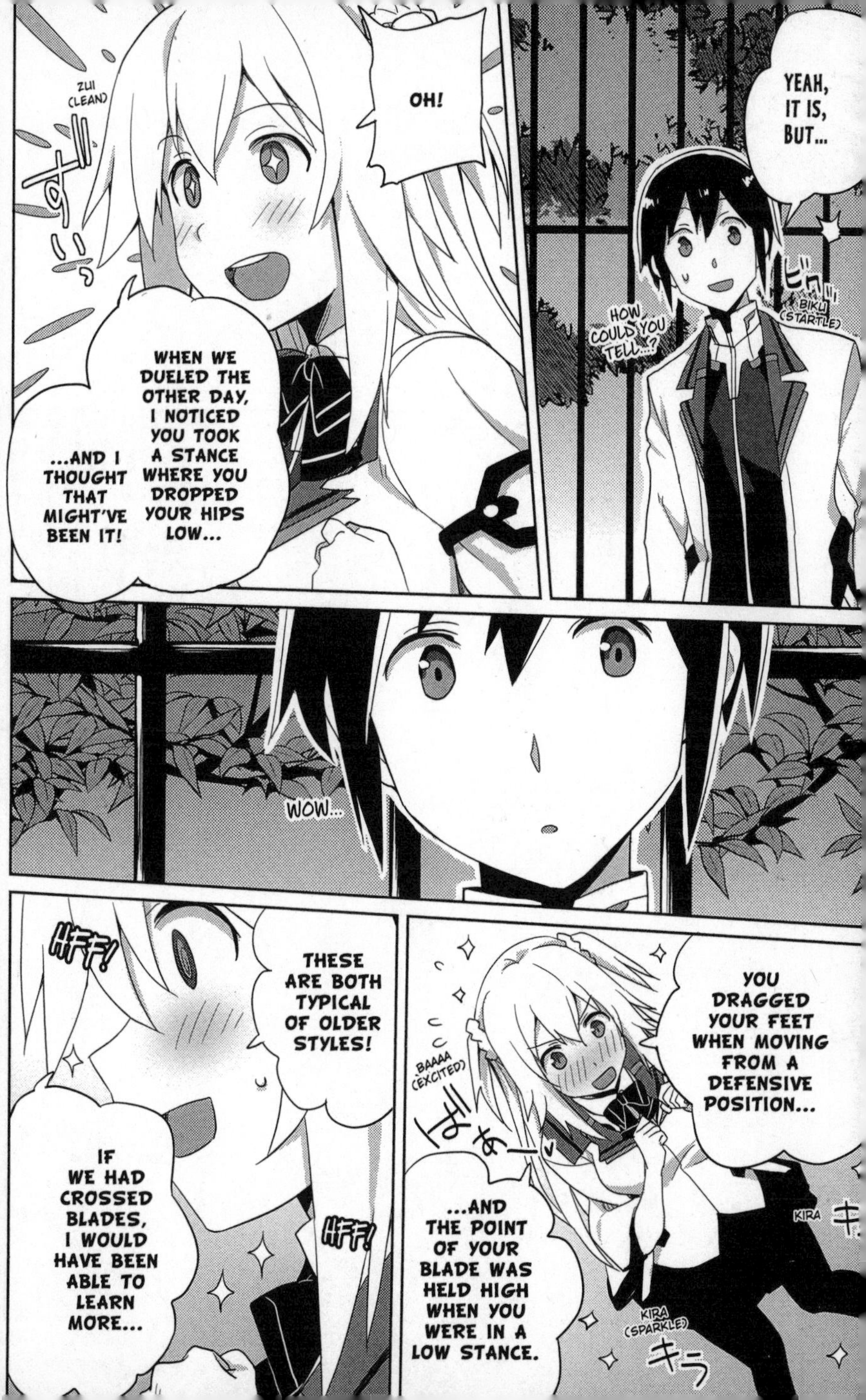
YEAH, IT IS, BUT...
BIKU (STARTLE)
HOW COULD YOU TELL...?
OH!
ZUI (LEAN)
WHEN WE DUELED THE OTHER DAY, I NOTICED YOU TOOK A STANCE WHERE YOU DROPPED YOUR HIPS LOW...
...AND I THOUGHT THAT MIGHT'VE BEEN IT!
WOW...
YOU DRAGGED YOUR FEET WHEN MOVING FROM A DEFENSIVE POSITION...
BAAAA (EXCITED)
KIRA
...AND THE POINT OF YOUR BLADE WAS HELD HIGH WHEN YOU WERE IN A LOW STANCE.
KIRA (SPARKLE)
HFF!
THESE ARE BOTH TYPICAL OF OLDER STYLES!
HFF!
IF WE HAD CROSSED BLADES, I WOULD HAVE BEEN ABLE TO LEARN MORE...

YOU KNOW ABOUT OUR STYLE?

THERE'S NO WAY I WOULDN'T KNOW ABOUT THE TOUDOU STYLE. SO PRECISE...

...IT'S LIKE FOLDING A PAPER CRANE, THEY SAY.

I MEAN, I DO A BIT OF SWORDPLAY MYSELF.

WELL, YEAH.

SPEAKING OF STYLES— YOURS IS AN OLDER ONE, ISN'T IT?

ズイ (ZUI) (CLEAN)

PAAA (BEAM)

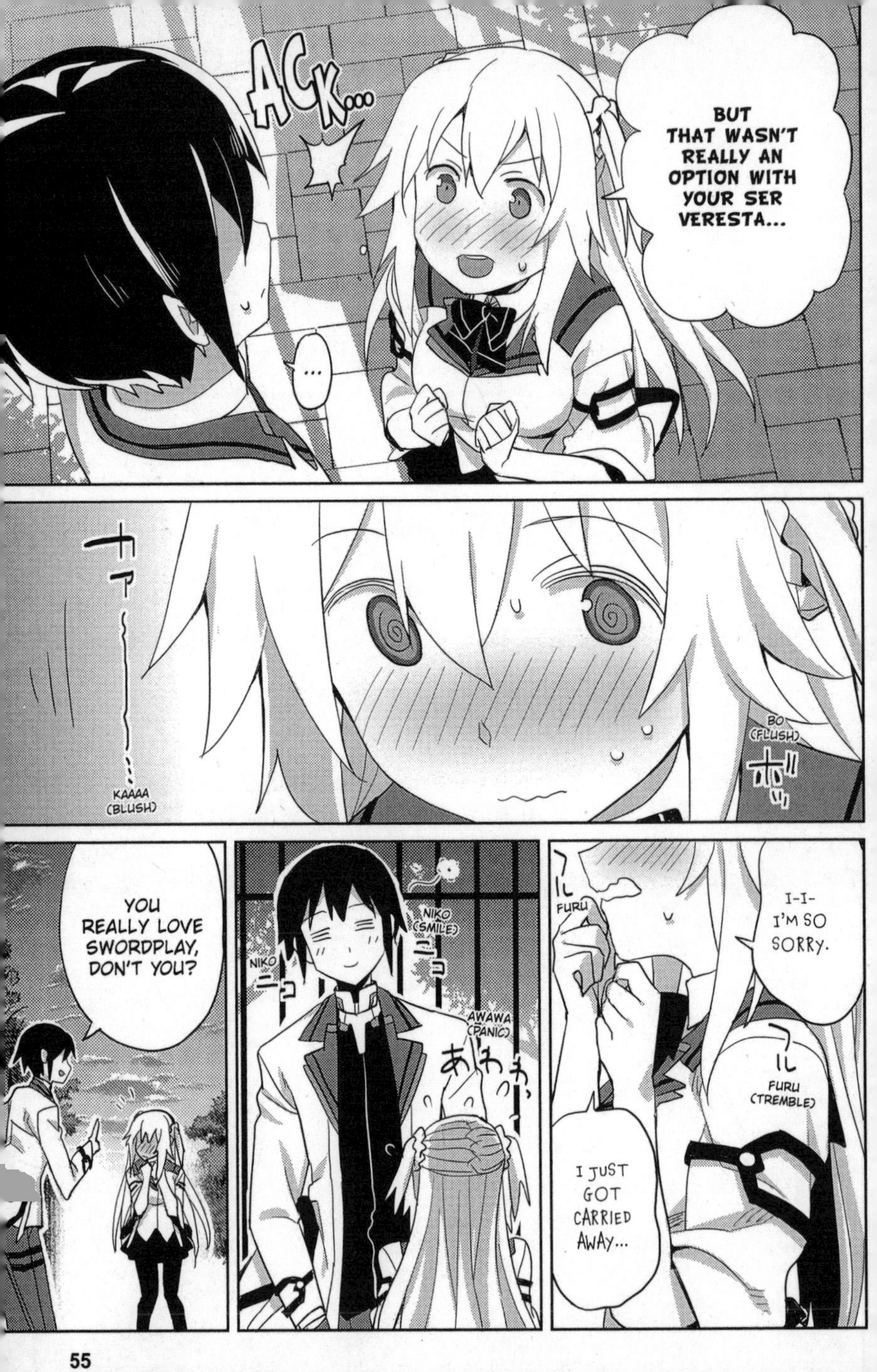
BUT THAT WASN'T REALLY AN OPTION WITH YOUR SER VERESTA...
ACK...
...
BO (FLUSH)
KAAAA (BLUSH)
I-I- I'M SO SORRY.
FURU
FURU (TREMBLE)
I JUST GOT CARRIED AWAY...
NIKO (SMILE)
NIKO
AWAWA (PANIC)
YOU REALLY LOVE SWORDPLAY, DON'T YOU?

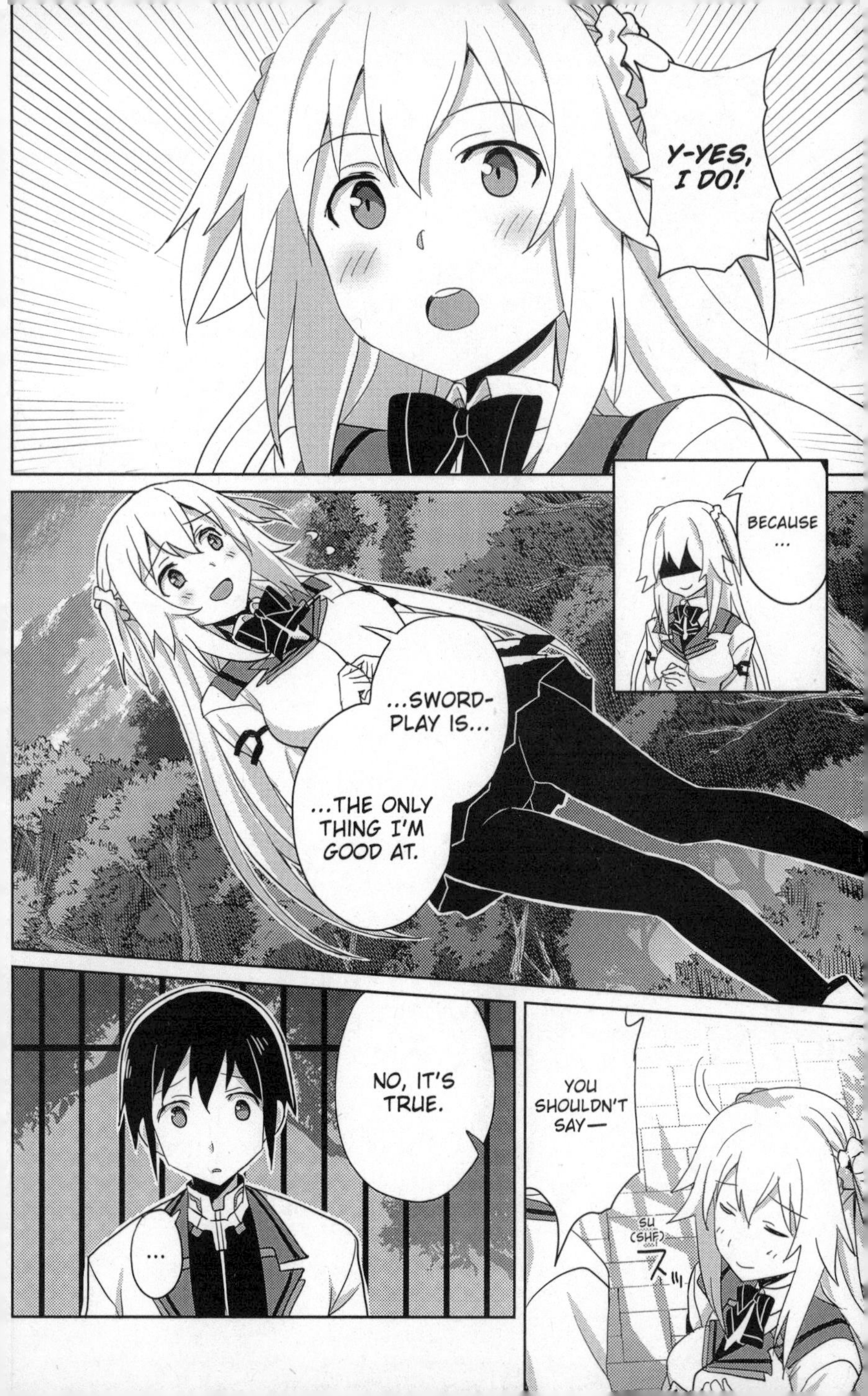
Y-YES, I DO!
BECAUSE...
...SWORD-PLAY IS...
...THE ONLY THING I'M GOOD AT.
YOU SHOULDN'T SAY—
SU (SHF)
NO, IT'S TRUE.
...

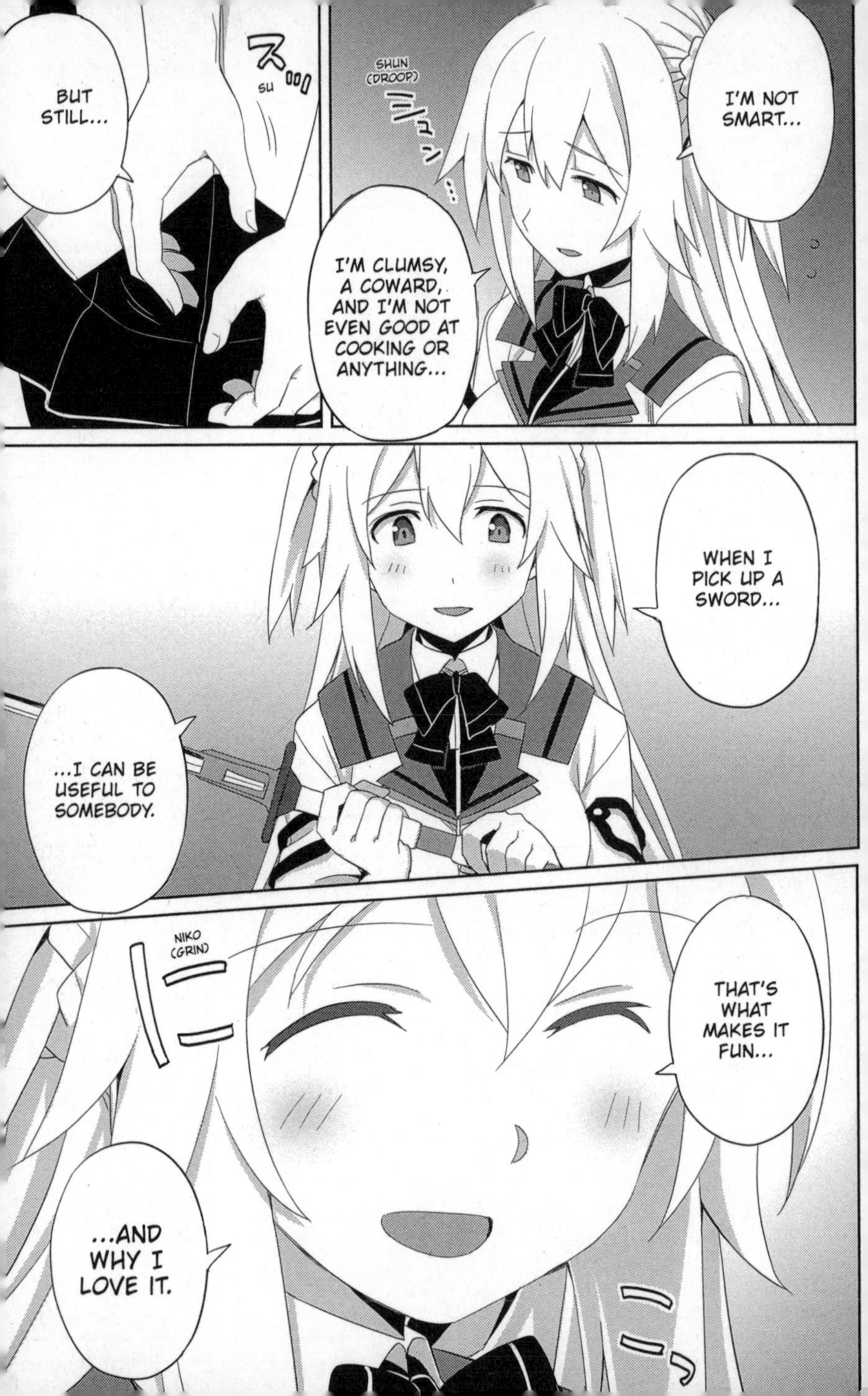
I'M NOT SMART...
SHUN (DROOP)
シュン…
I'M CLUMSY, A COWARD, AND I'M NOT EVEN GOOD AT COOKING OR ANYTHING...
ス
SU
BUT STILL...
WHEN I PICK UP A SWORD...
...I CAN BE USEFUL TO SOMEBODY.
THAT'S WHAT MAKES IT FUN...
NIKO (GRIN)
...AND WHY I LOVE IT.

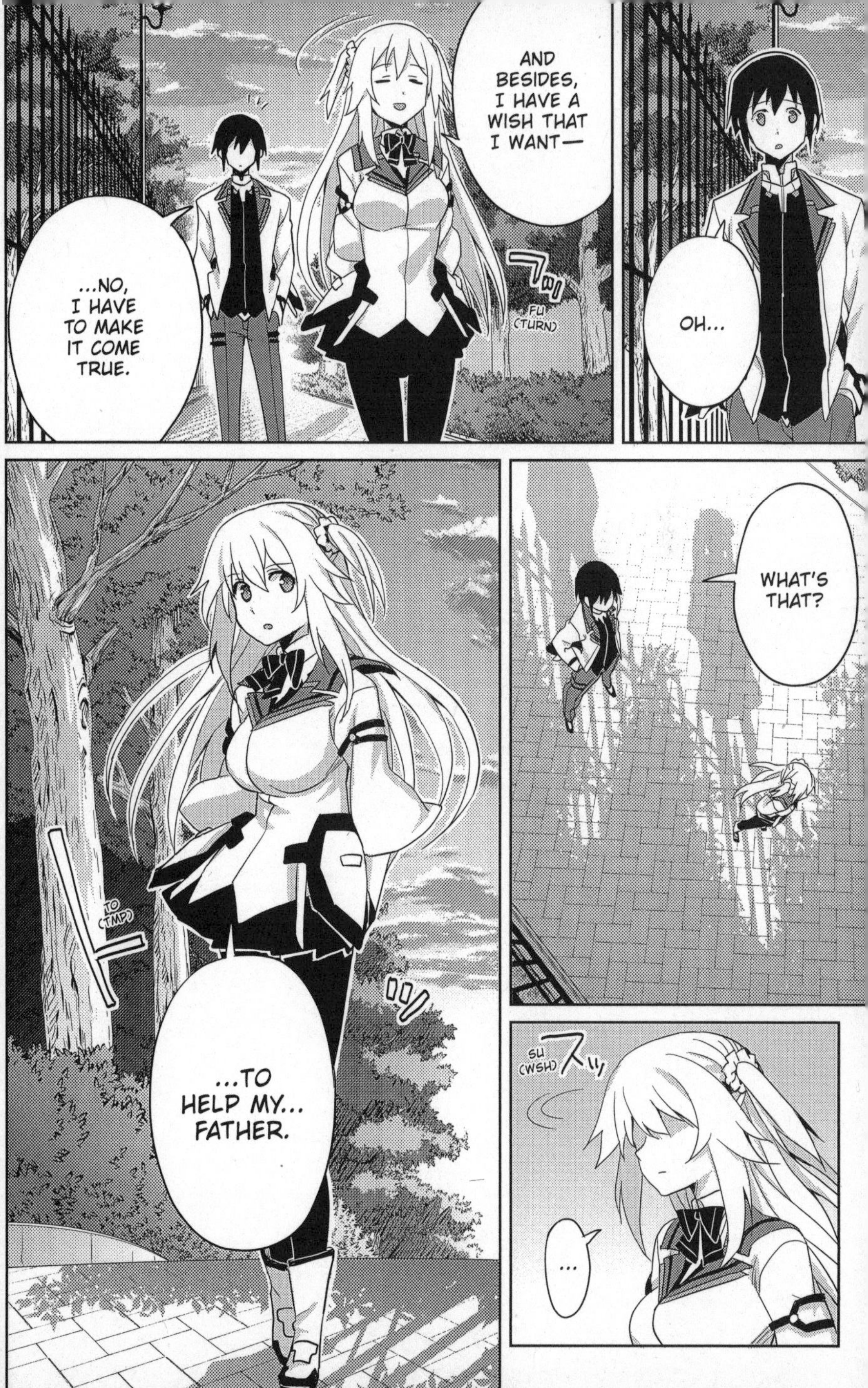
OH...
AND BESIDES, I HAVE A WISH THAT I WANT—
FU (TURN)
...NO, I HAVE TO MAKE IT COME TRUE.
WHAT'S THAT?
SU (WSH)
...
TO (TMP)
...TO HELP MY... FATHER.

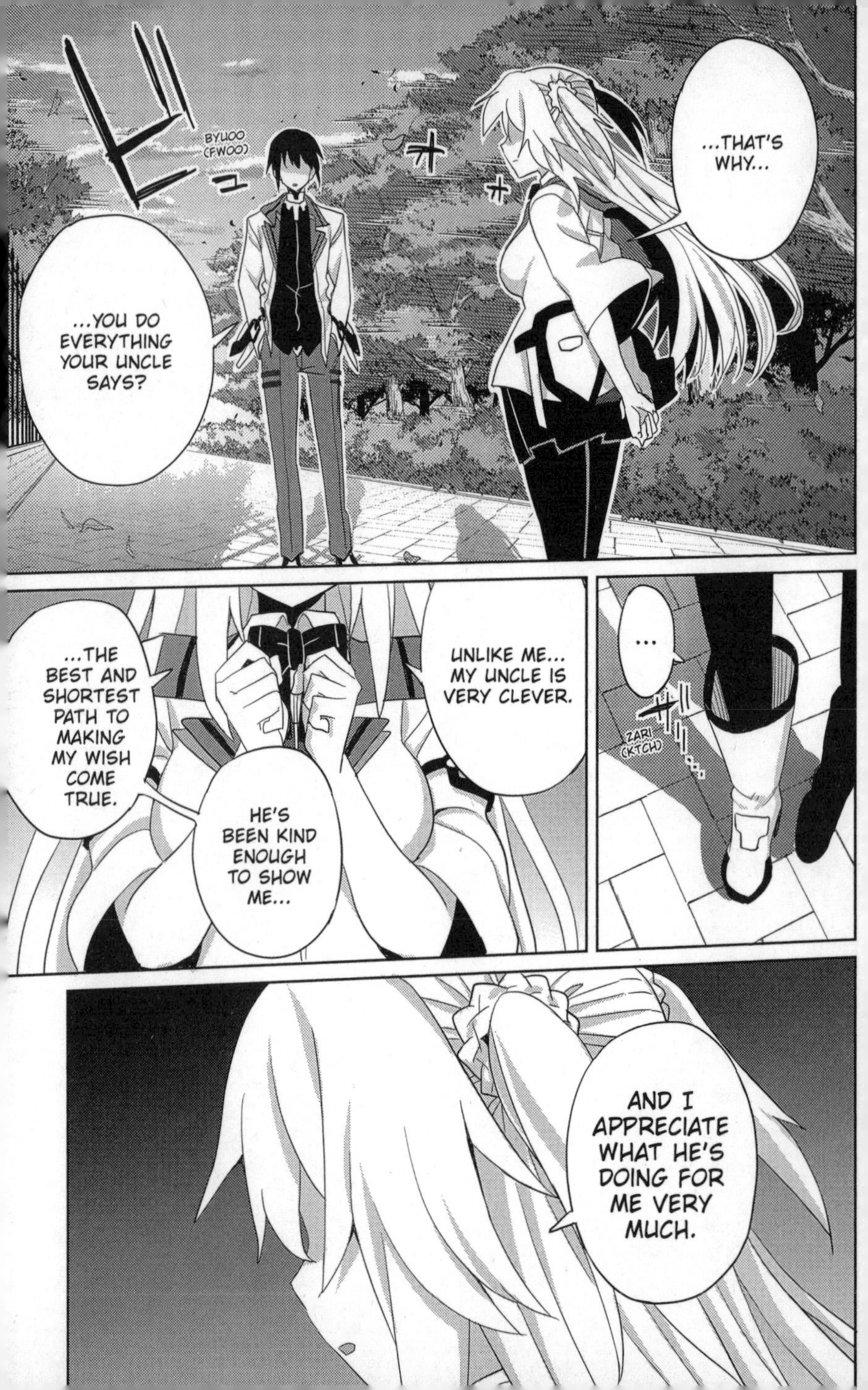
...THAT'S WHY...
BYUOO (FWOO)
...YOU DO EVERYTHING YOUR UNCLE SAYS?
...
ZARI (KTCH)
UNLIKE ME... MY UNCLE IS VERY CLEVER.
HE'S BEEN KIND ENOUGH TO SHOW ME...
...THE BEST AND SHORTEST PATH TO MAKING MY WISH COME TRUE.
AND I APPRECIATE WHAT HE'S DOING FOR ME VERY MUCH.

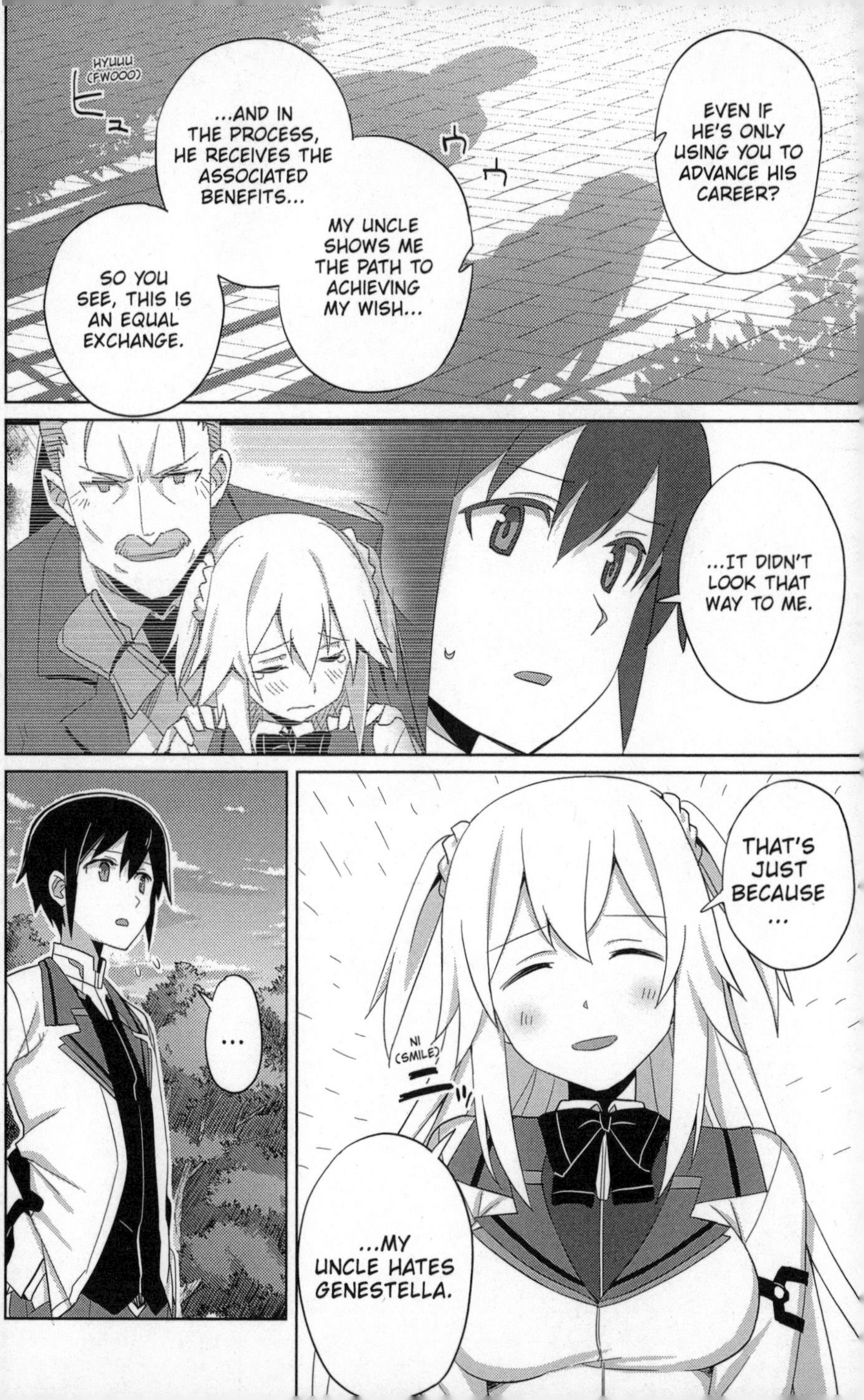
EVEN IF HE'S ONLY USING YOU TO ADVANCE HIS CAREER?
MY UNCLE SHOWS ME THE PATH TO ACHIEVING MY WISH...
...AND IN THE PROCESS, HE RECEIVES THE ASSOCIATED BENEFITS...
HYUUU (FWOOO)
SO YOU SEE, THIS IS AN EQUAL EXCHANGE.
...IT DIDN'T LOOK THAT WAY TO ME.
THAT'S JUST BECAUSE ...
NI (SMILE)
...MY UNCLE HATES GENESTELLA.
...

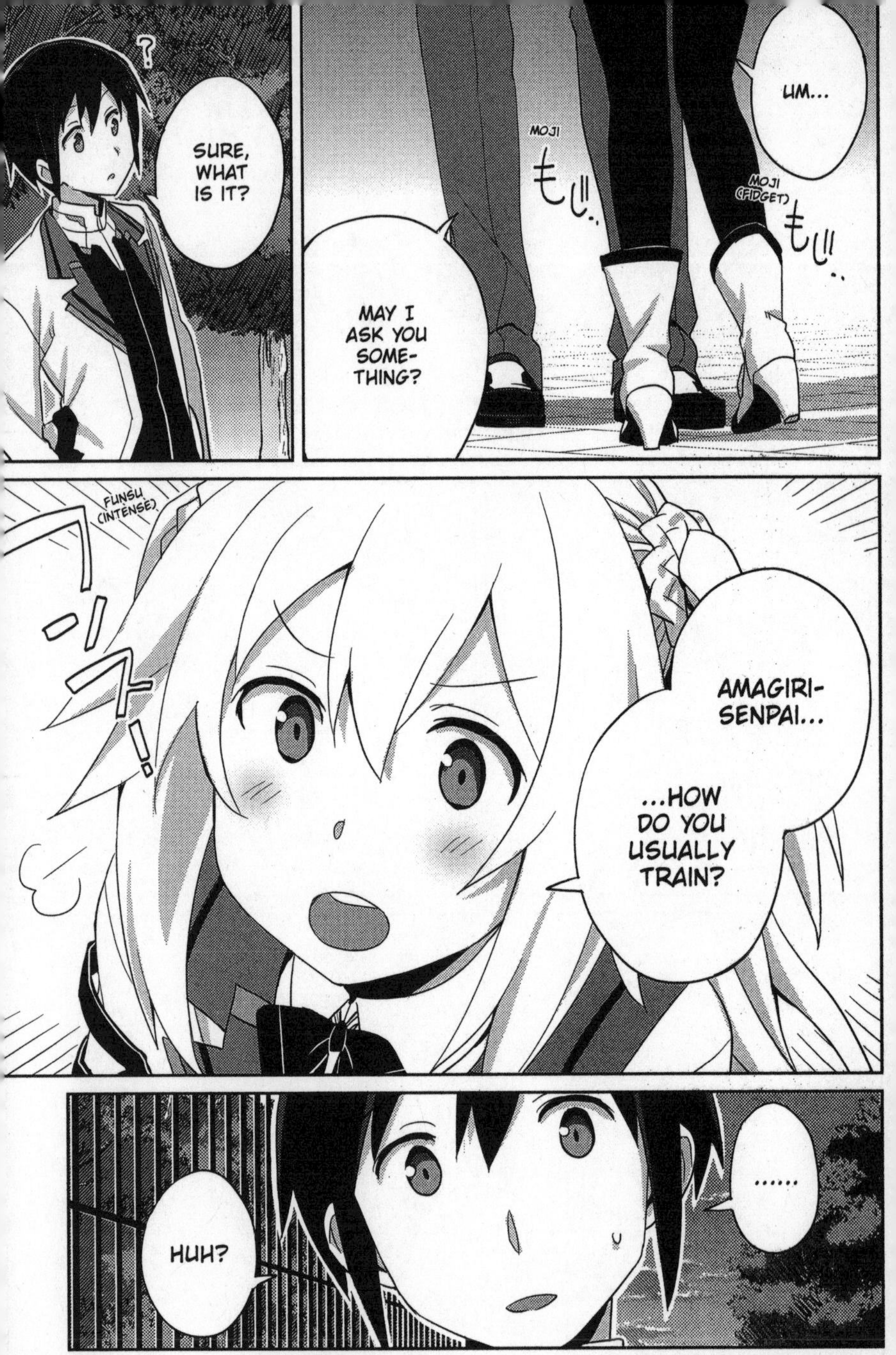
UM...
MOJI (FIDGET)
もじ..
MOJI
もじ..
MAY I ASK YOU SOME-THING?
?
SURE, WHAT IS IT?
AMAGIRI-SENPAI...
...HOW DO YOU USUALLY TRAIN?
FUNSU (INTENSE)
フンス!
......
HUH?

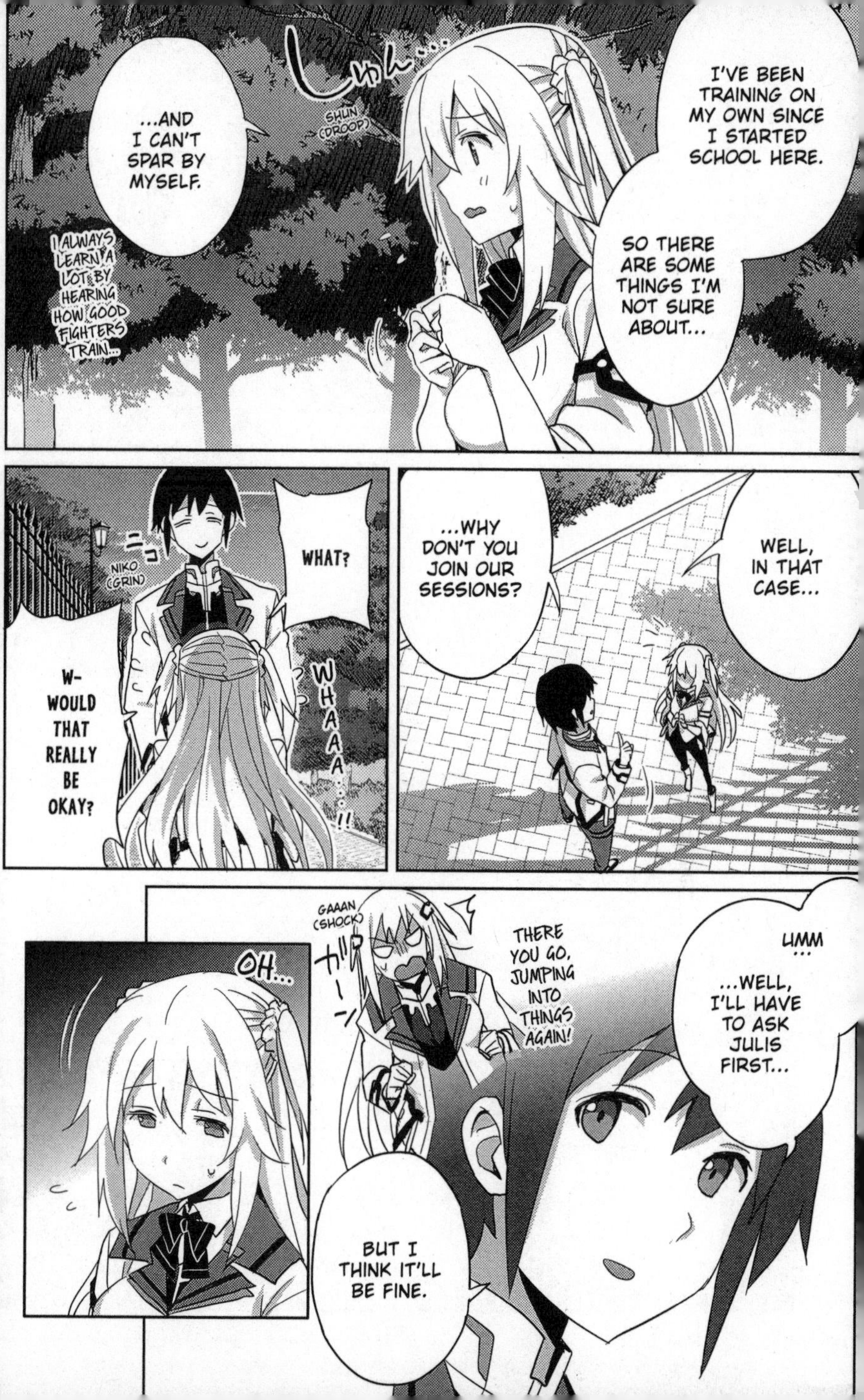
I'VE BEEN TRAINING ON MY OWN SINCE I STARTED SCHOOL HERE.
SO THERE ARE SOME THINGS I'M NOT SURE ABOUT...
しゅん...
SHUN (DROOP)
...AND I CAN'T SPAR BY MYSELF.
I ALWAYS LEARN A LOT BY HEARING HOW GOOD FIGHTERS TRAIN...
WELL, IN THAT CASE...
...WHY DON'T YOU JOIN OUR SESSIONS?
WHAT?
NIKO (GRIN)
W-WOULD THAT REALLY BE OKAY?
WHAAAA...!!
UMM...
...WELL, I'LL HAVE TO ASK JULIS FIRST...
BUT I THINK IT'LL BE FINE.
GAAAN (SHOCK)
THERE YOU GO, JUMPING INTO THINGS AGAIN!
OH...

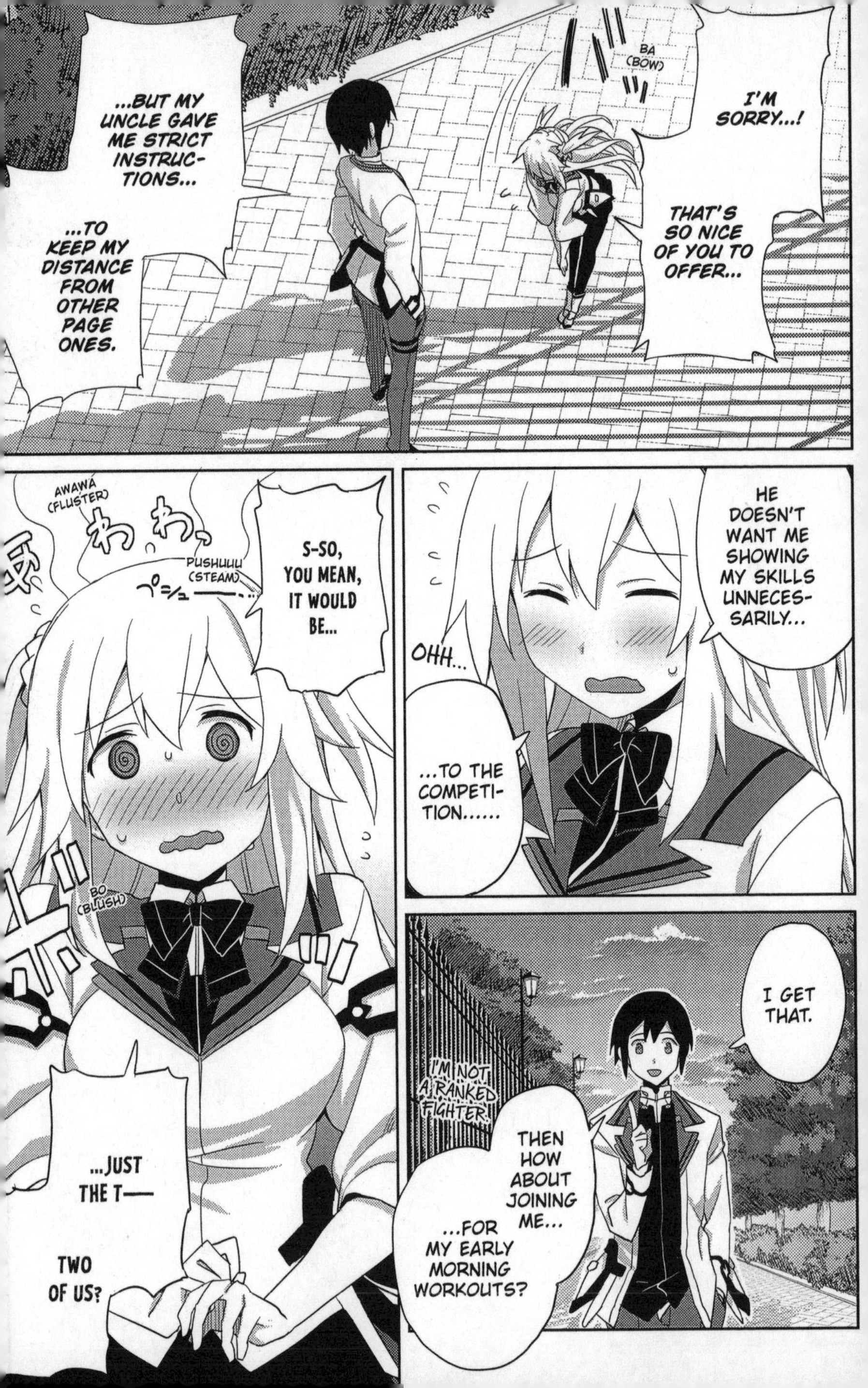
BA (BOW)
I'M SORRY...!
THAT'S SO NICE OF YOU TO OFFER...
...BUT MY UNCLE GAVE ME STRICT INSTRUCTIONS...
...TO KEEP MY DISTANCE FROM OTHER PAGE ONES.
HE DOESN'T WANT ME SHOWING MY SKILLS UNNECESSARILY...
OHH...
...TO THE COMPETITION......
I GET THAT.
I'M NOT A RANKED FIGHTER.
THEN HOW ABOUT JOINING ME...
...FOR MY EARLY MORNING WORKOUTS?
AWAWA (FLUSTER)
PUSHUUU (STEAM)
S-SO, YOU MEAN, IT WOULD BE...
BO (BLUSH)
...JUST THE T—
TWO OF US?

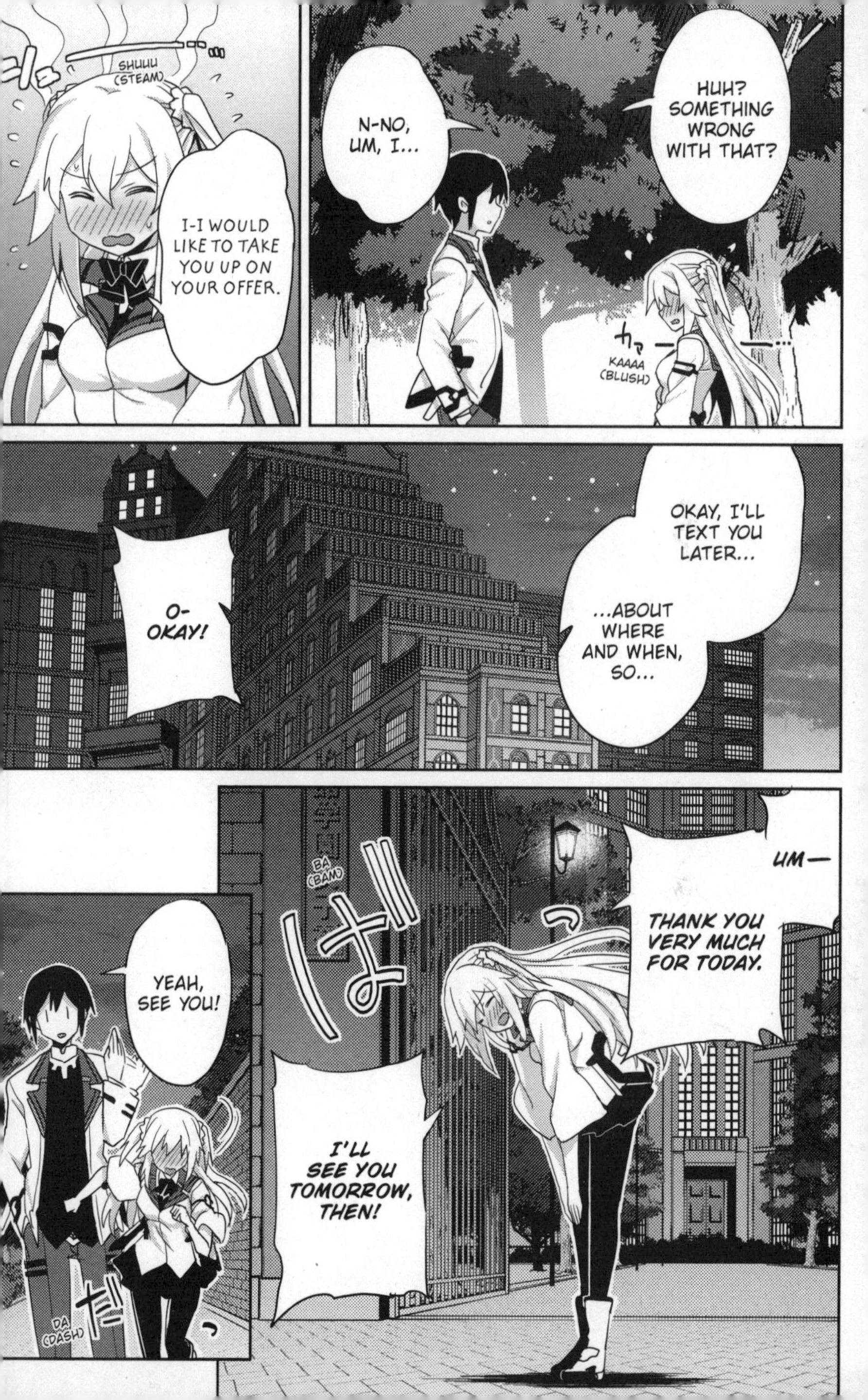
HUH? SOMETHING WRONG WITH THAT?
N-NO, UM, I...
KAAAA (BLUSH)
SHUUU (STEAM)
I-I WOULD LIKE TO TAKE YOU UP ON YOUR OFFER.
OKAY, I'LL TEXT YOU LATER...
...ABOUT WHERE AND WHEN, SO...
O-OKAY!
UM—
THANK YOU VERY MUCH FOR TODAY.
BA (BAM)
I'LL SEE YOU TOMORROW, THEN!
YEAH, SEE YOU!
DA (DASH)

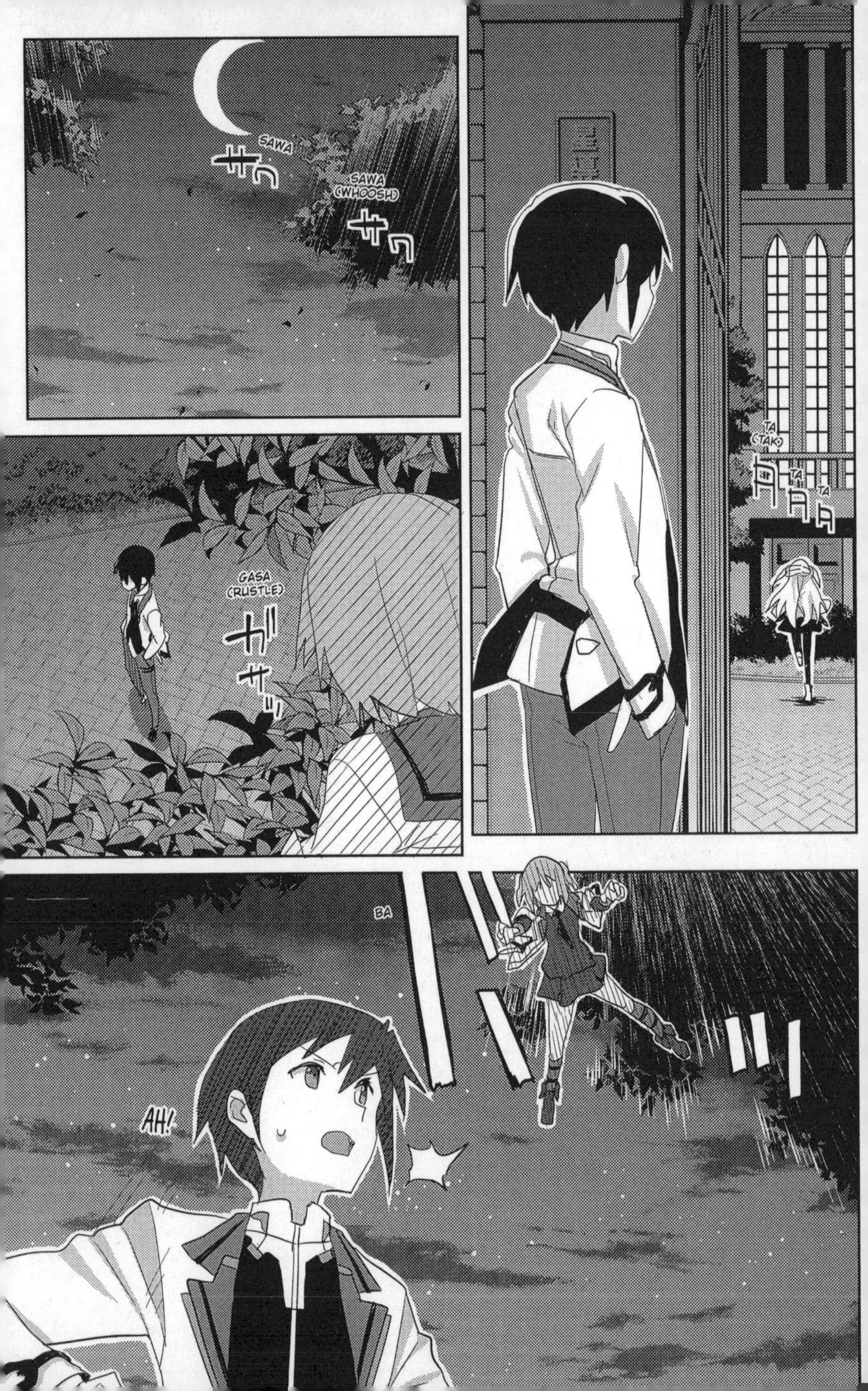
TA (TAK)
TA
TA
SAWA
SAWA (WHOOSH)
GASA (RUSTLE)
BA
AH!

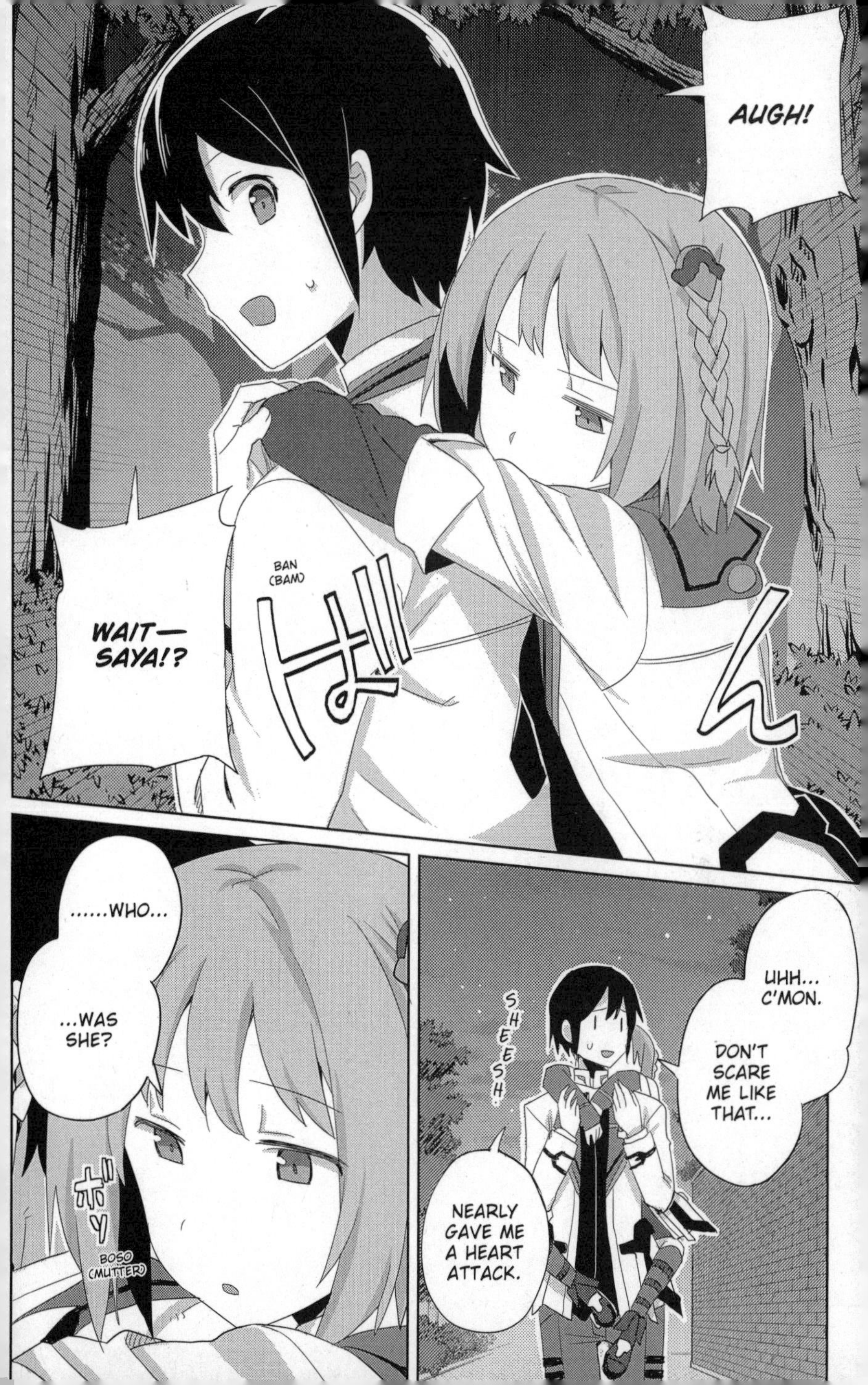
AUGH!
BAN (BAM)
WAIT— SAYA!?
UHH... C'MON.
DON'T SCARE ME LIKE THAT...
SHEESH.
NEARLY GAVE ME A HEART ATTACK.
......WHO...
...WAS SHE?
BOSO (MUTTER)

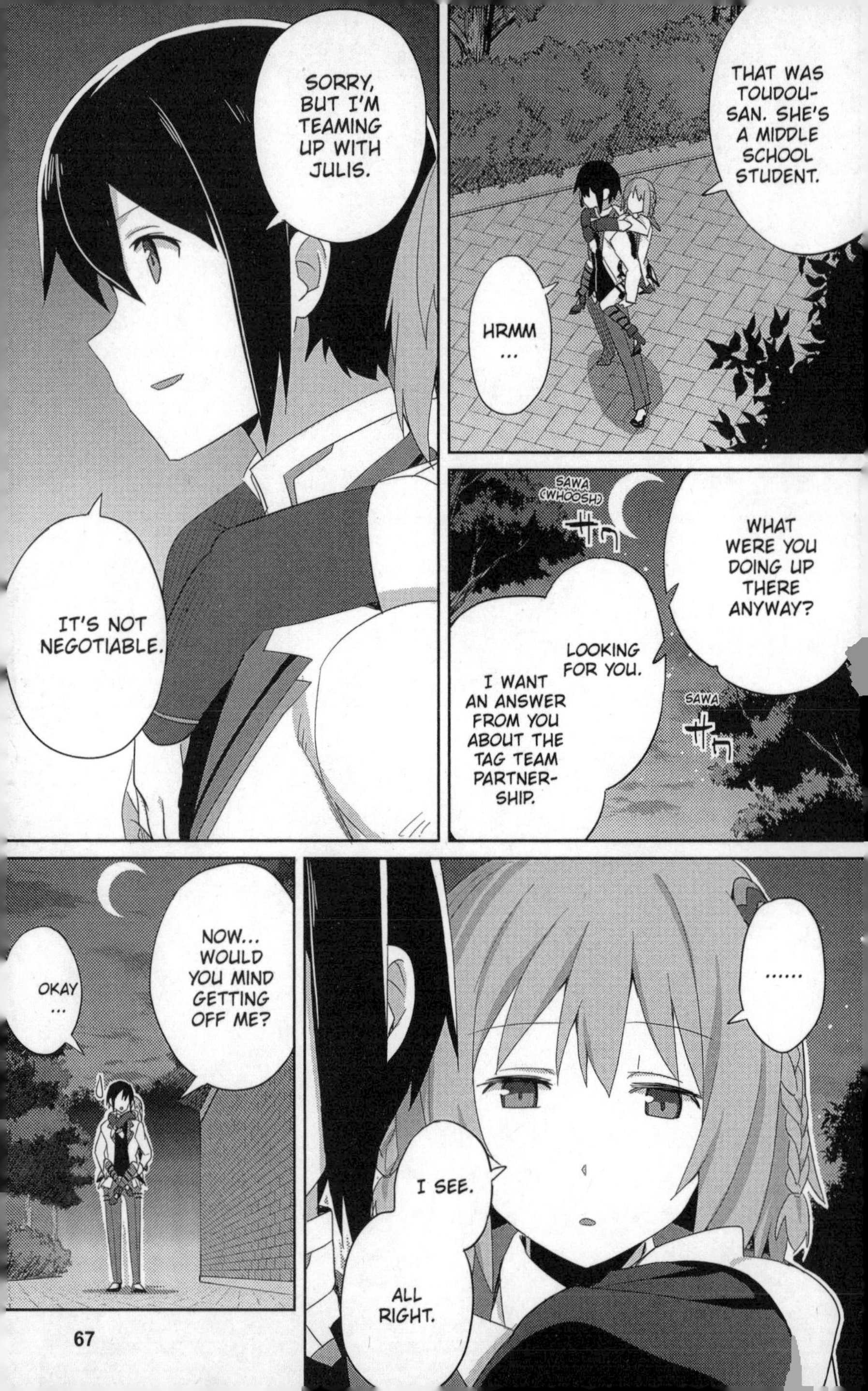
THAT WAS TOUDOU-SAN. SHE'S A MIDDLE SCHOOL STUDENT.
HRMM...
SAWA (WHOOSH)
WHAT WERE YOU DOING UP THERE ANYWAY?
LOOKING FOR YOU.
I WANT AN ANSWER FROM YOU ABOUT THE TAG TEAM PARTNER-SHIP.
SAWA
SORRY, BUT I'M TEAMING UP WITH JULIS.
IT'S NOT NEGOTIABLE.
......
I SEE.
ALL RIGHT.
NOW... WOULD YOU MIND GETTING OFF ME?
OKAY...

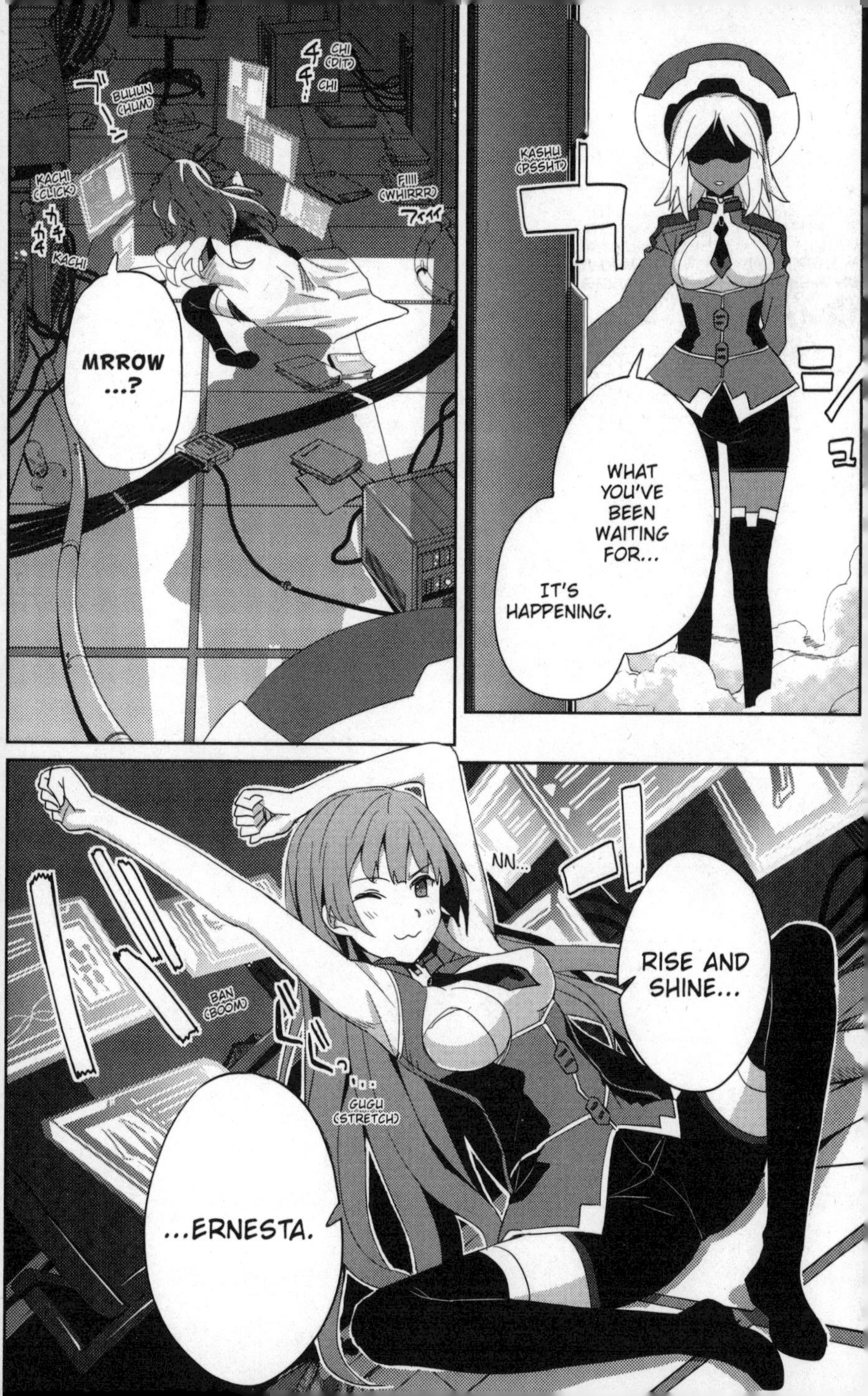

KASHU (PSSHT)
WHAT YOU'VE BEEN WAITING FOR...
IT'S HAPPENING.
BUUUN (HUM)
CHI (DIT)
CHI
KACHI (CLICK)
KACHI
FIII (WHIRRR)
MRROW ...?
NN...
RISE AND SHINE...
BAN (BOOM)
GUGU (STRETCH)
...ERNESTA.

THE
ASTERISK WAR

KAAAA
(BLUSH)

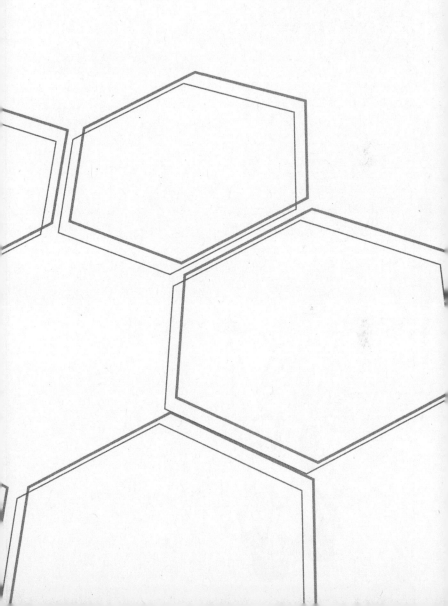

THE
ASTERISK WAR

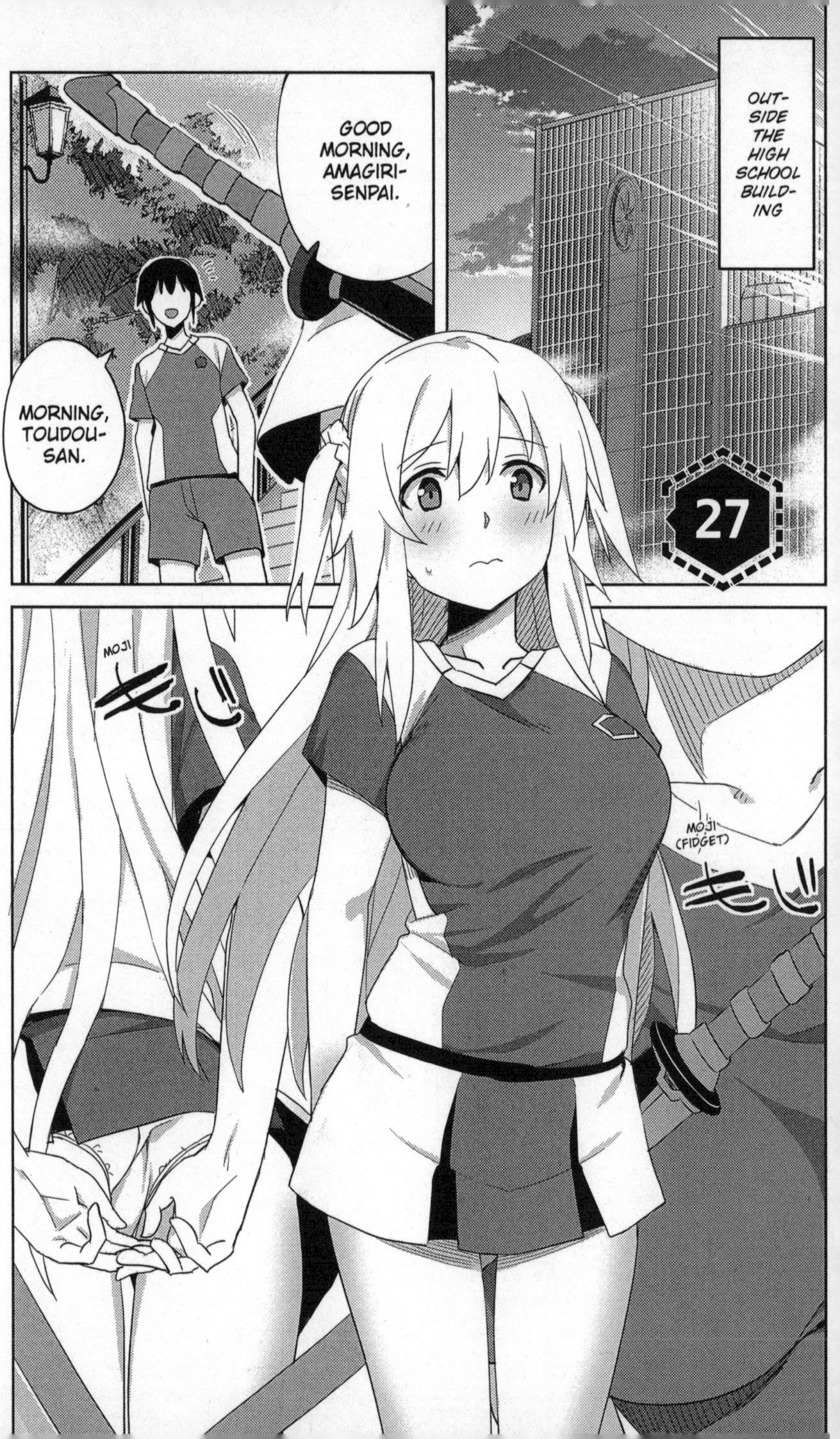

OUT-SIDE THE HIGH SCHOOL BUILD-ING
27
GOOD MORNING, AMAGIRI-SENPAI.
MORNING, TOUDOU-SAN.
MOJI (FIDGET)
もじ
MOJI
もじ

OKAY, SO LET'S START WITH A RUN......

OH, ACTUALLY WE SHOULD STRETCH FIRST.

RIGHT!

GUGUUU (STREEETCH)

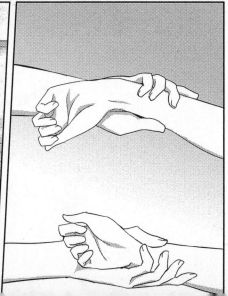

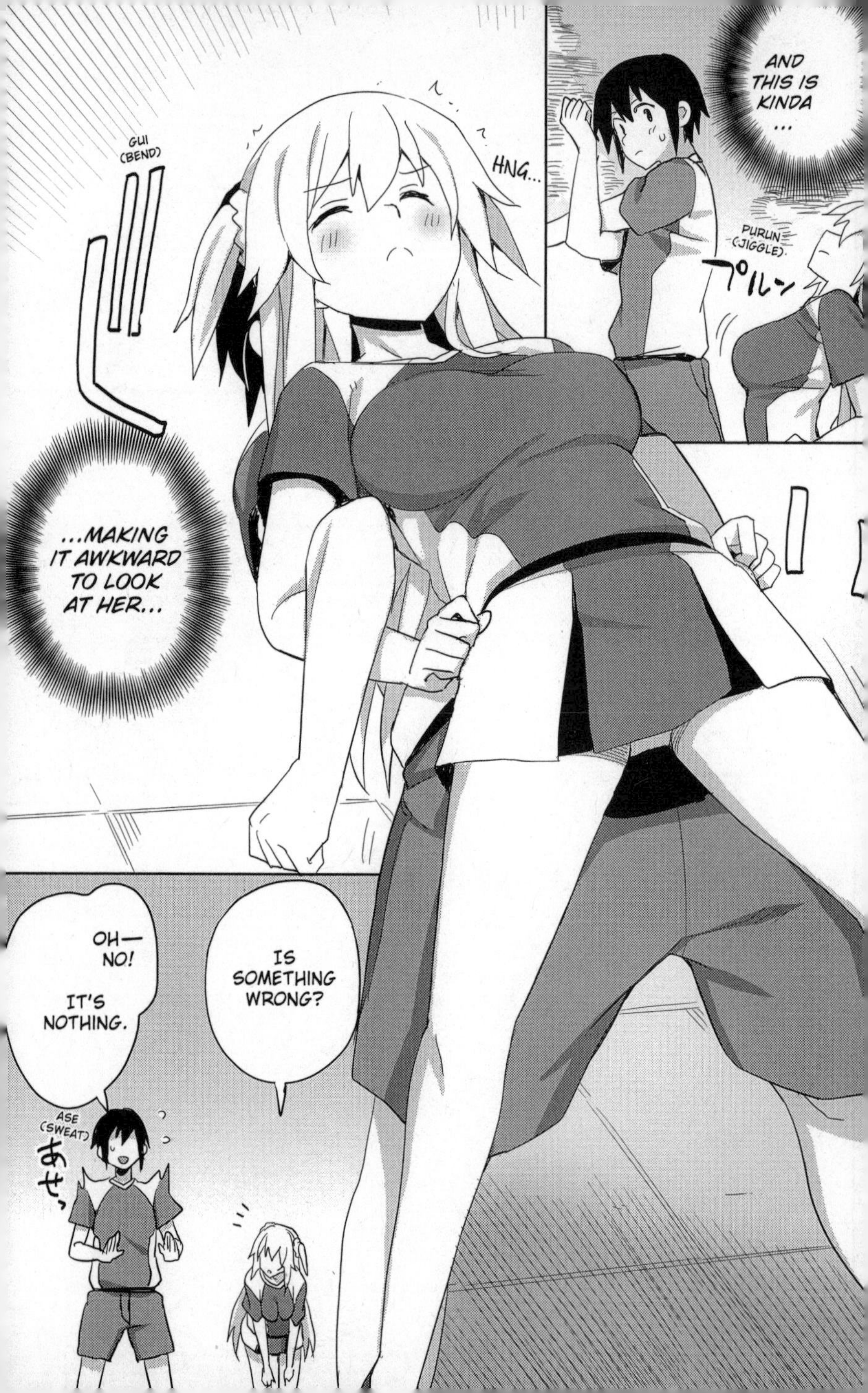
AND THIS IS KINDA ...
PURUN (JIGGLE)
プルン
HNG...
GUI (BEND)
...MAKING IT AWKWARD TO LOOK AT HER...
IS SOMETHING WRONG?
OH—NO!
IT'S NOTHING.
ASE (SWEAT)
あせ

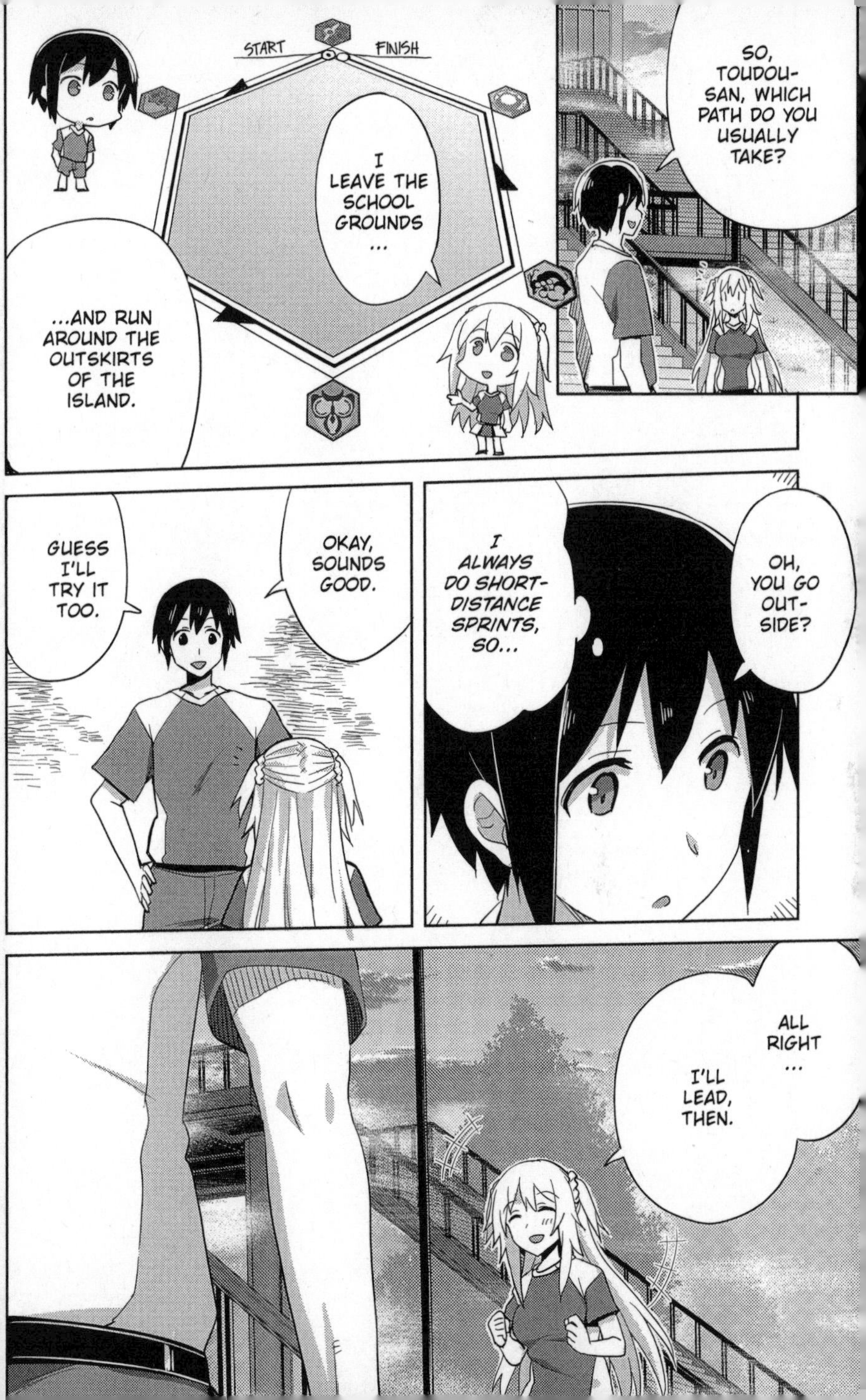
SO, TOUDOU-SAN, WHICH PATH DO YOU USUALLY TAKE?
START
FINISH
I LEAVE THE SCHOOL GROUNDS...
...AND RUN AROUND THE OUTSKIRTS OF THE ISLAND.
OH, YOU GO OUT-SIDE?
I ALWAYS DO SHORT-DISTANCE SPRINTS, SO...
OKAY, SOUNDS GOOD.
GUESS I'LL TRY IT TOO.
ALL RIGHT...
I'LL LEAD, THEN.

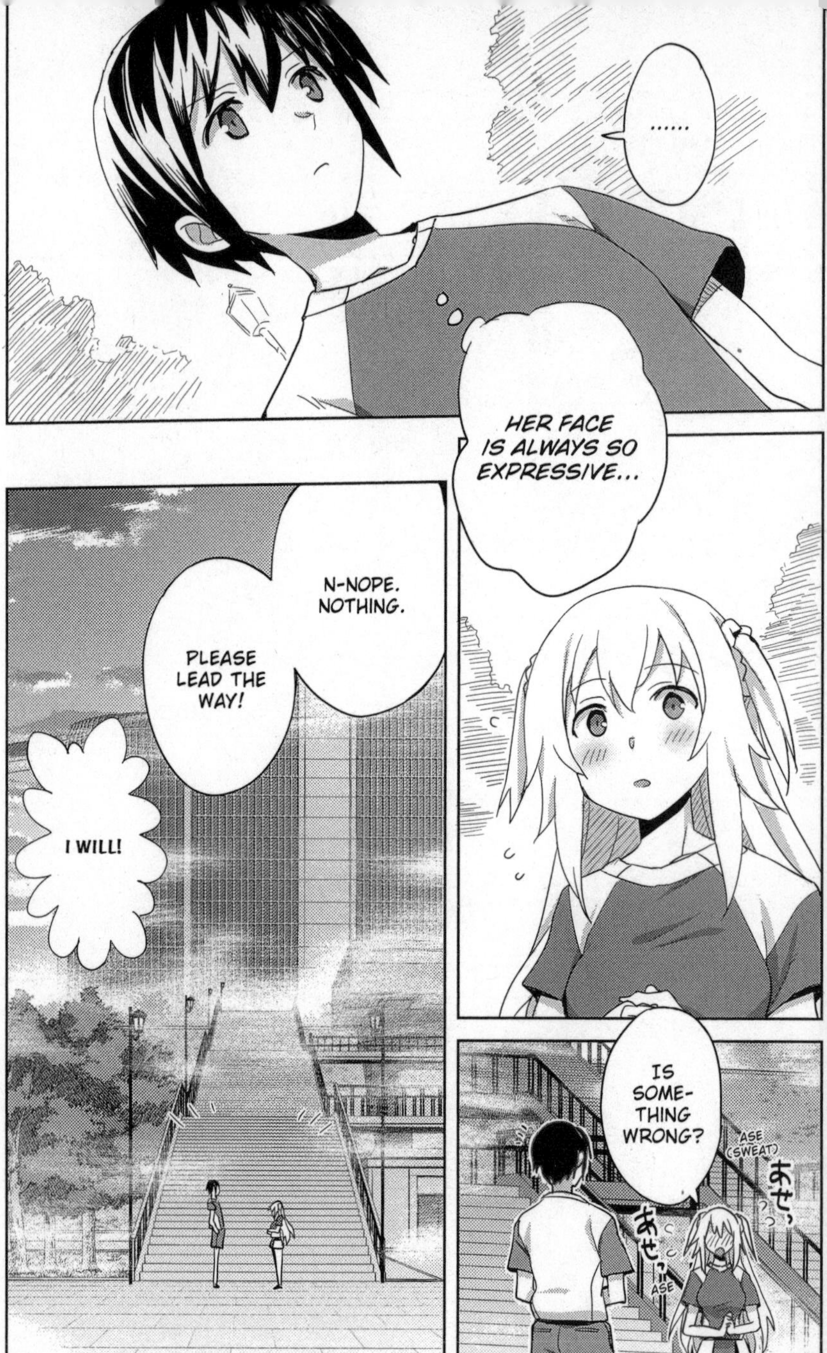
......
HER FACE IS ALWAYS SO EXPRESSIVE...
IS SOME-THING WRONG?
ASE (SWEAT)
あせ
あせ
ASE
N-NOPE. NOTHING.
PLEASE LEAD THE WAY!
I WILL!

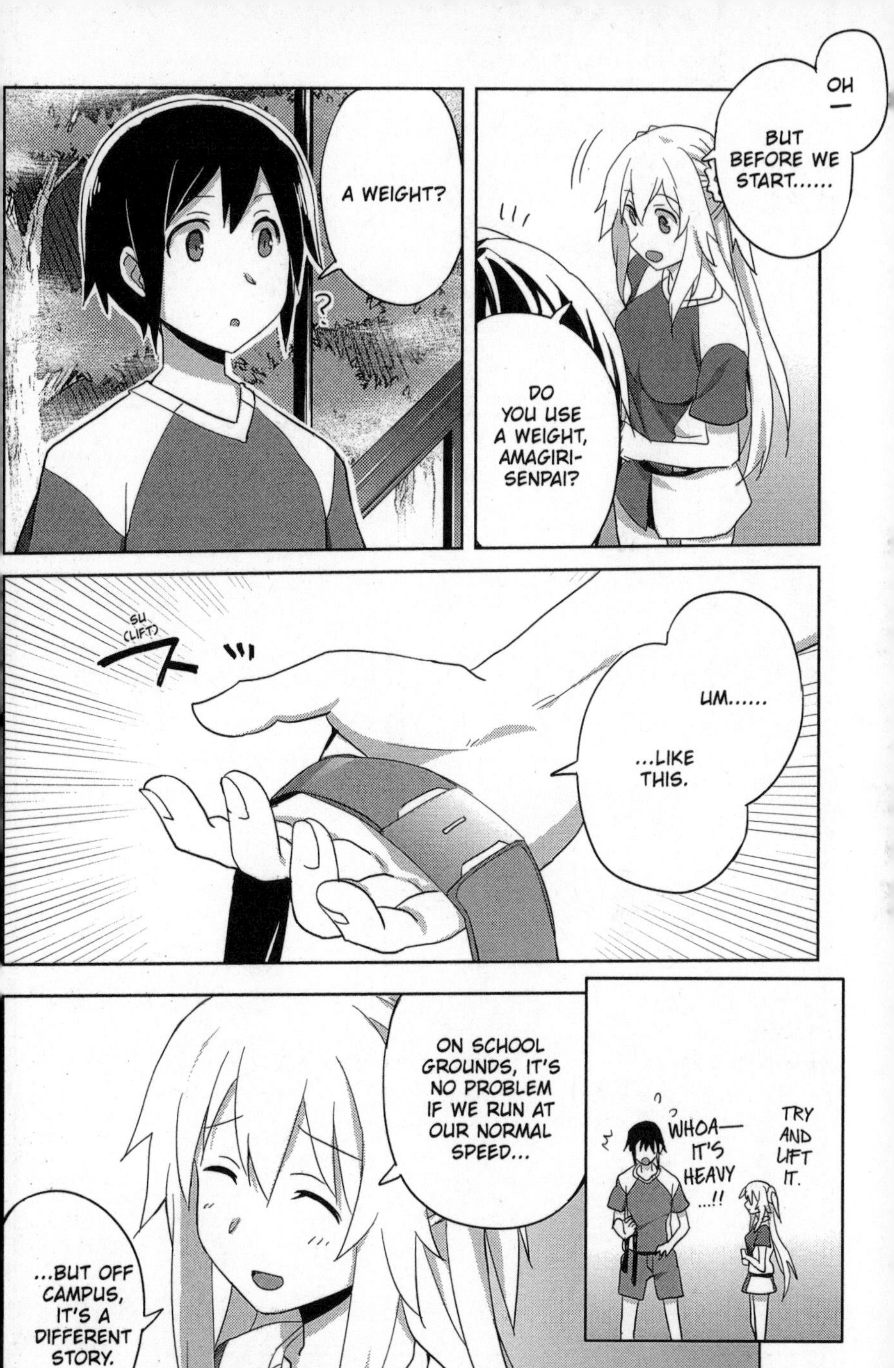

OH— BUT BEFORE WE START......
DO YOU USE A WEIGHT, AMAGIRI-SENPAI?
A WEIGHT?
SU (LIFT)
UM...... ...LIKE THIS.
TRY AND LIFT IT.
WHOA— IT'S HEAVY ...!!
ON SCHOOL GROUNDS, IT'S NO PROBLEM IF WE RUN AT OUR NORMAL SPEED...
...BUT OFF CAMPUS, IT'S A DIFFERENT STORY.

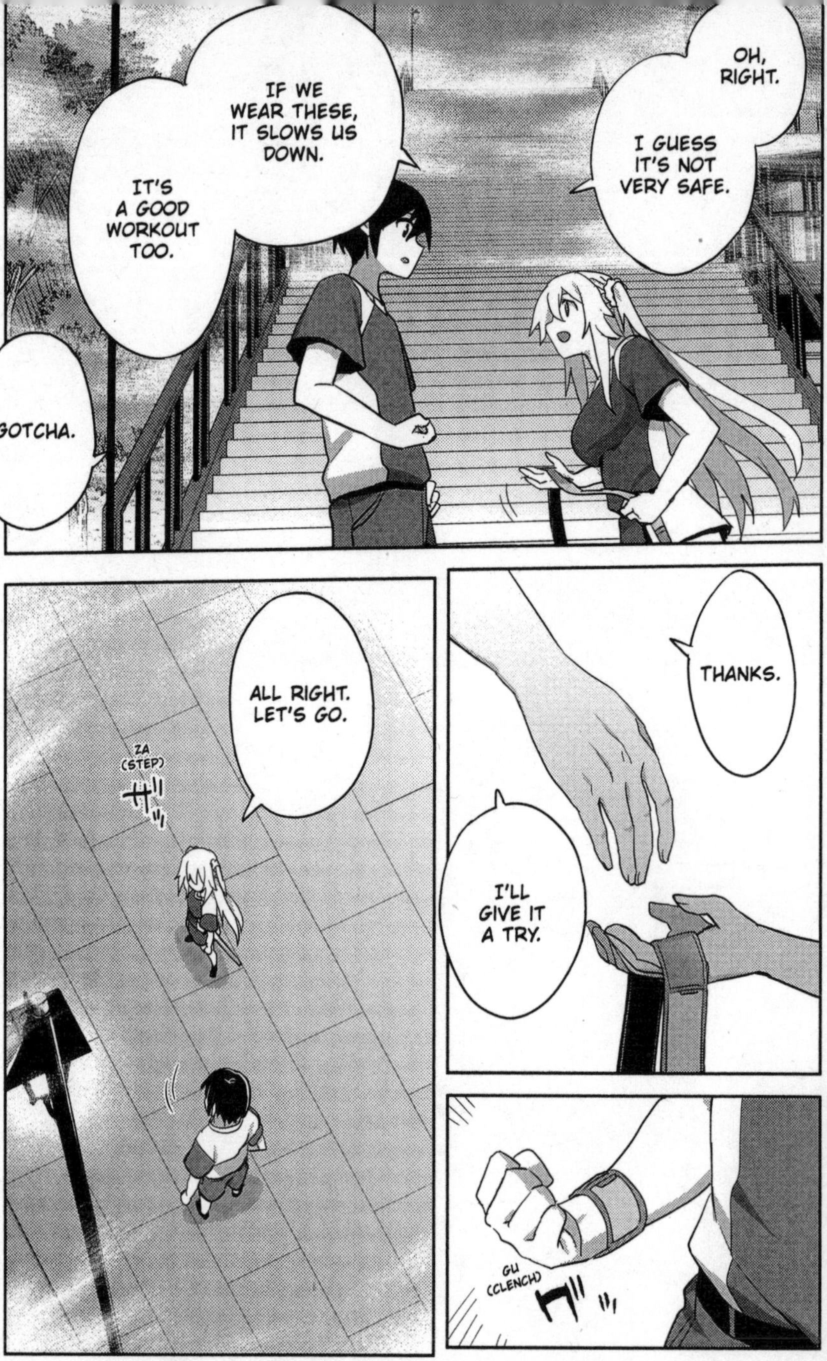
OH, RIGHT.
I GUESS IT'S NOT VERY SAFE.
IF WE WEAR THESE, IT SLOWS US DOWN.
IT'S A GOOD WORKOUT TOO.
GOTCHA.
THANKS.
I'LL GIVE IT A TRY.
GU (CLENCH)
ALL RIGHT. LET'S GO.
ZA (STEP)

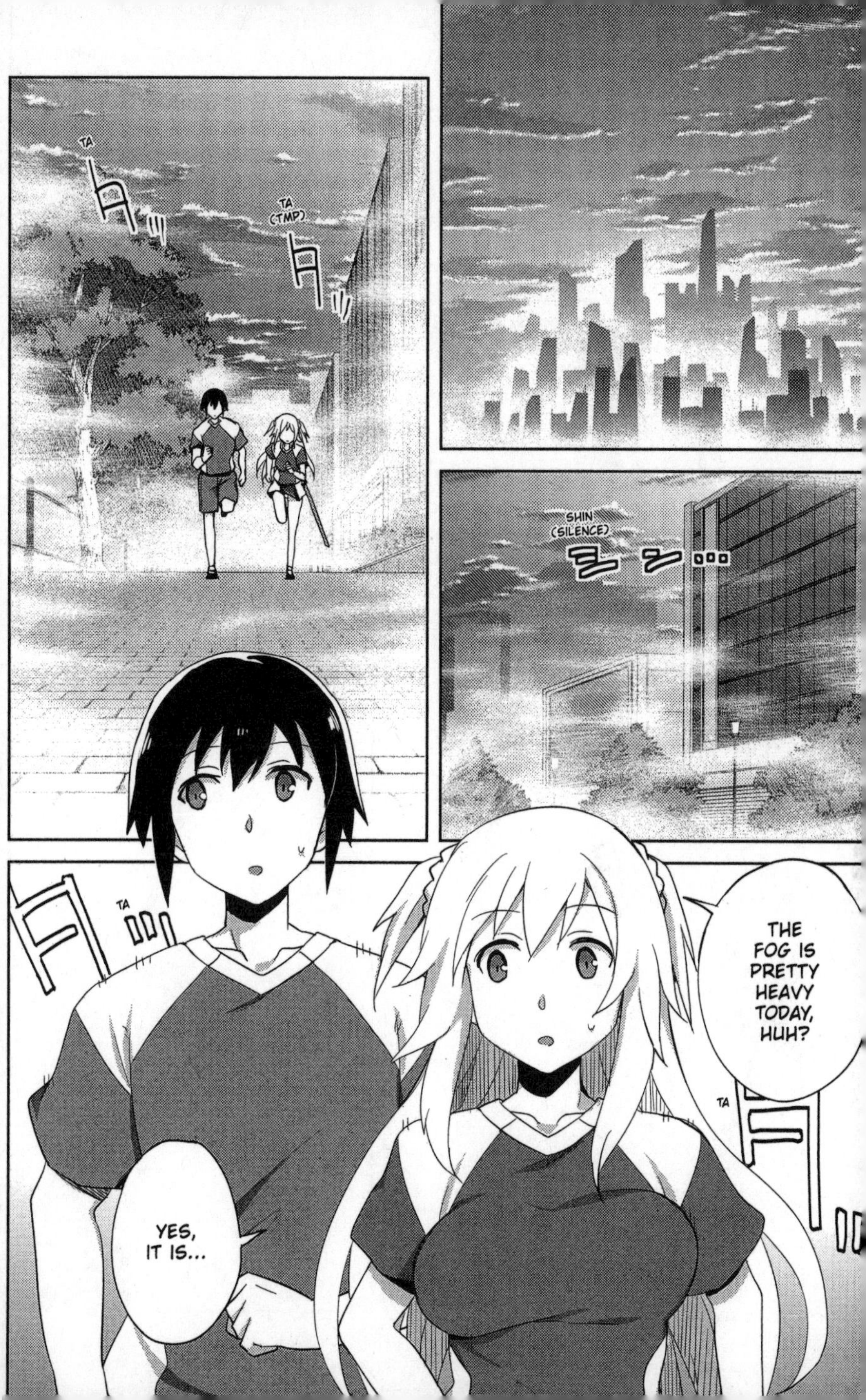
SHIN (SILENCE)
TA
TA (TMP)
THE FOG IS PRETTY HEAVY TODAY, HUH?
TA
TA
YES, IT IS...

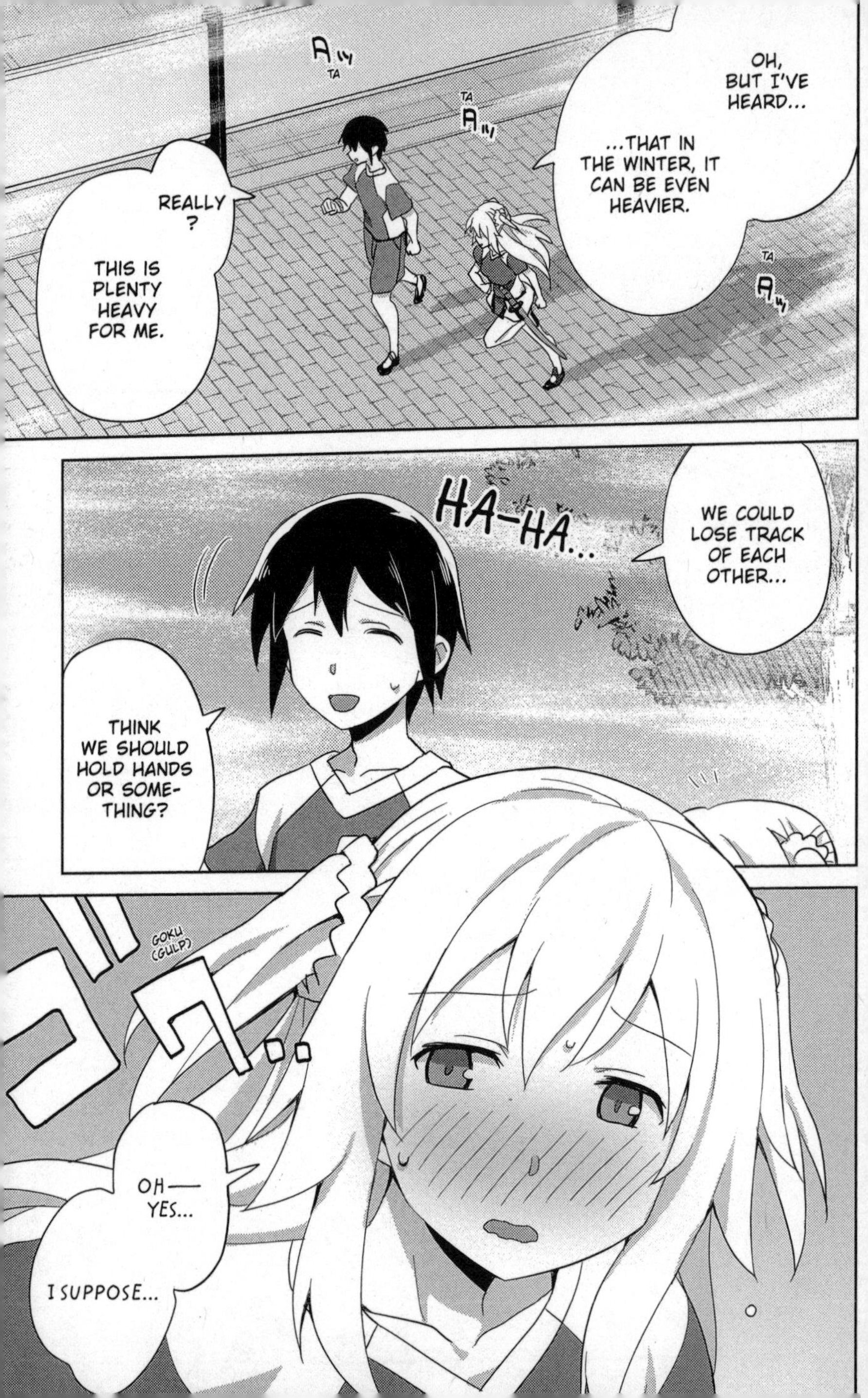
OH, BUT I'VE HEARD...
...THAT IN THE WINTER, IT CAN BE EVEN HEAVIER.
TA
TA
TA
REALLY?
THIS IS PLENTY HEAVY FOR ME.
WE COULD LOSE TRACK OF EACH OTHER...
HA-HA...
THINK WE SHOULD HOLD HANDS OR SOME-THING?
GOKU (GULP)
OH— YES...
I SUPPOSE...

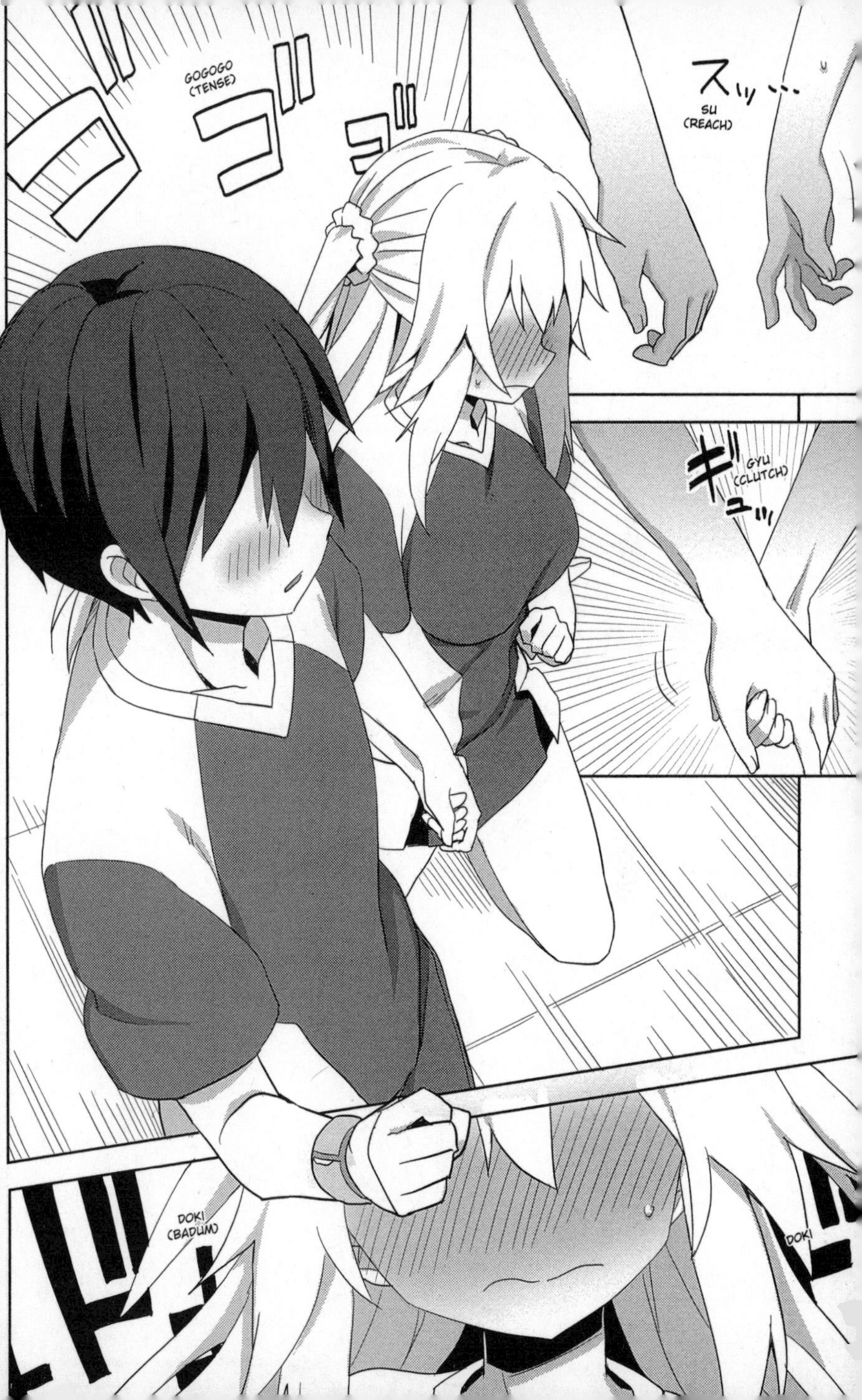

スッ…
SU
(REACH)
ギュッ
GYU
(CLUTCH)
ゴゴゴ
GOGOGO
(TENSE)
DOKI
(BADUM)
DOKI

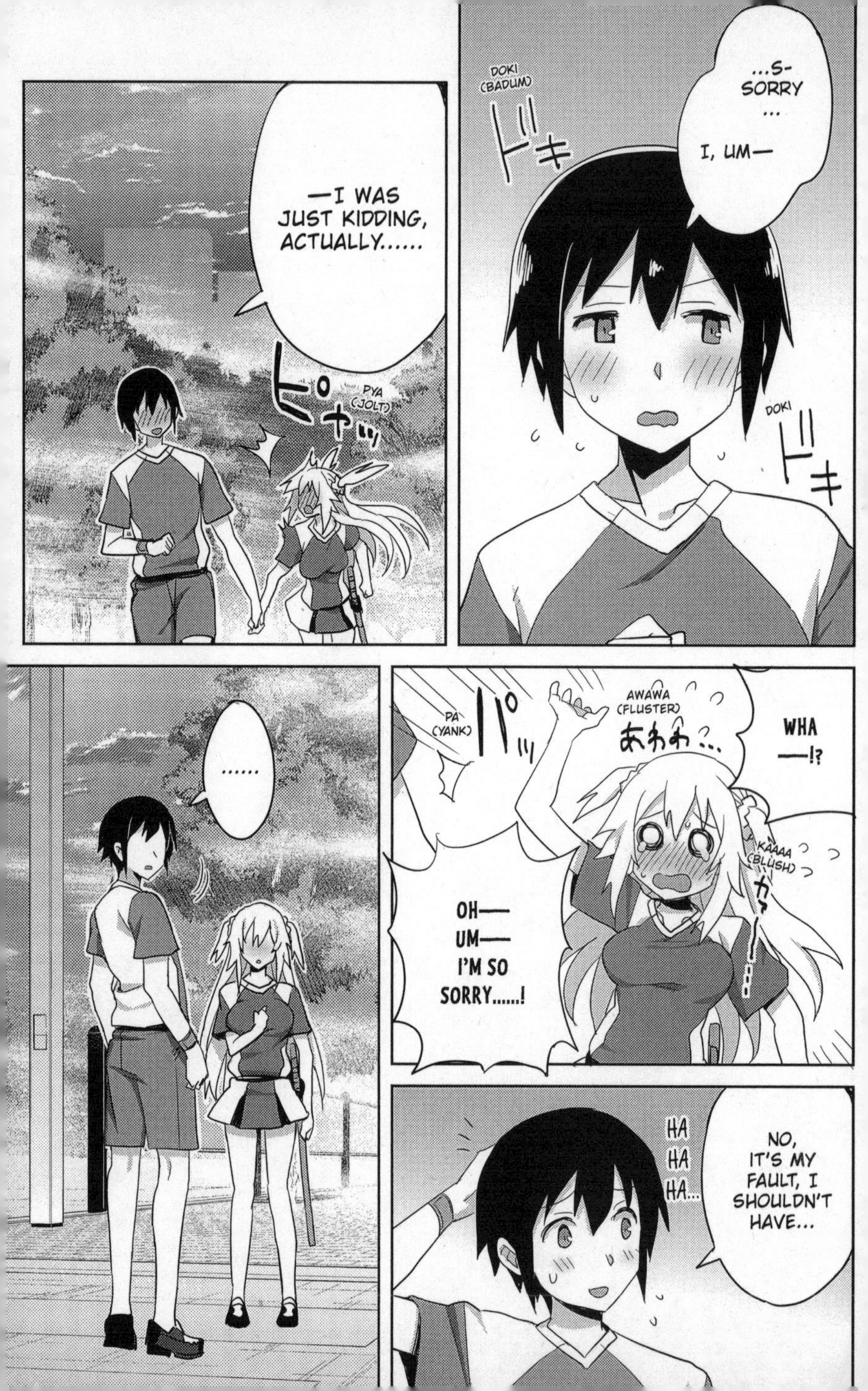
...S-SORRY ... I, UM—
DOKI (BADUM)
ドキ
DOKI
ドキ
—I WAS JUST KIDDING, ACTUALLY......
PYA (JOLT)
ピャッ
WHA—!?
AWAWA (FLUSTER)
あわわ…
PA (YANK)
パッ
KAAAA (BLUSH)
カァ
OH— UM— I'M SO SORRY......!
NO, IT'S MY FAULT, I SHOULDN'T HAVE...
HA HA HA...
......

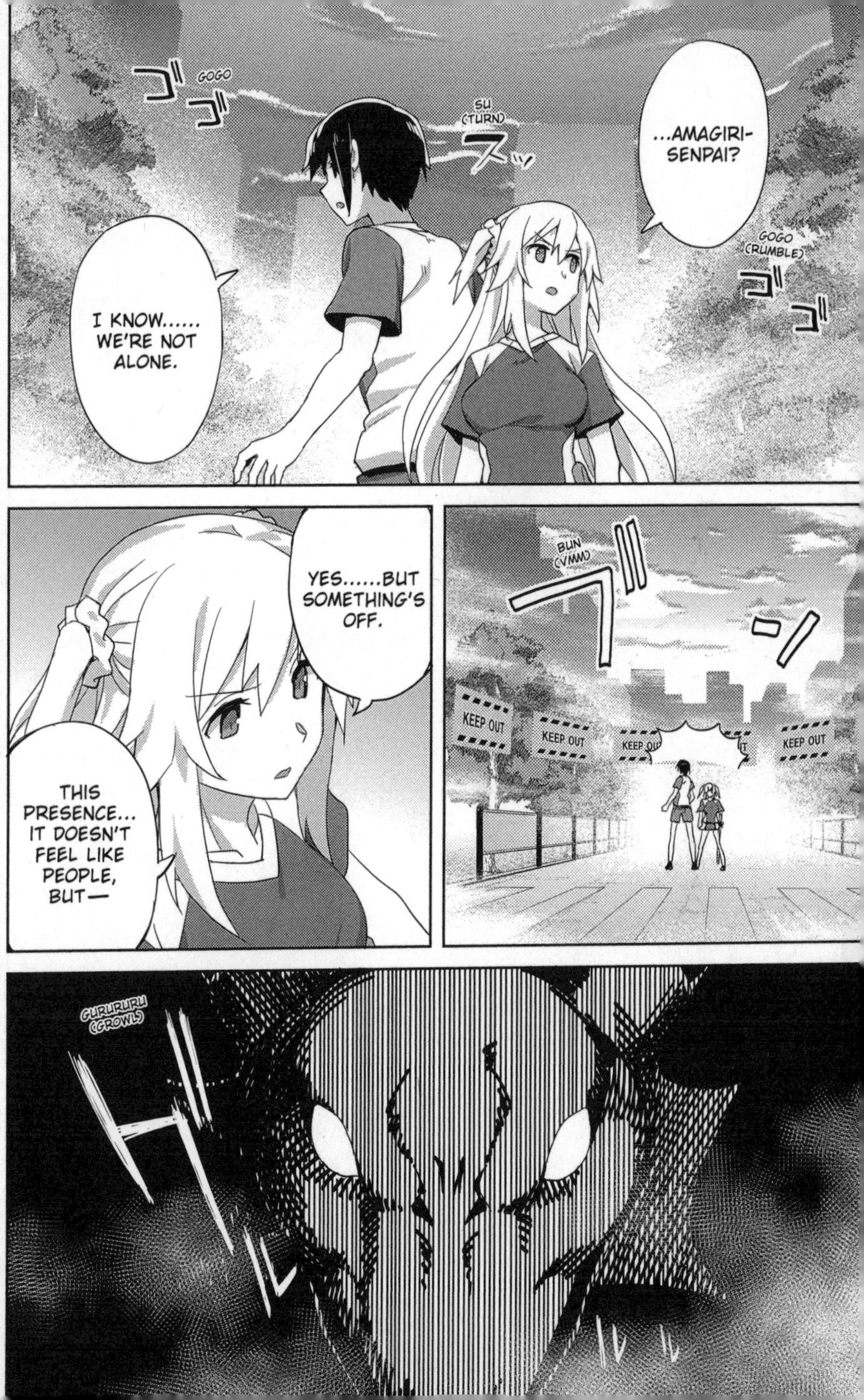
GOGO
SU (TURN)
...AMAGIRI-SENPAI?
GOGO (RUMBLE)
I KNOW...... WE'RE NOT ALONE.
BUN (VMM)
KEEP OUT
KEEP OUT
KEEP OUT
KEEP OUT
YES......BUT SOMETHING'S OFF.
THIS PRESENCE... IT DOESN'T FEEL LIKE PEOPLE, BUT—
GURURURU (GROWL)

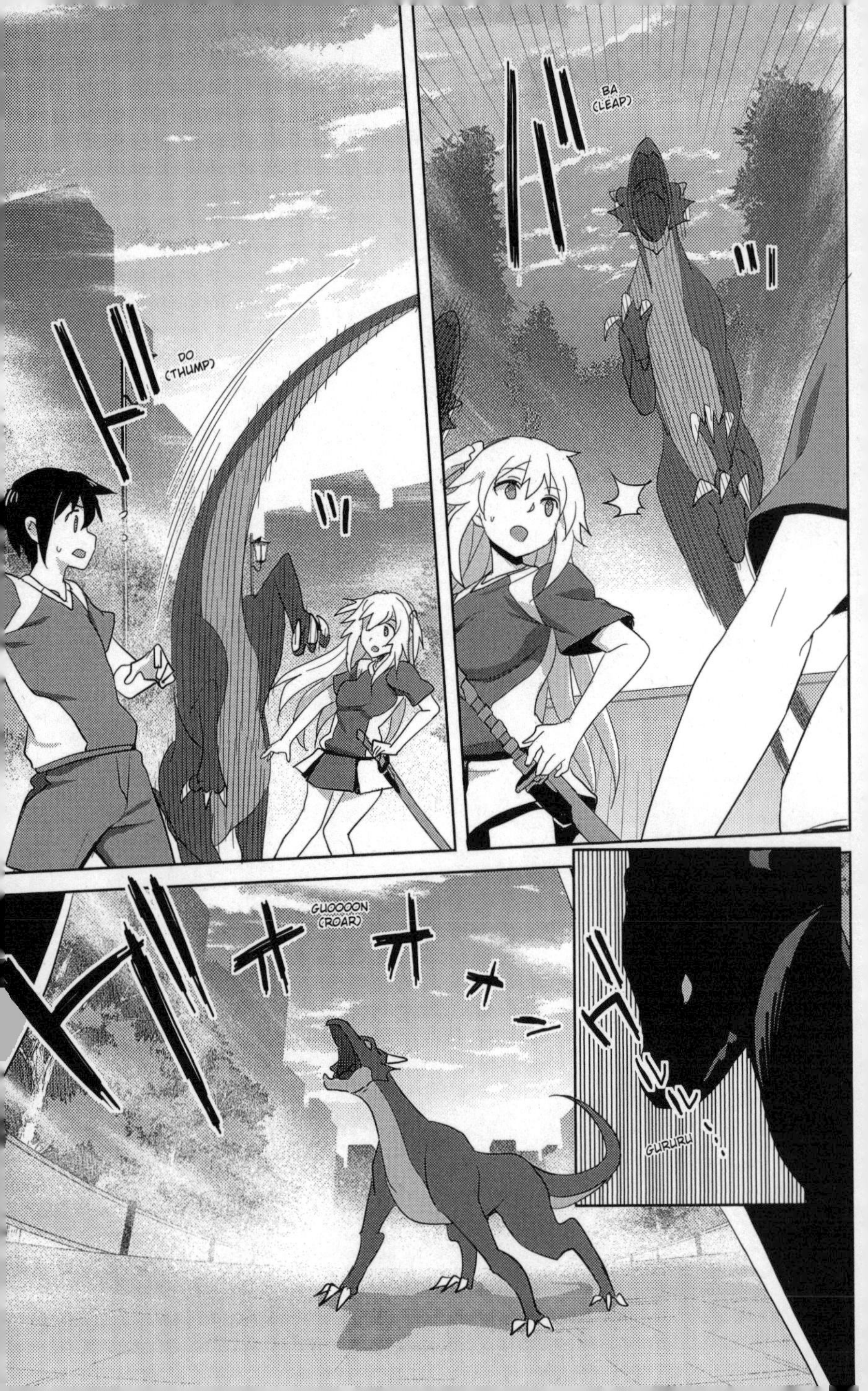
BA
(LEAP)
DO
(THUMP)
GURURU
GUOOOON
(ROAR)

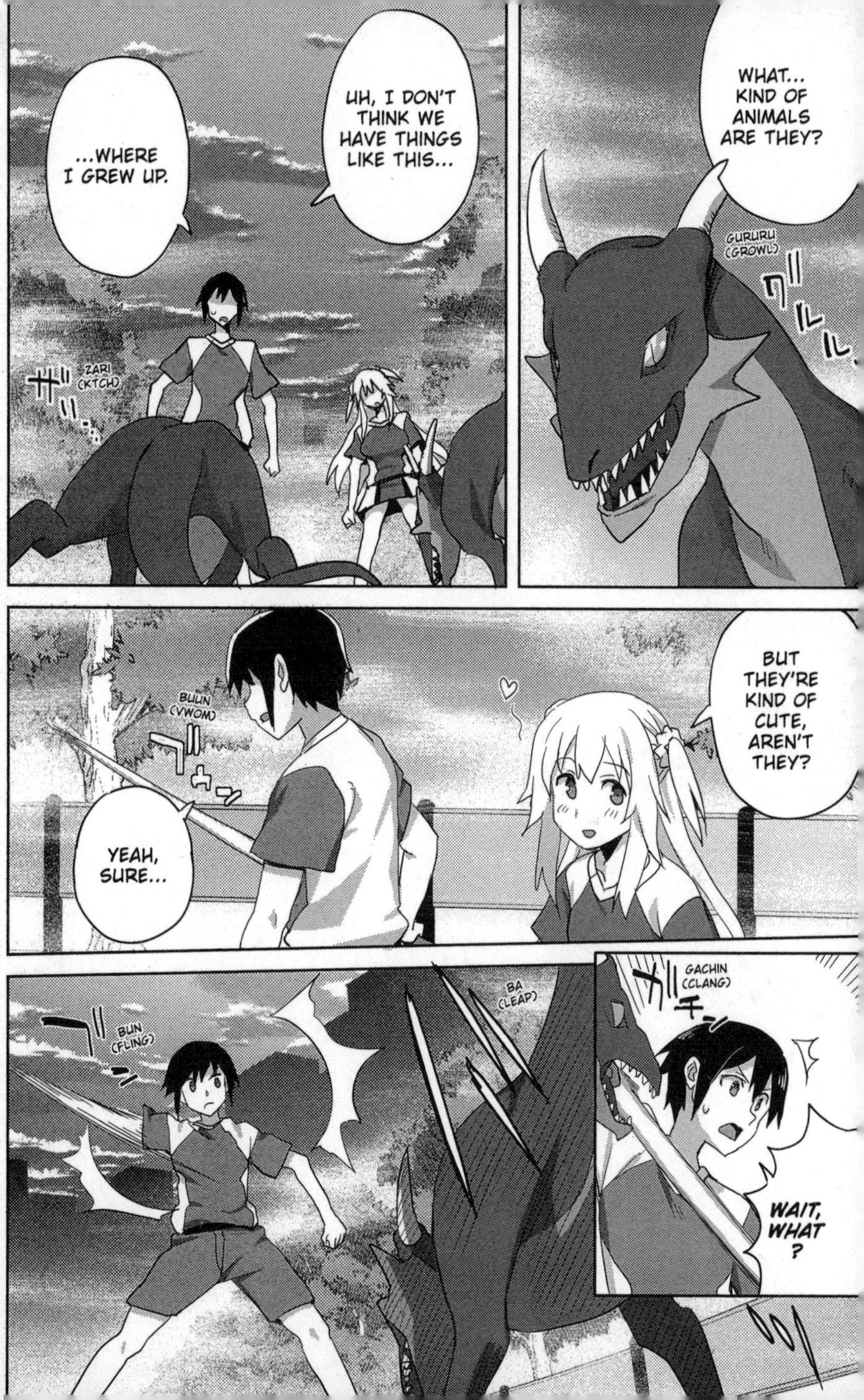
WHAT... KIND OF ANIMALS ARE THEY?
GURURU (GROWL)
UH, I DON'T THINK WE HAVE THINGS LIKE THIS...
...WHERE I GREW UP.
ZARI (KTCH)
BUT THEY'RE KIND OF CUTE, AREN'T THEY?
BUUN (VWOM)
YEAH, SURE...
GACHIN (CLANG)
WAIT, WHAT?
BA (LEAP)
BUN (FLING)

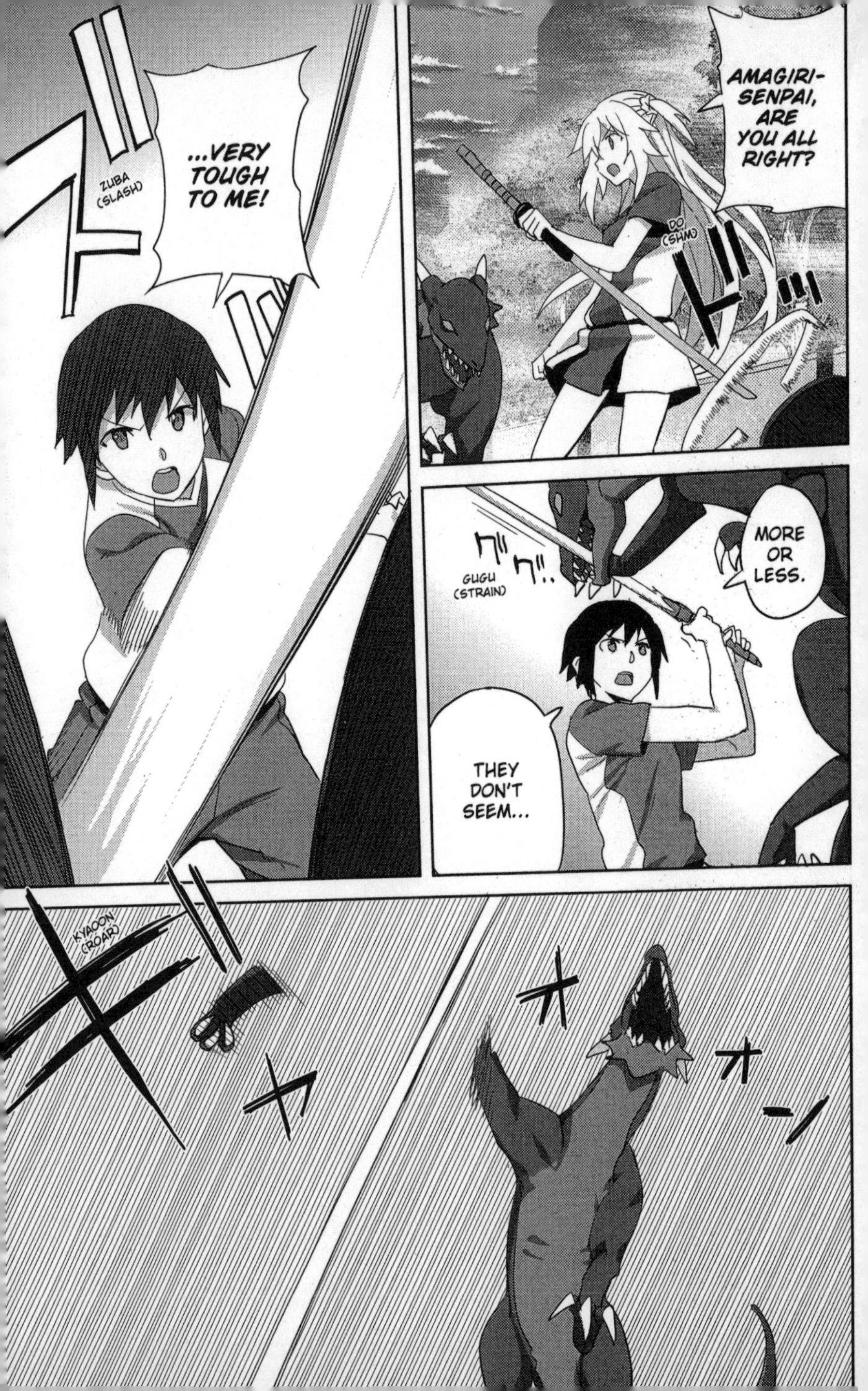

AMAGIRI-SENPAI, ARE YOU ALL RIGHT?
DO (SHM)
MORE OR LESS.
GUGU (STRAIN)
THEY DON'T SEEM...
ZUBA (SLASH)
...VERY TOUGH TO ME!
KYAOON (ROAR)

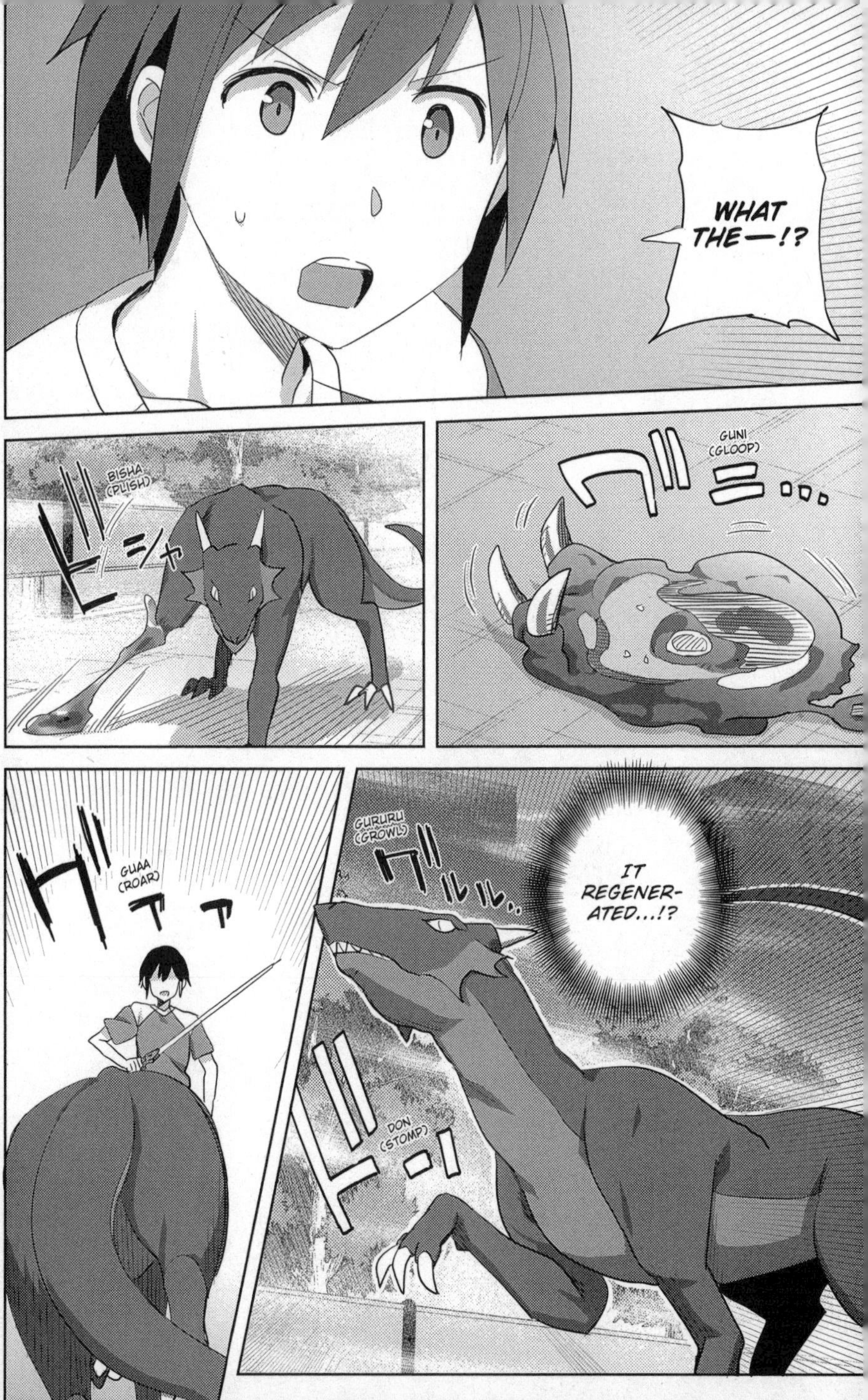
WHAT THE—!?
GUNI (GLOOP)
BISHA (PLISH)
GURURU (GROWL)
IT REGENERATED...!?
DON (STOMP)
GUAA (ROAR)

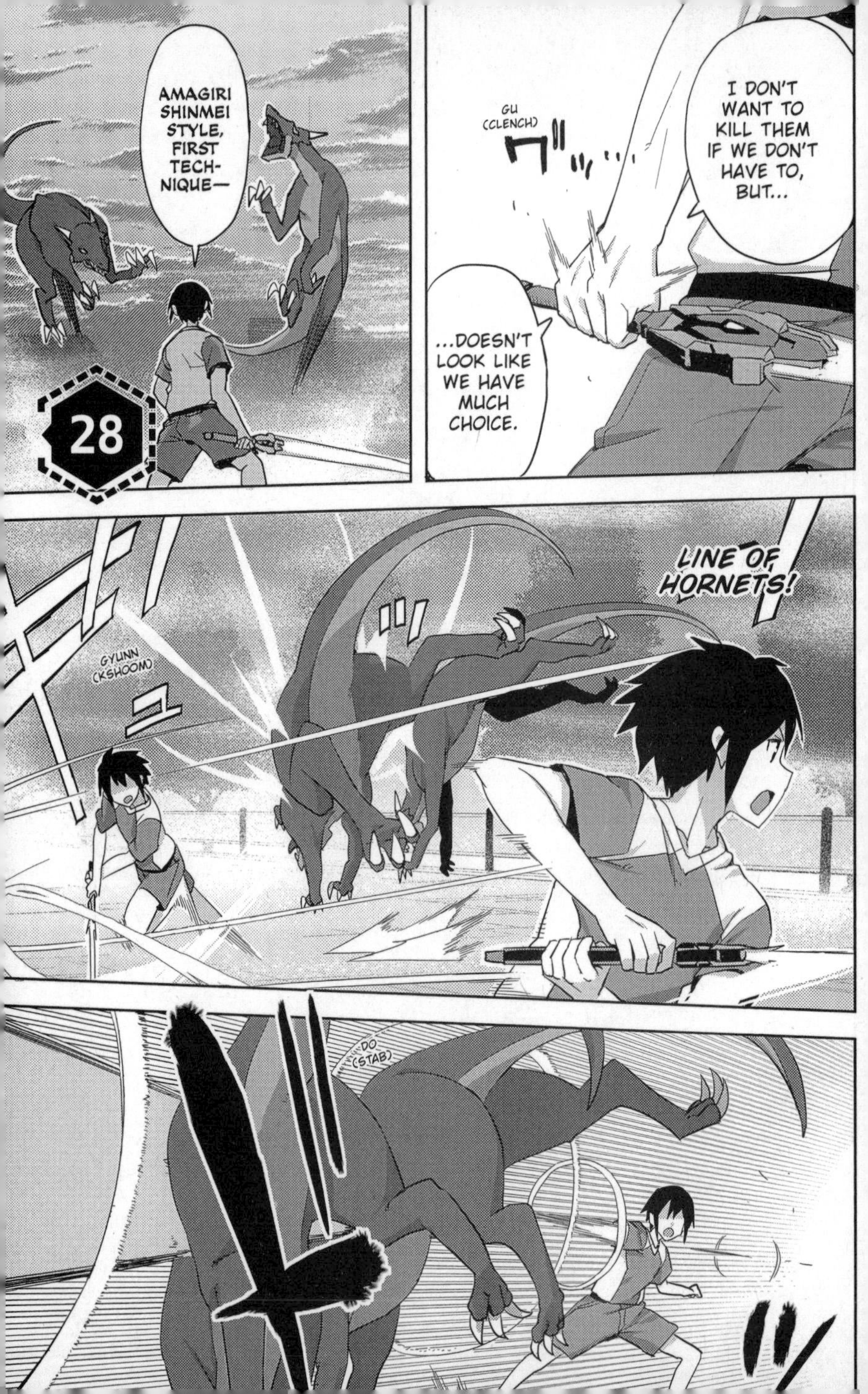
I DON'T WANT TO KILL THEM IF WE DON'T HAVE TO, BUT...
GU (CLENCH)
...DOESN'T LOOK LIKE WE HAVE MUCH CHOICE.
AMAGIRI SHINMEI STYLE, FIRST TECHNIQUE—
28
LINE OF HORNETS!
GYUNN (KSHOOM)
DO (STAB)

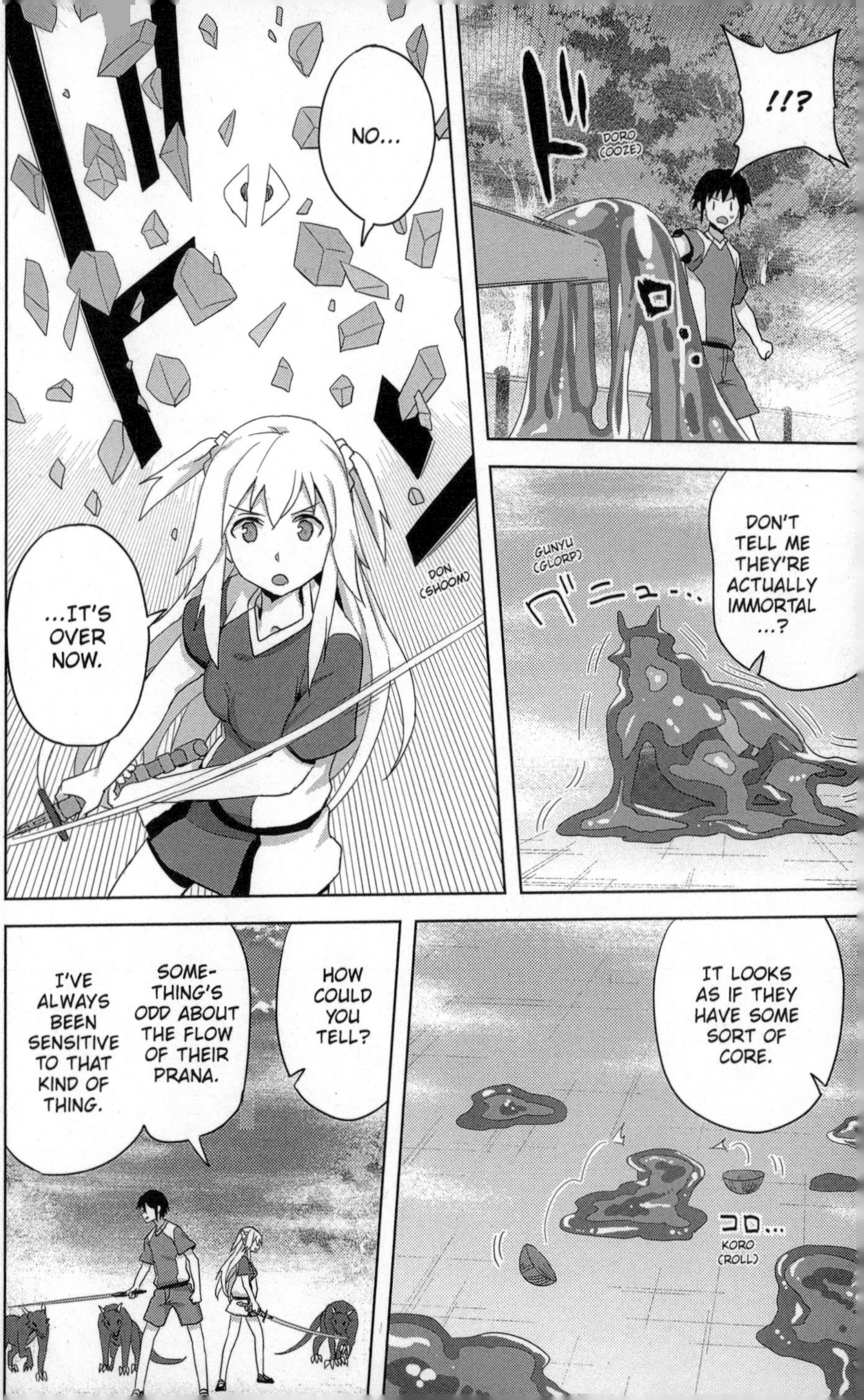

ド
DORO (COOZE)
!!?
グニュ…
GUNYU (GLORP)
DON'T TELL ME THEY'RE ACTUALLY IMMORTAL …?
NO…
DON (SHOOM)
…IT'S OVER NOW.
IT LOOKS AS IF THEY HAVE SOME SORT OF CORE.
コロ…
KORO (ROLL)
HOW COULD YOU TELL?
SOME-THING'S ODD ABOUT THE FLOW OF THEIR PRANA.
I'VE ALWAYS BEEN SENSITIVE TO THAT KIND OF THING.

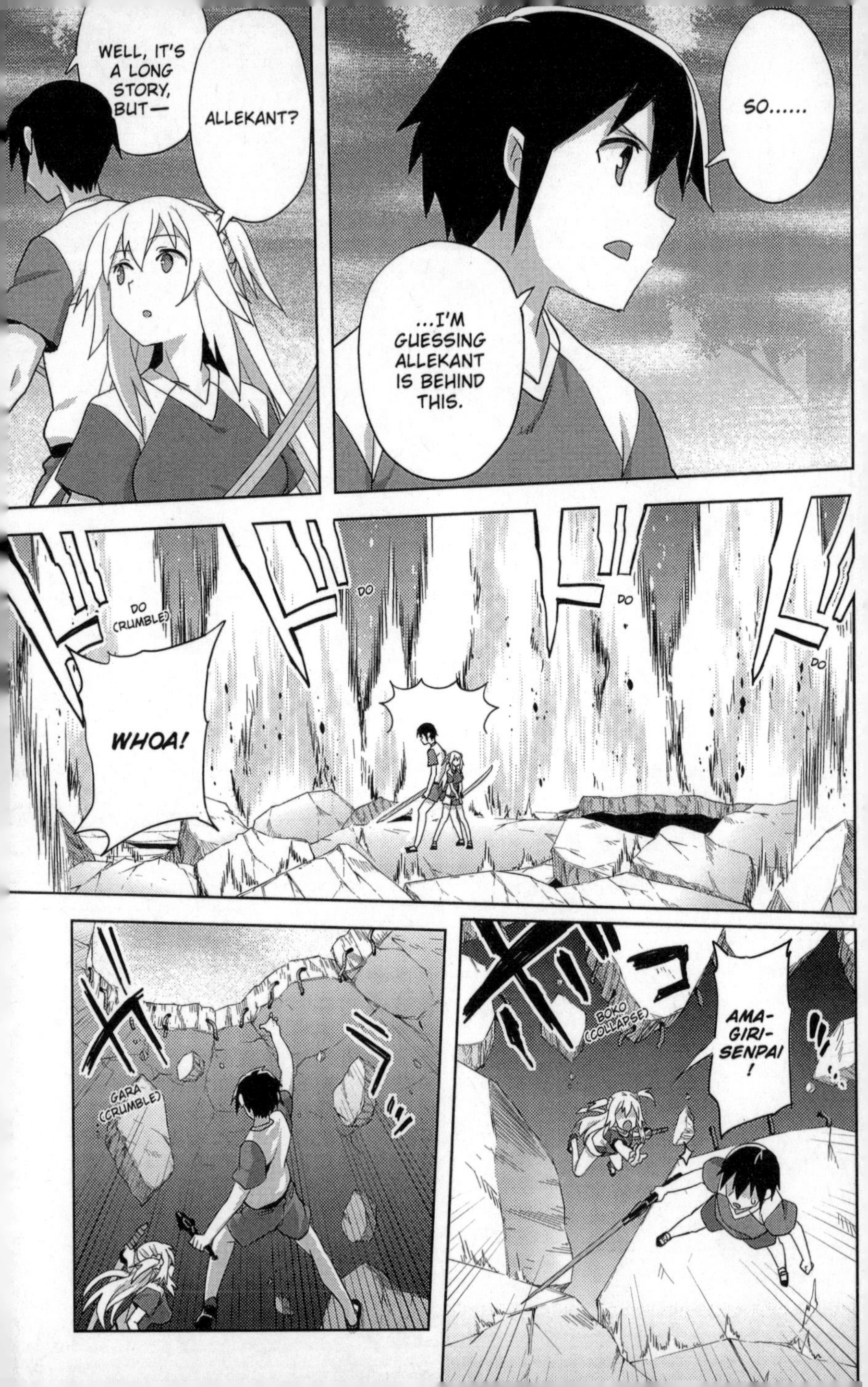
SO......
...I'M GUESSING ALLEKANT IS BEHIND THIS.
ALLEKANT?
WELL, IT'S A LONG STORY, BUT—
DO
DO
DO
DO (RUMBLE)
WHOA!
BOKO (COLLAPSE)
AMA-GIRI-SENPAI!
GARA (CRUMBLE)

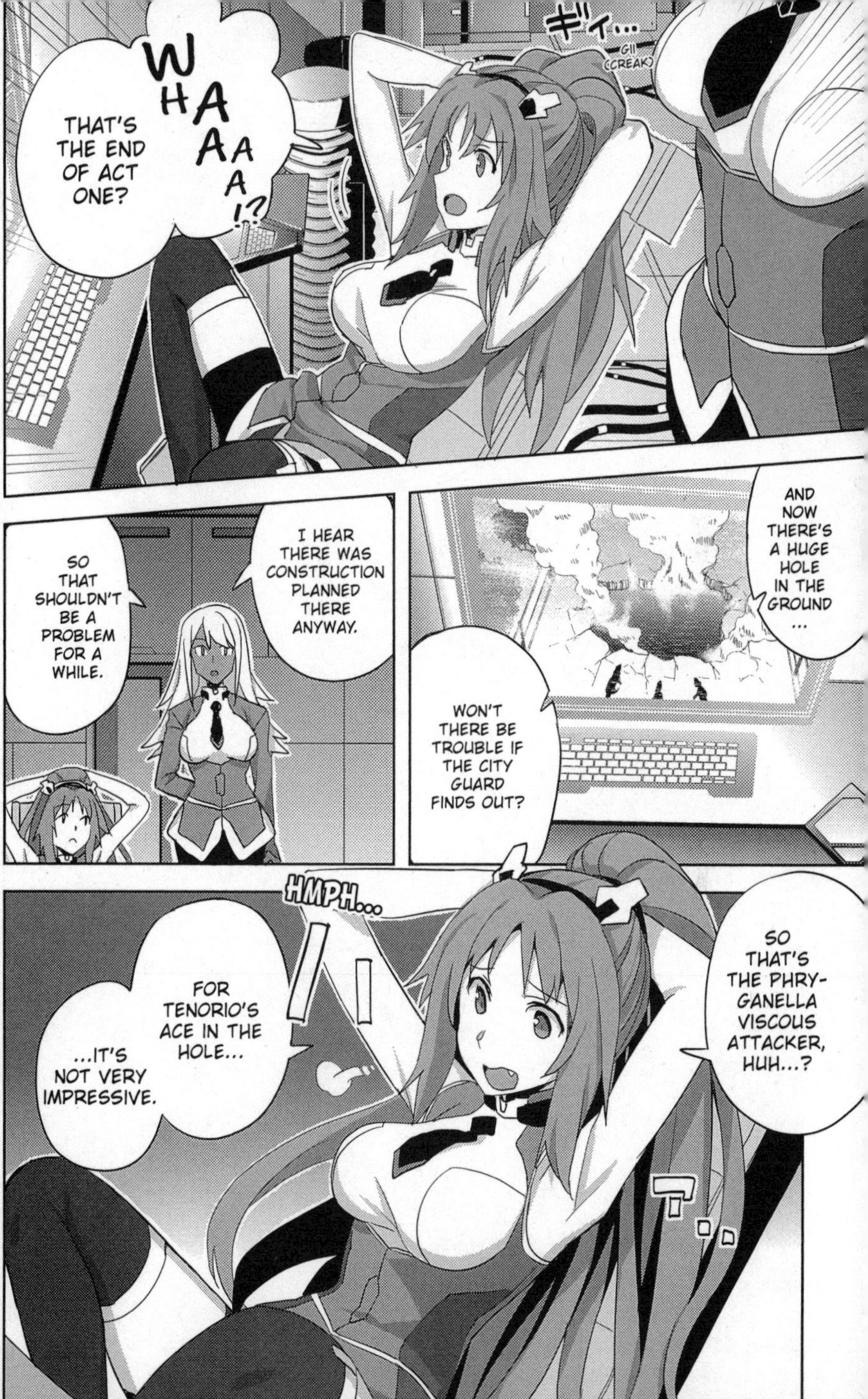
ギィ…
GII (CREAK)
WHAAAAA!?
THAT'S THE END OF ACT ONE?
AND NOW THERE'S A HUGE HOLE IN THE GROUND...
WON'T THERE BE TROUBLE IF THE CITY GUARD FINDS OUT?
I HEAR THERE WAS CONSTRUCTION PLANNED THERE ANYWAY.
SO THAT SHOULDN'T BE A PROBLEM FOR A WHILE.
SO THAT'S THE PHRY-GANELLA VISCOUS ATTACKER, HUH...?
HMPH...
FOR TENORIO'S ACE IN THE HOLE...
...IT'S NOT VERY IMPRESSIVE.

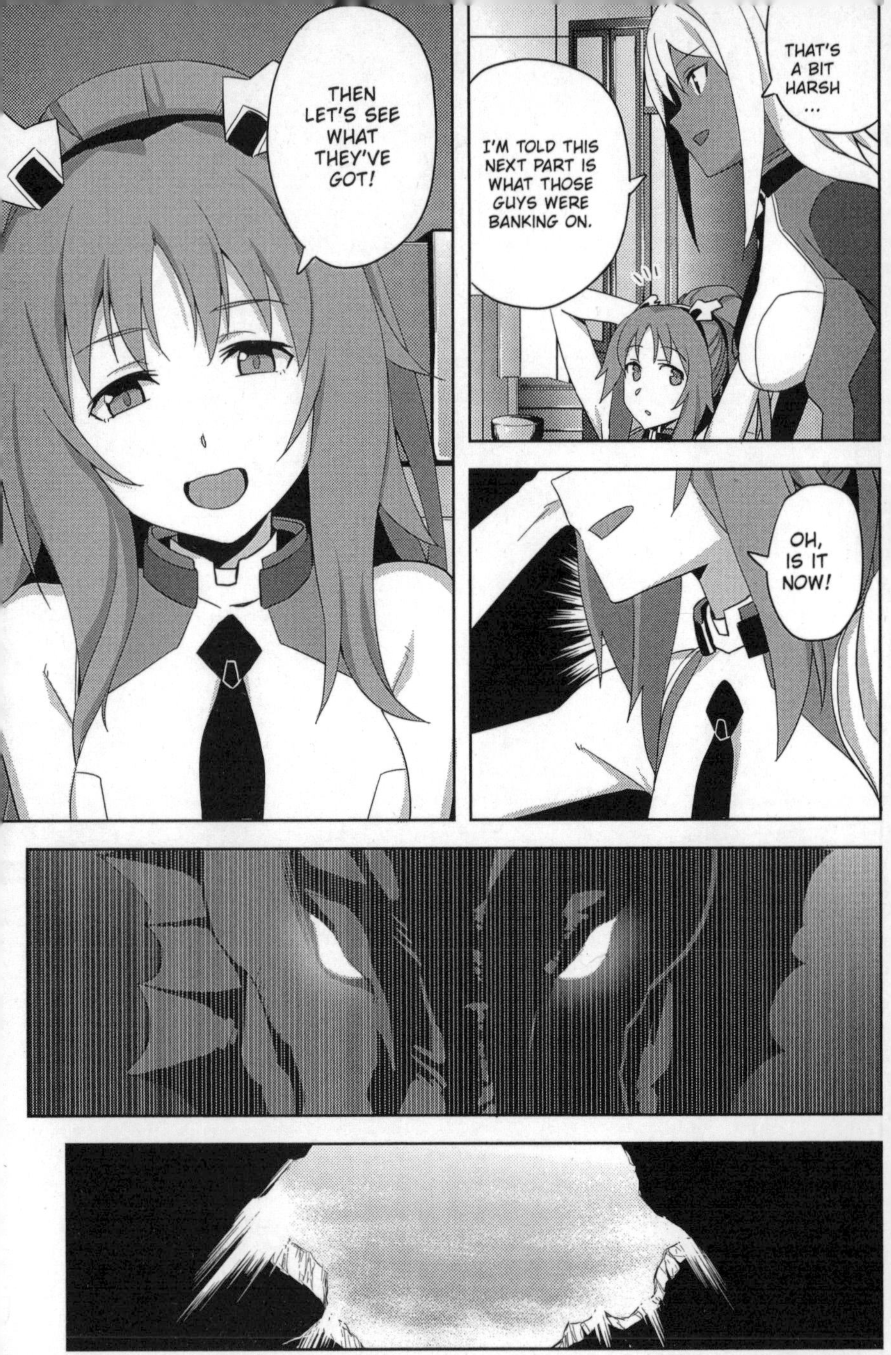
THAT'S A BIT HARSH...
I'M TOLD THIS NEXT PART IS WHAT THOSE GUYS WERE BANKING ON.
OH, IS IT NOW!
THEN LET'S SEE WHAT THEY'VE GOT!

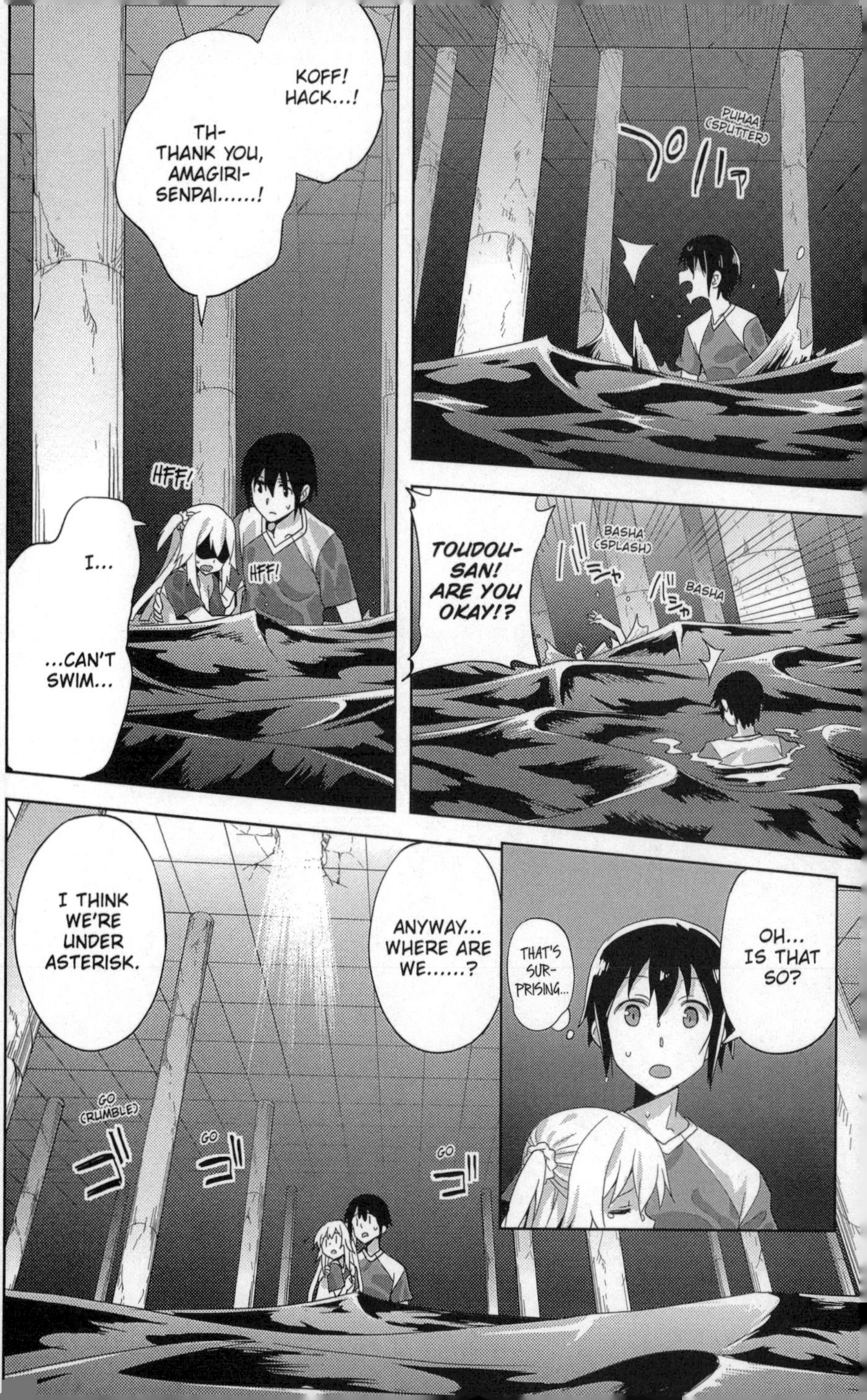
PUHAA (SPUTTER)
TOUDOU-SAN! ARE YOU OKAY!?
BASHA (SPLASH)
BASHA
KOFF! HACK...!
TH-THANK YOU, AMAGIRI-SENPAI......!
HFF!
HFF!
I...
...CAN'T SWIM...
OH... IS THAT SO?
THAT'S SUR-PRISING...
ANYWAY... WHERE ARE WE......?
I THINK WE'RE UNDER ASTERISK.
GO
GO
GO (RUMBLE)

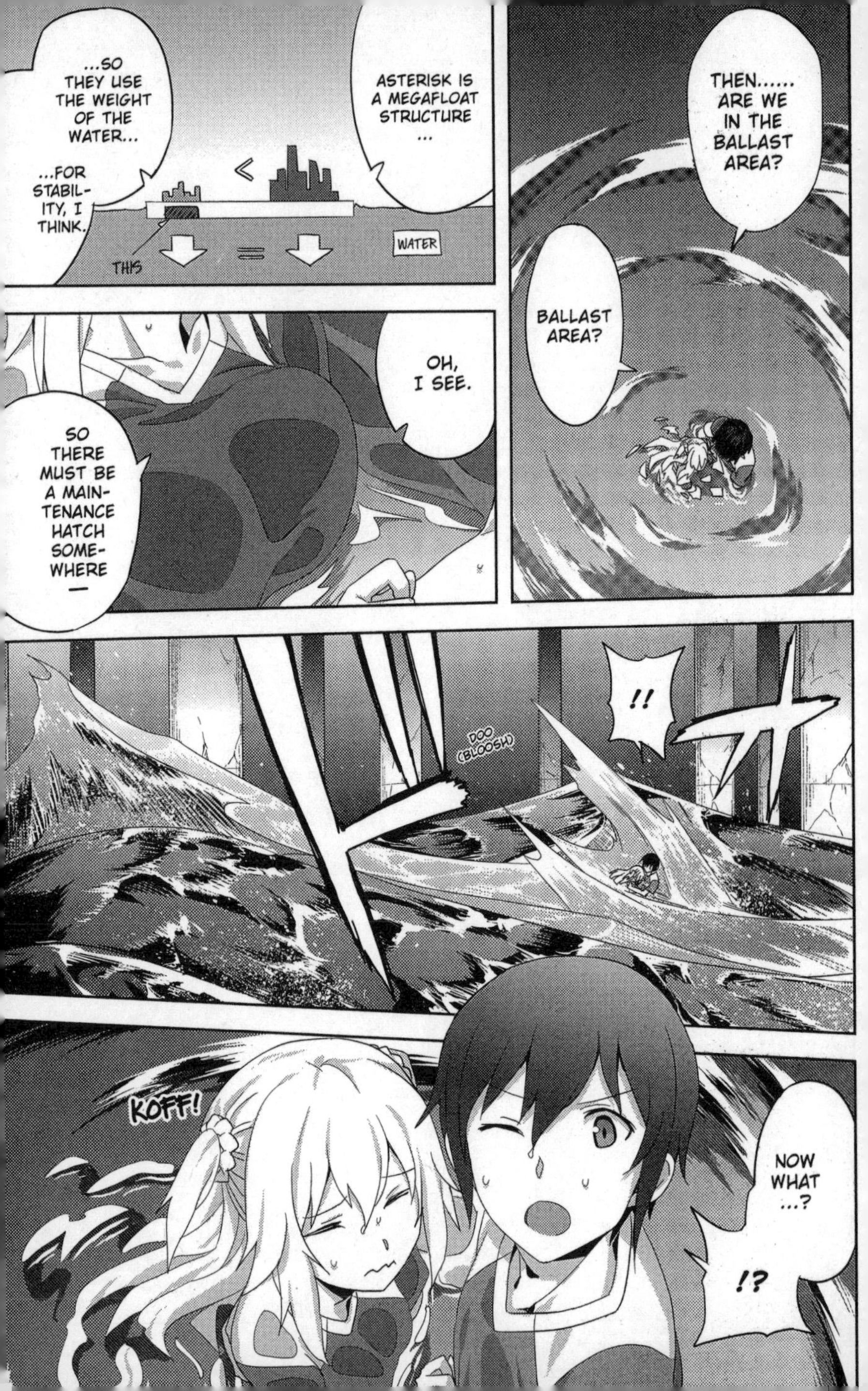
THEN...... ARE WE IN THE BALLAST AREA?
BALLAST AREA?
ASTERISK IS A MEGAFLOAT STRUCTURE ...
...SO THEY USE THE WEIGHT OF THE WATER...
...FOR STABILITY, I THINK.
THIS
WATER
OH, I SEE.
SO THERE MUST BE A MAINTENANCE HATCH SOMEWHERE—
!!
DOO (BLOOSH)
NOW WHAT ...?
!?
KOFF!

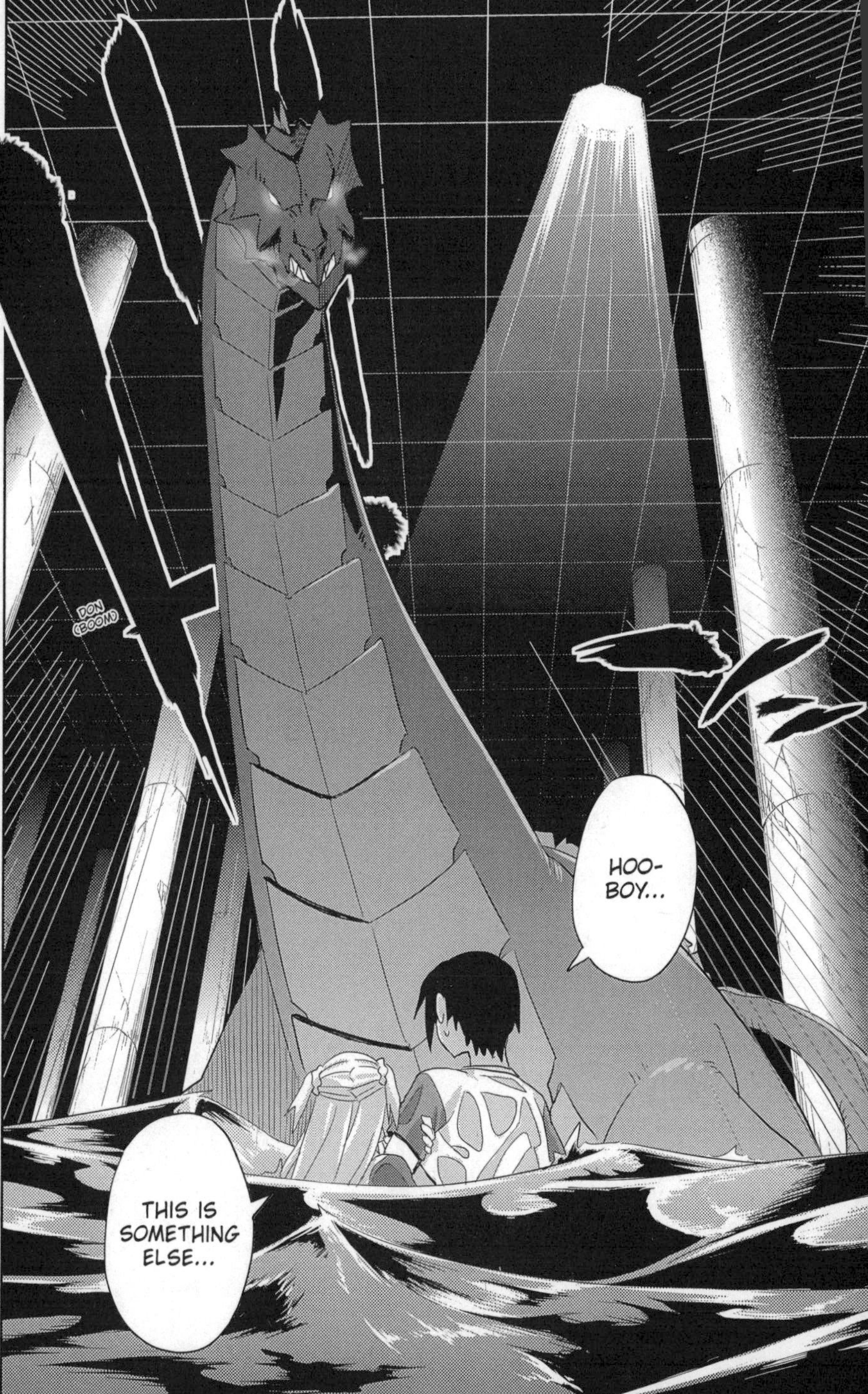
HOO-BOY...
DON (BOOM)
THIS IS SOMETHING ELSE...

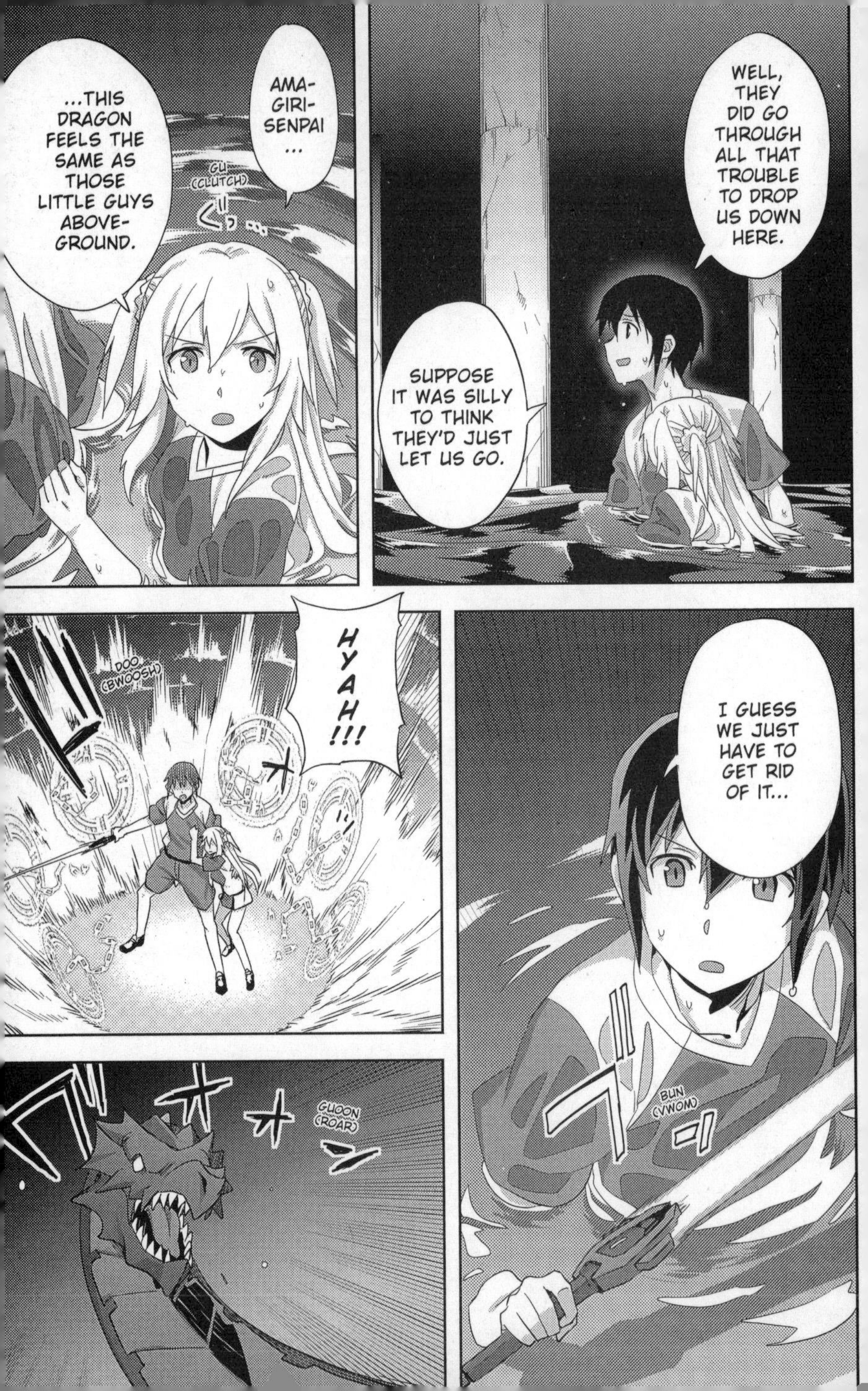
WELL, THEY DID GO THROUGH ALL THAT TROUBLE TO DROP US DOWN HERE.
SUPPOSE IT WAS SILLY TO THINK THEY'D JUST LET US GO.
AMA-GIRI-SENPAI...
GU (CLUTCH)
...THIS DRAGON FEELS THE SAME AS THOSE LITTLE GUYS ABOVE-GROUND.
I GUESS WE JUST HAVE TO GET RID OF IT...
BUN (VWOM)
HYAH!!!
DOO (BWOOSH)
GUOON (ROAR)

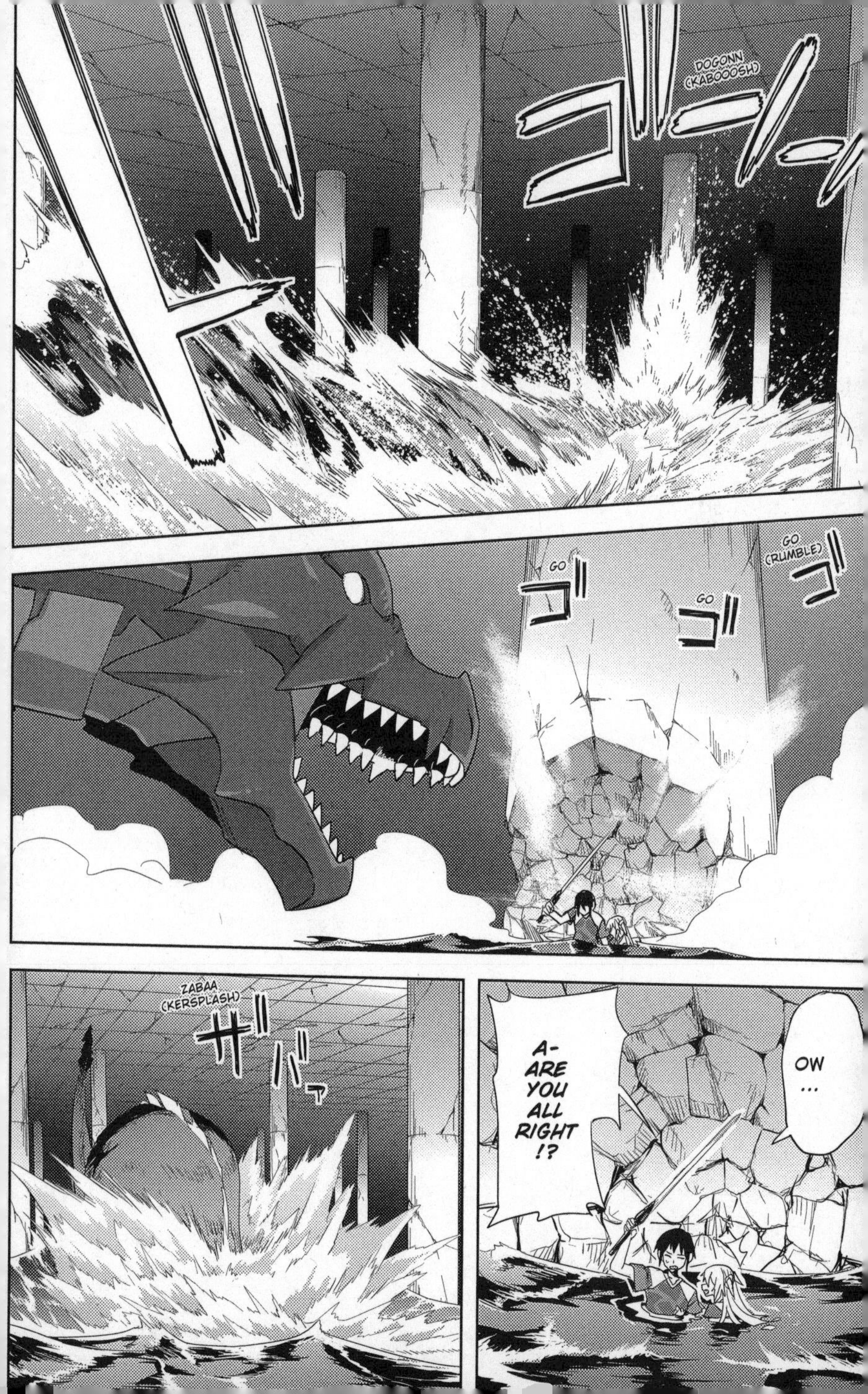
DOGONN (KABOOOSH)
GO (RUMBLE)
GO
GO
OW ...
A- ARE YOU ALL RIGHT !?
ZABAA (KERSPLASH)

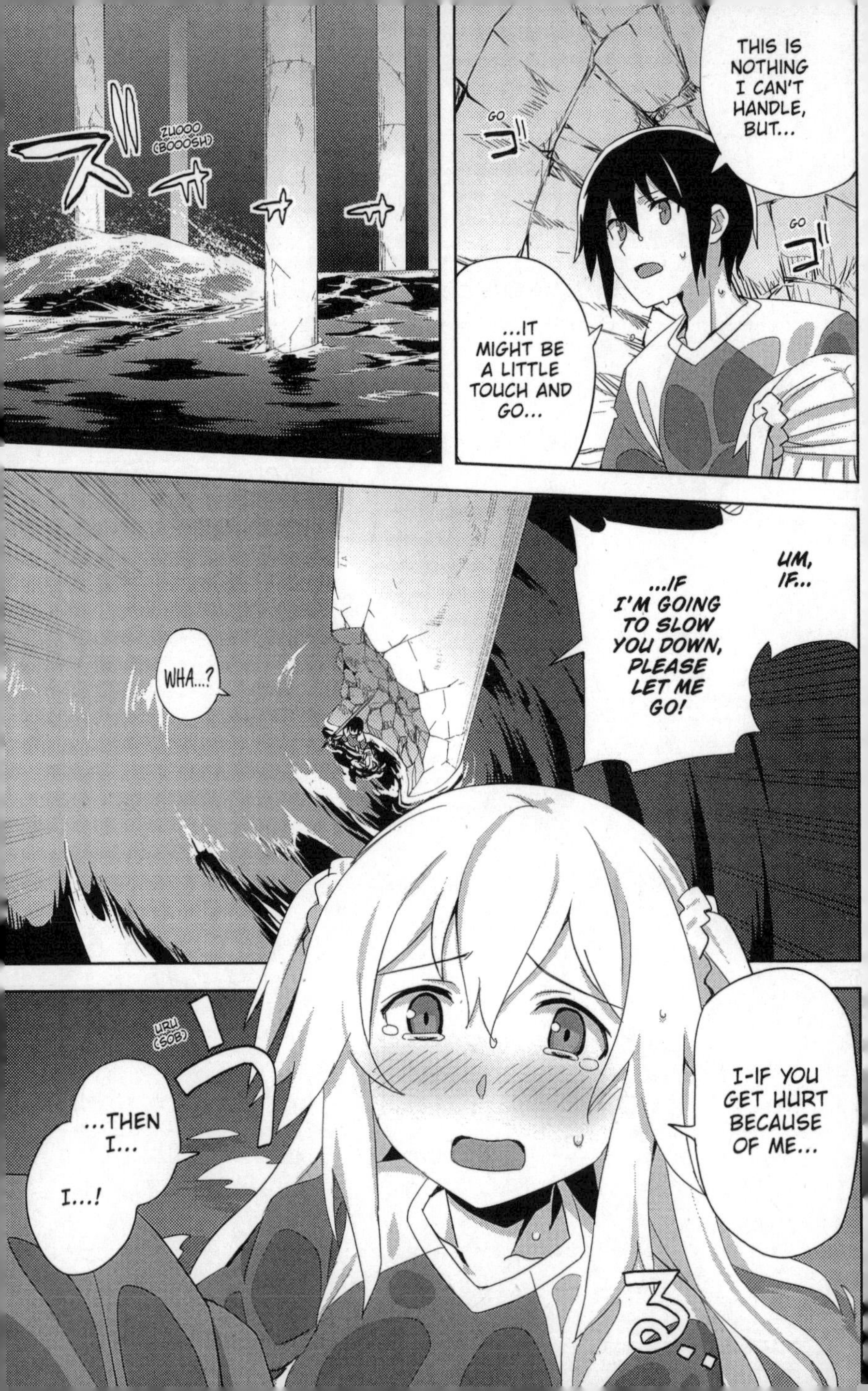
THIS IS NOTHING I CAN'T HANDLE, BUT...
GO
GO
...IT MIGHT BE A LITTLE TOUCH AND GO...
ZUOOO (BOOOSH)
UM, IF...
...IF I'M GOING TO SLOW YOU DOWN, PLEASE LET ME GO!
WHA...?
I-IF YOU GET HURT BECAUSE OF ME...
URU (SOB)
...THEN I...
I...!

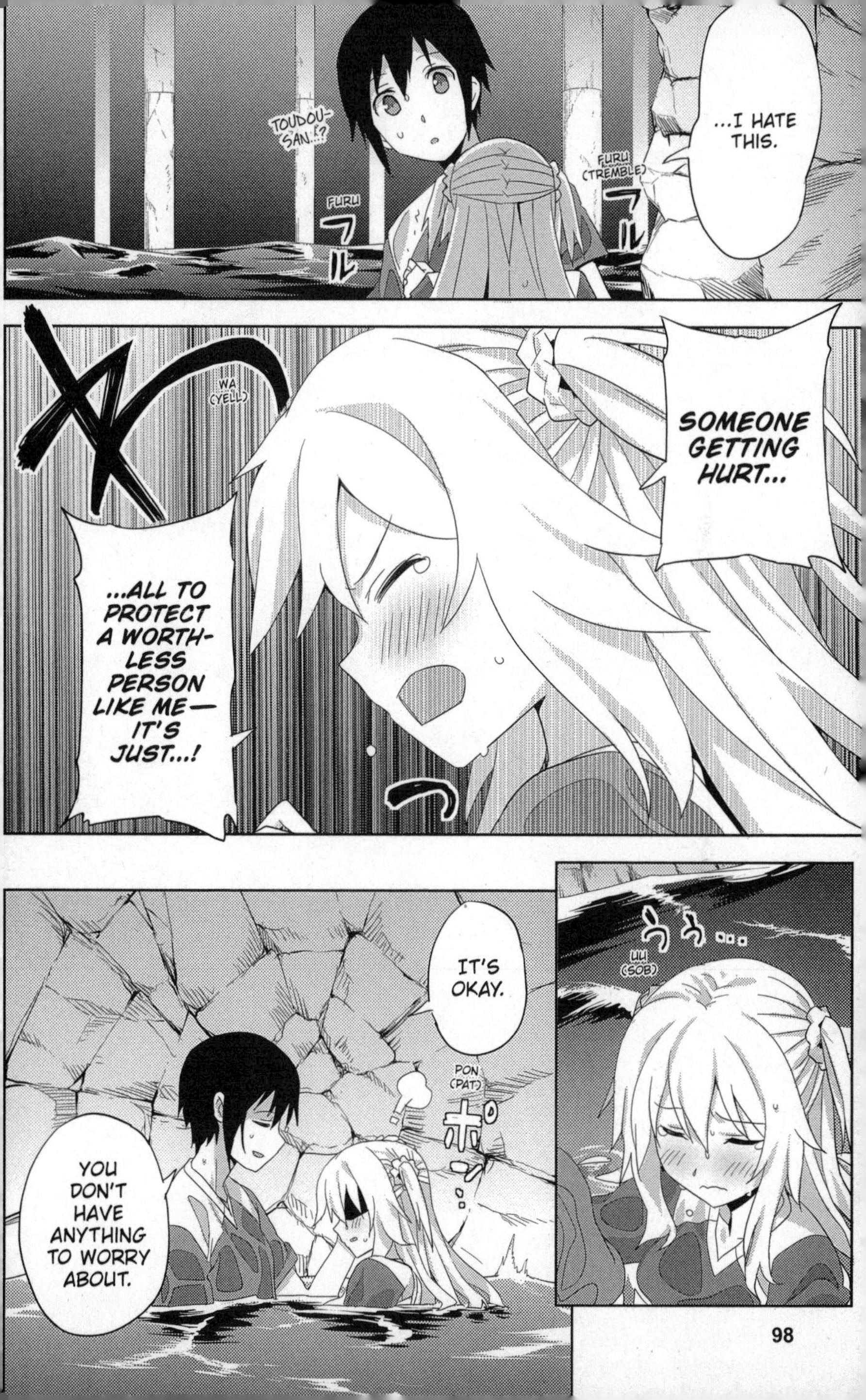
...I HATE THIS.
FURU (TREMBLE)
TOUDOU-SAN...?
FURU
SOMEONE GETTING HURT...
WA (YELL)
...ALL TO PROTECT A WORTH-LESS PERSON LIKE ME— IT'S JUST...!
UU (SOB)
IT'S OKAY.
PON (PAT)
YOU DON'T HAVE ANYTHING TO WORRY ABOUT.

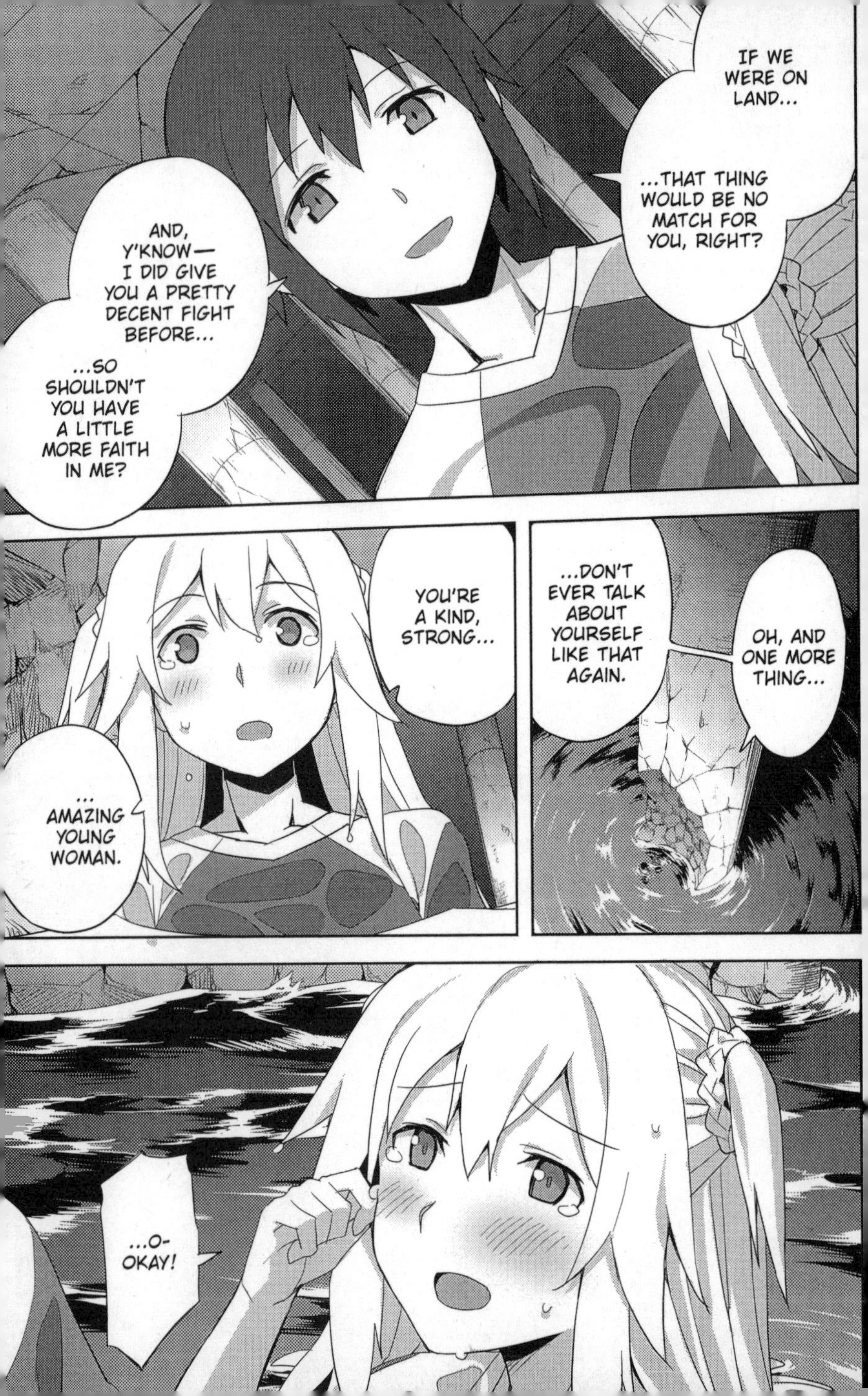
IF WE WERE ON LAND...
...THAT THING WOULD BE NO MATCH FOR YOU, RIGHT?
AND, Y'KNOW— I DID GIVE YOU A PRETTY DECENT FIGHT BEFORE...
...SO SHOULDN'T YOU HAVE A LITTLE MORE FAITH IN ME?
OH, AND ONE MORE THING...
...DON'T EVER TALK ABOUT YOURSELF LIKE THAT AGAIN.
YOU'RE A KIND, STRONG...
... AMAZING YOUNG WOMAN.
...O- OKAY!

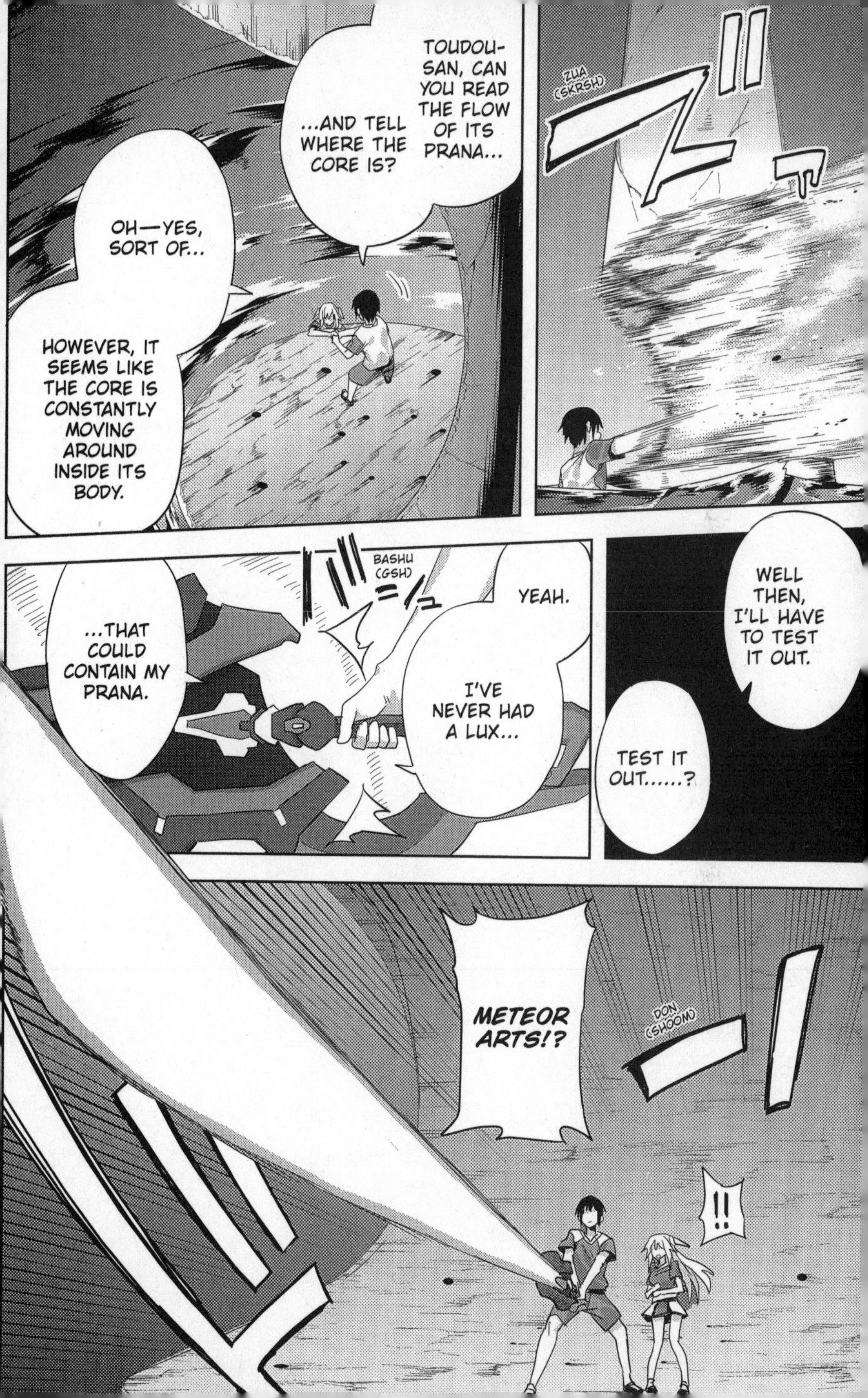
ZUA (SKRSH)
TOUDOU-SAN, CAN YOU READ THE FLOW OF ITS PRANA...
...AND TELL WHERE THE CORE IS?
OH—YES, SORT OF...
HOWEVER, IT SEEMS LIKE THE CORE IS CONSTANTLY MOVING AROUND INSIDE ITS BODY.
WELL THEN, I'LL HAVE TO TEST IT OUT.
TEST IT OUT......?
BASHU (GSH)
YEAH.
I'VE NEVER HAD A LUX...
...THAT COULD CONTAIN MY PRANA.
DON (SHOOM)
METEOR ARTS!?
!!

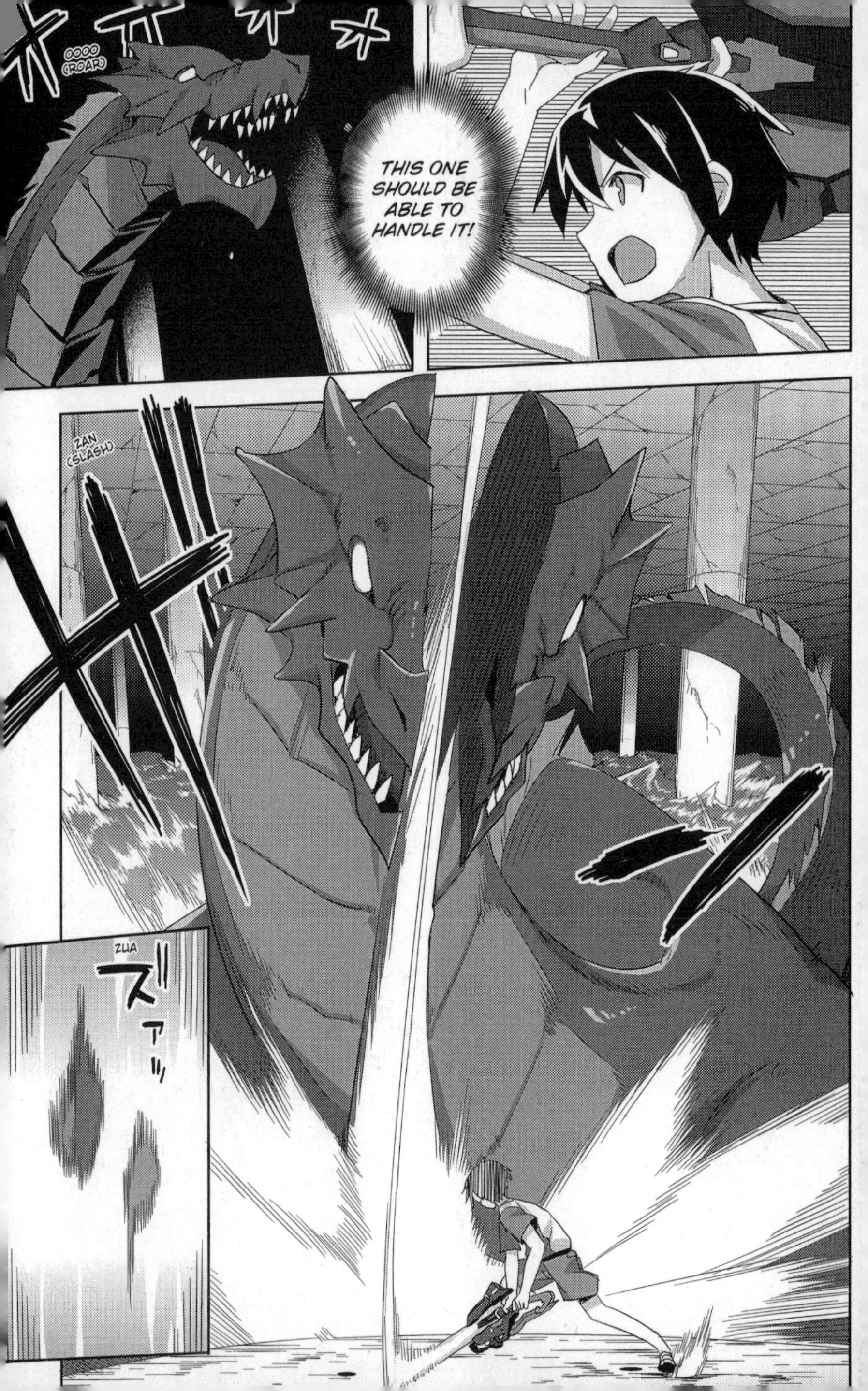
THIS ONE SHOULD BE ABLE TO HANDLE IT!
OOOO (ROAR)
ZAN (SLASH)
ZUA

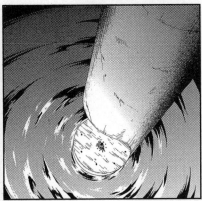

...SO YOU CAN ONLY FIGHT AT FULL POWER...

BICHO
(DRIP)
ピ
チ
ャ
...

...FOR FIVE MINUTES?

I THINK I COULD GO LONGER IF I PUSHED IT...

BUT EVEN THEN I PROBABLY WOULDN'T LAST TEN MINUTES.

YEAH.

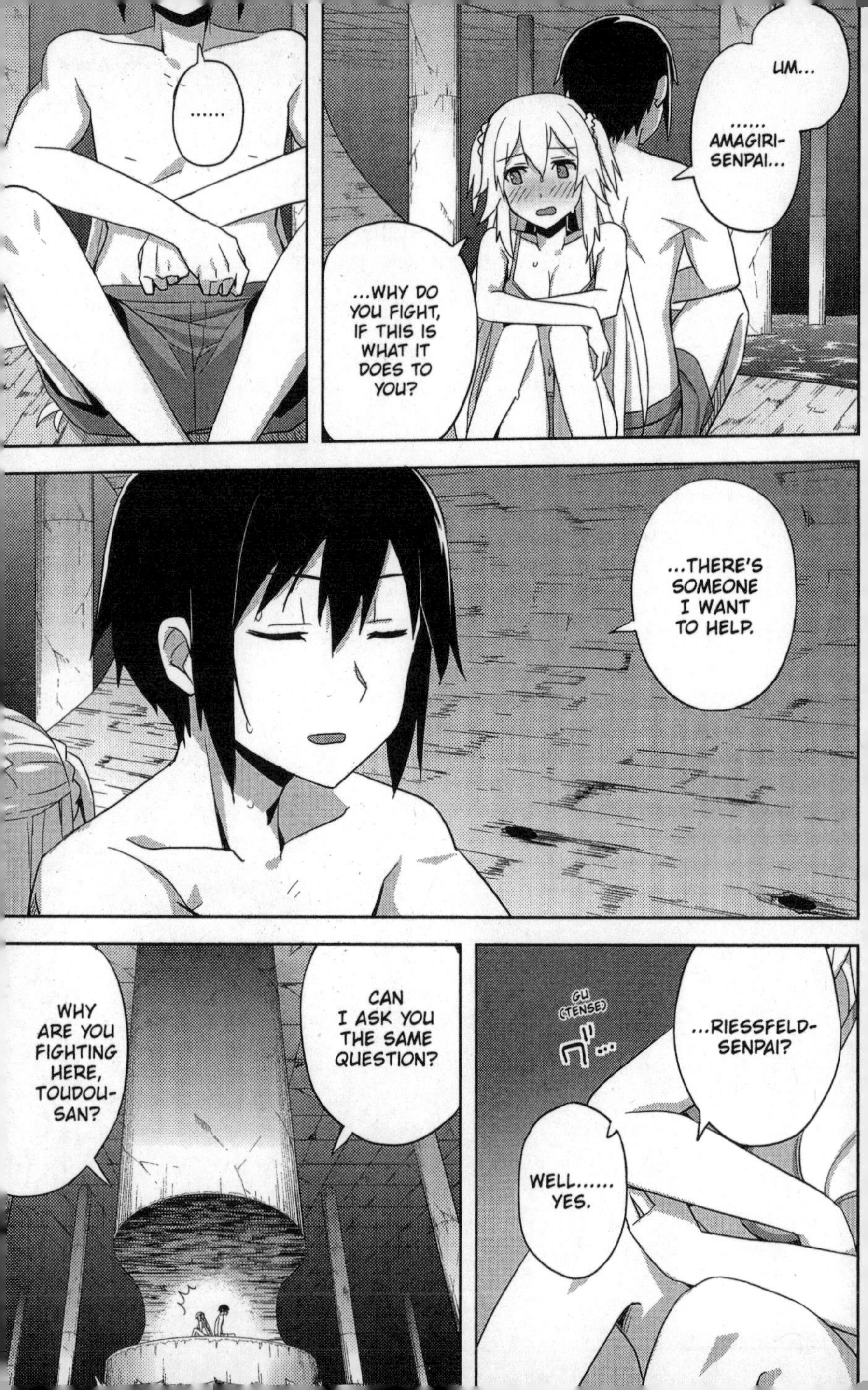
UM...
......AMAGIRI-SENPAI...
...WHY DO YOU FIGHT, IF THIS IS WHAT IT DOES TO YOU?
......
...THERE'S SOMEONE I WANT TO HELP.
GU (TENSE)
...RIESSFELD-SENPAI?
WELL...... YES.
CAN I ASK YOU THE SAME QUESTION?
WHY ARE YOU FIGHTING HERE, TOUDOU-SAN?

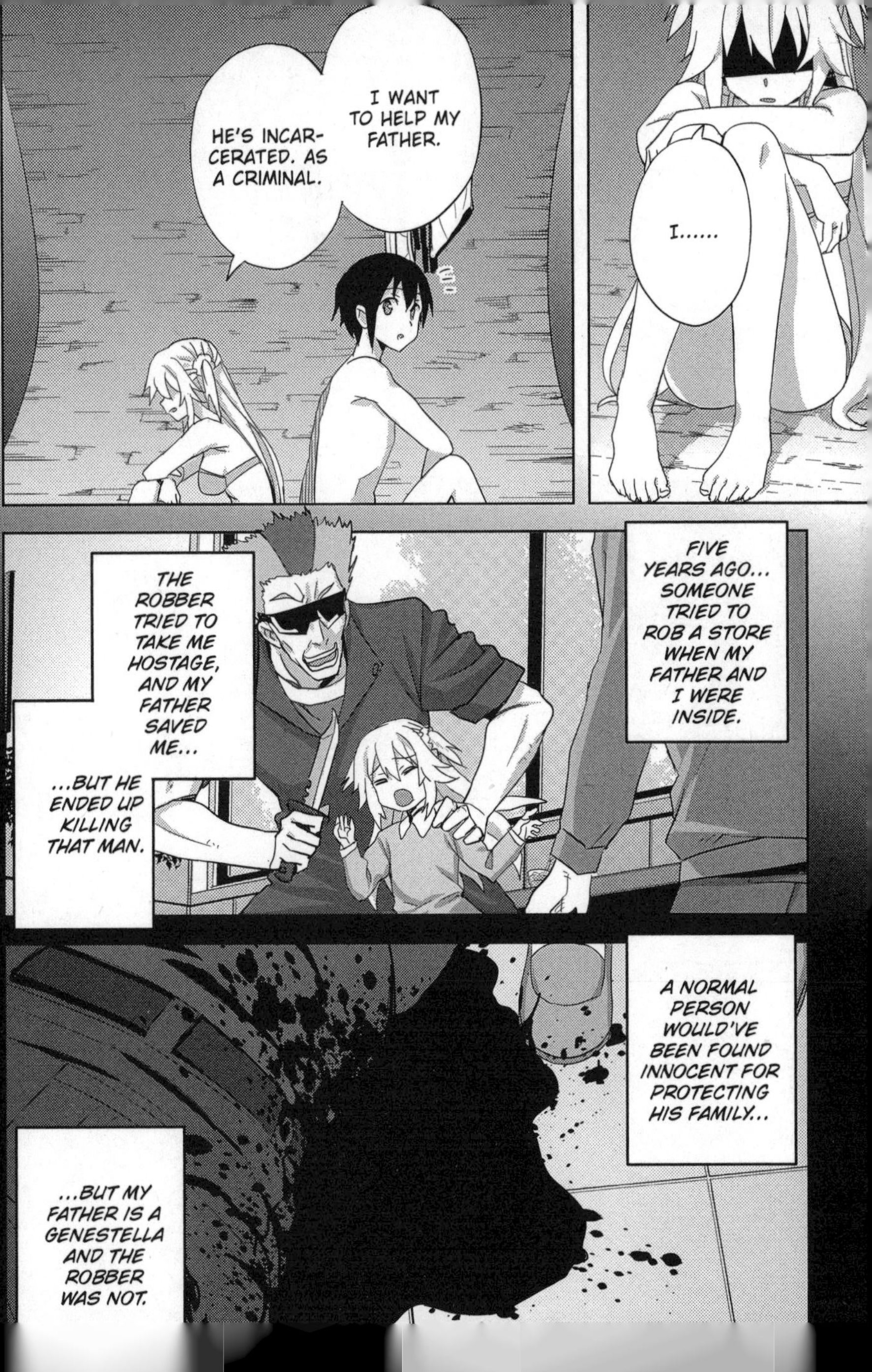
I......
I WANT TO HELP MY FATHER.
HE'S INCARCERATED. AS A CRIMINAL.
FIVE YEARS AGO... SOMEONE TRIED TO ROB A STORE WHEN MY FATHER AND I WERE INSIDE.
THE ROBBER TRIED TO TAKE ME HOSTAGE, AND MY FATHER SAVED ME...
...BUT HE ENDED UP KILLING THAT MAN.
A NORMAL PERSON WOULD'VE BEEN FOUND INNOCENT FOR PROTECTING HIS FAMILY...
...BUT MY FATHER IS A GENESTELLA AND THE ROBBER WAS NOT.

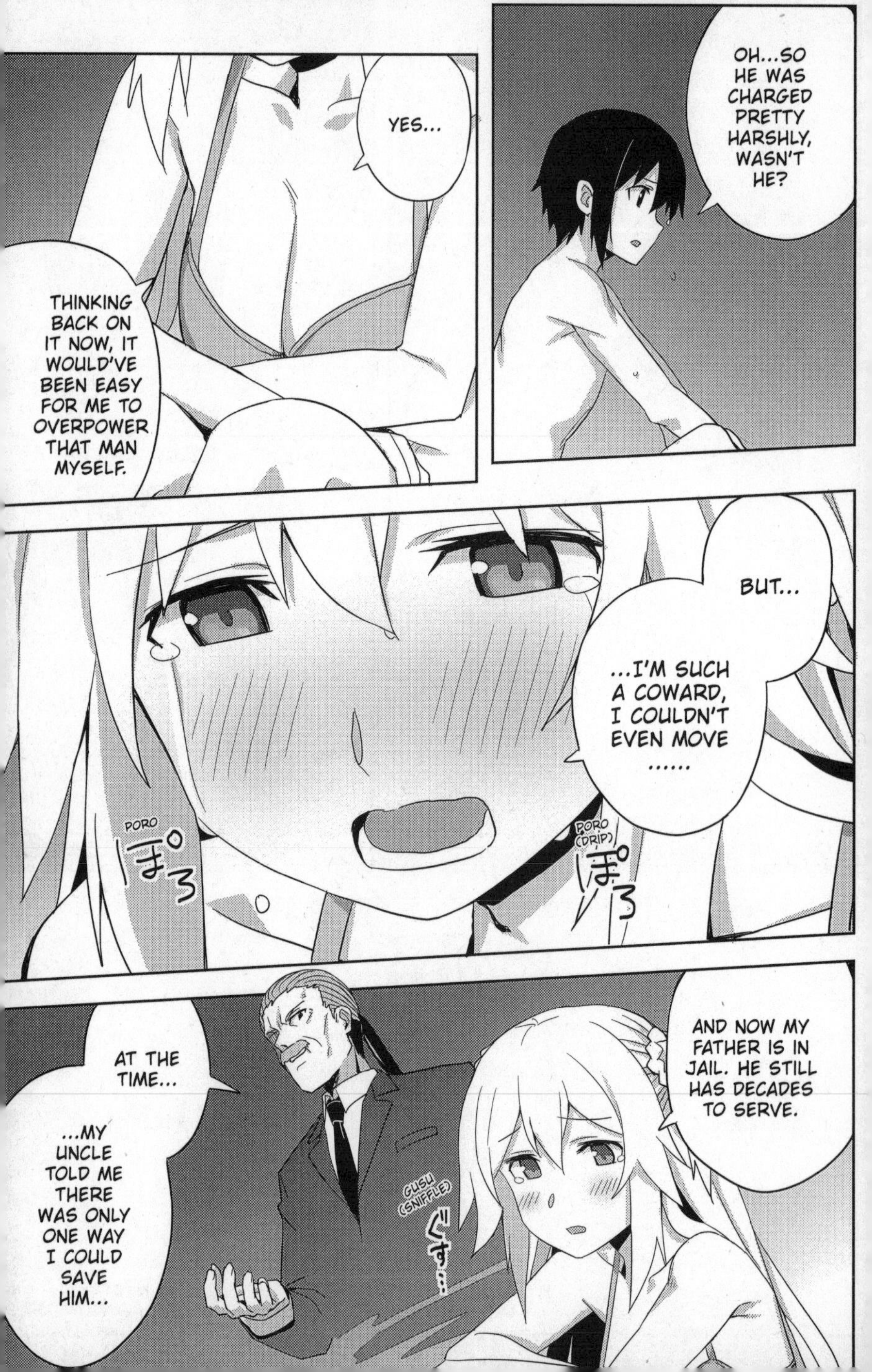
OH...SO HE WAS CHARGED PRETTY HARSHLY, WASN'T HE?
YES...
THINKING BACK ON IT NOW, IT WOULD'VE BEEN EASY FOR ME TO OVERPOWER THAT MAN MYSELF.
BUT...
...I'M SUCH A COWARD, I COULDN'T EVEN MOVE ......
PORO (DRIP)
ぽろ
PORO
ぽろ
AND NOW MY FATHER IS IN JAIL. HE STILL HAS DECADES TO SERVE.
GUSU (SNIFFLE)
ぐす...
AT THE TIME...
...MY UNCLE TOLD ME THERE WAS ONLY ONE WAY I COULD SAVE HIM...

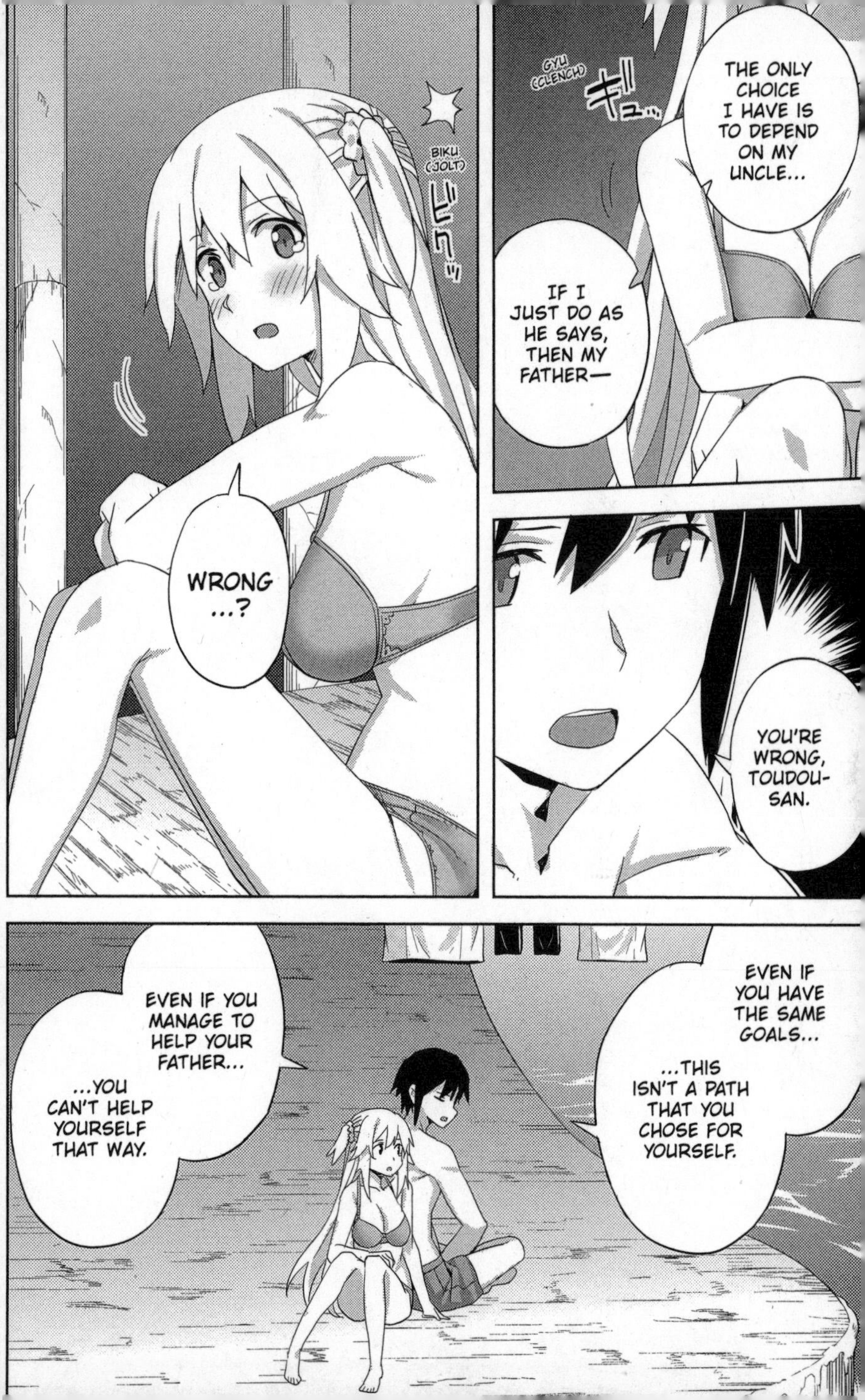
GYU (CLENCH)
ギュ…
THE ONLY CHOICE I HAVE IS TO DEPEND ON MY UNCLE...
IF I JUST DO AS HE SAYS, THEN MY FATHER—
YOU'RE WRONG, TOUDOU-SAN.
BIKU (JOLT)
ビクッ
WRONG ...?
EVEN IF YOU HAVE THE SAME GOALS...
...THIS ISN'T A PATH THAT YOU CHOSE FOR YOURSELF.
EVEN IF YOU MANAGE TO HELP YOUR FATHER...
...YOU CAN'T HELP YOURSELF THAT WAY.

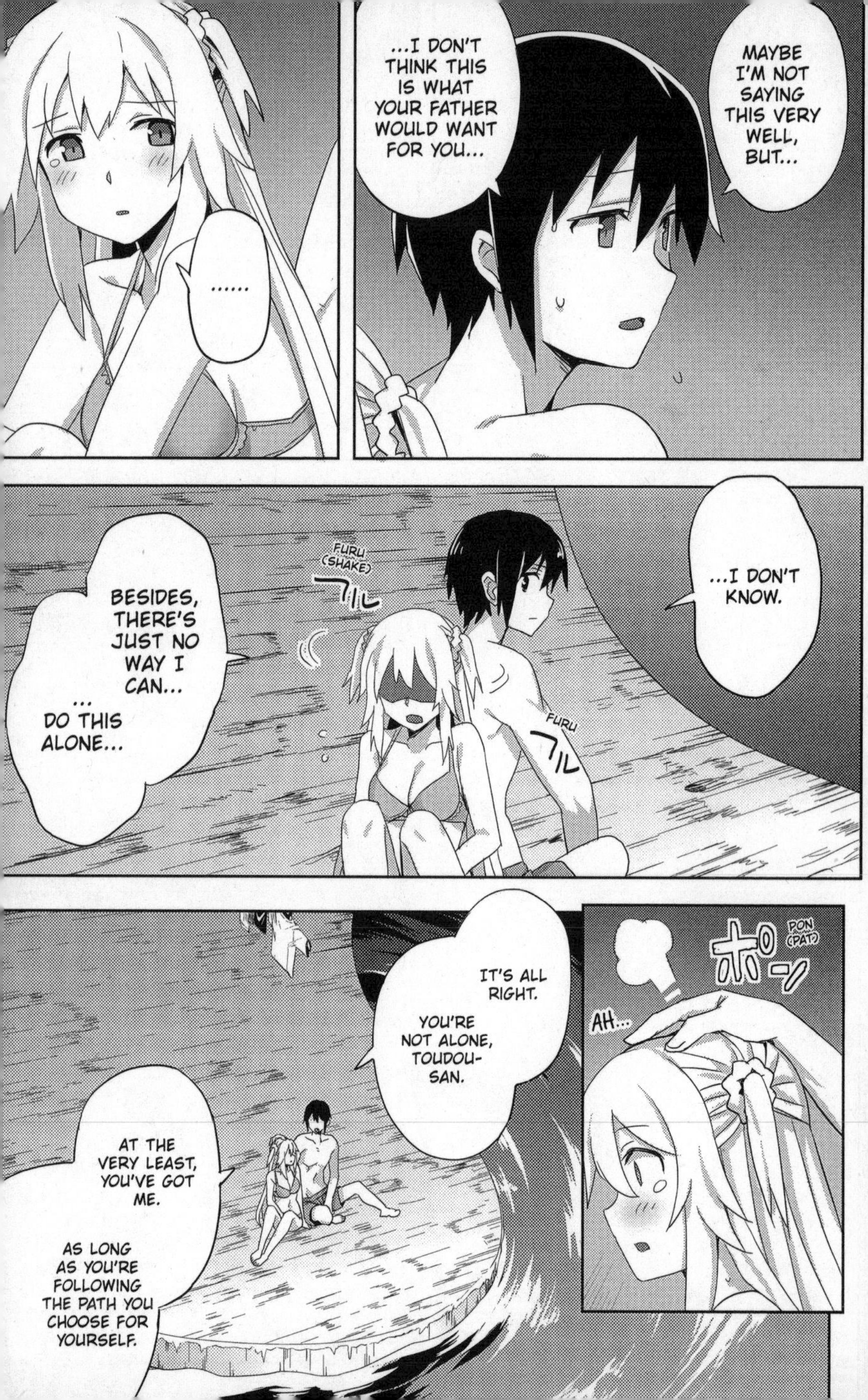
MAYBE I'M NOT SAYING THIS VERY WELL, BUT...
...I DON'T THINK THIS IS WHAT YOUR FATHER WOULD WANT FOR YOU...
......
...I DON'T KNOW.
FURU
FURU (SHAKE)
BESIDES, THERE'S JUST NO WAY I CAN... ... DO THIS ALONE...
PON (PAT)
AH...
IT'S ALL RIGHT.
YOU'RE NOT ALONE, TOUDOU-SAN.
AT THE VERY LEAST, YOU'VE GOT ME.
AS LONG AS YOU'RE FOLLOWING THE PATH YOU CHOOSE FOR YOURSELF.

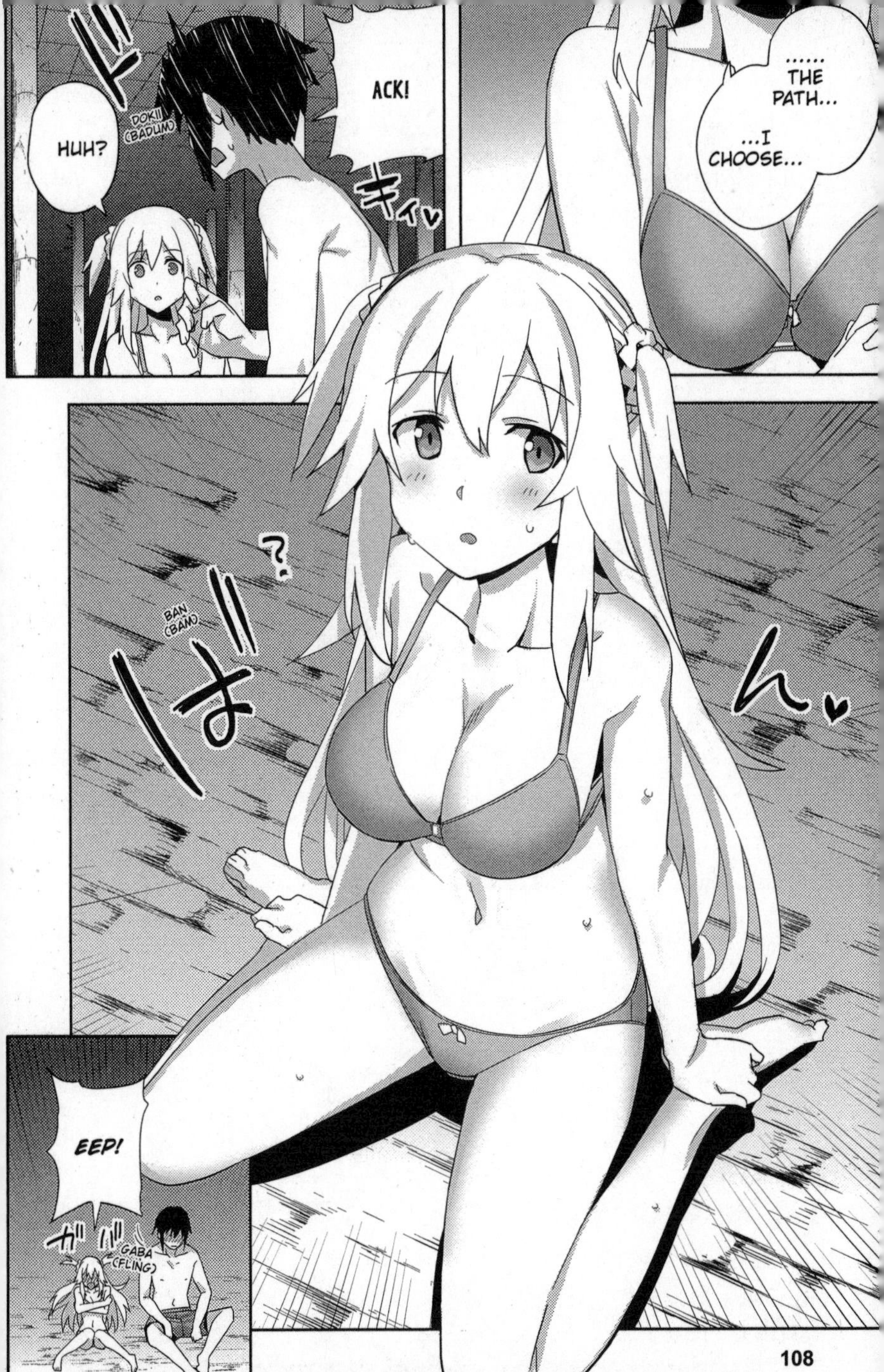

......
THE PATH...
...I CHOOSE...
ACK!
DOKI! (BADUM)
HUH?
?
BAN (BAM)
EEP!
GABA (FLING)

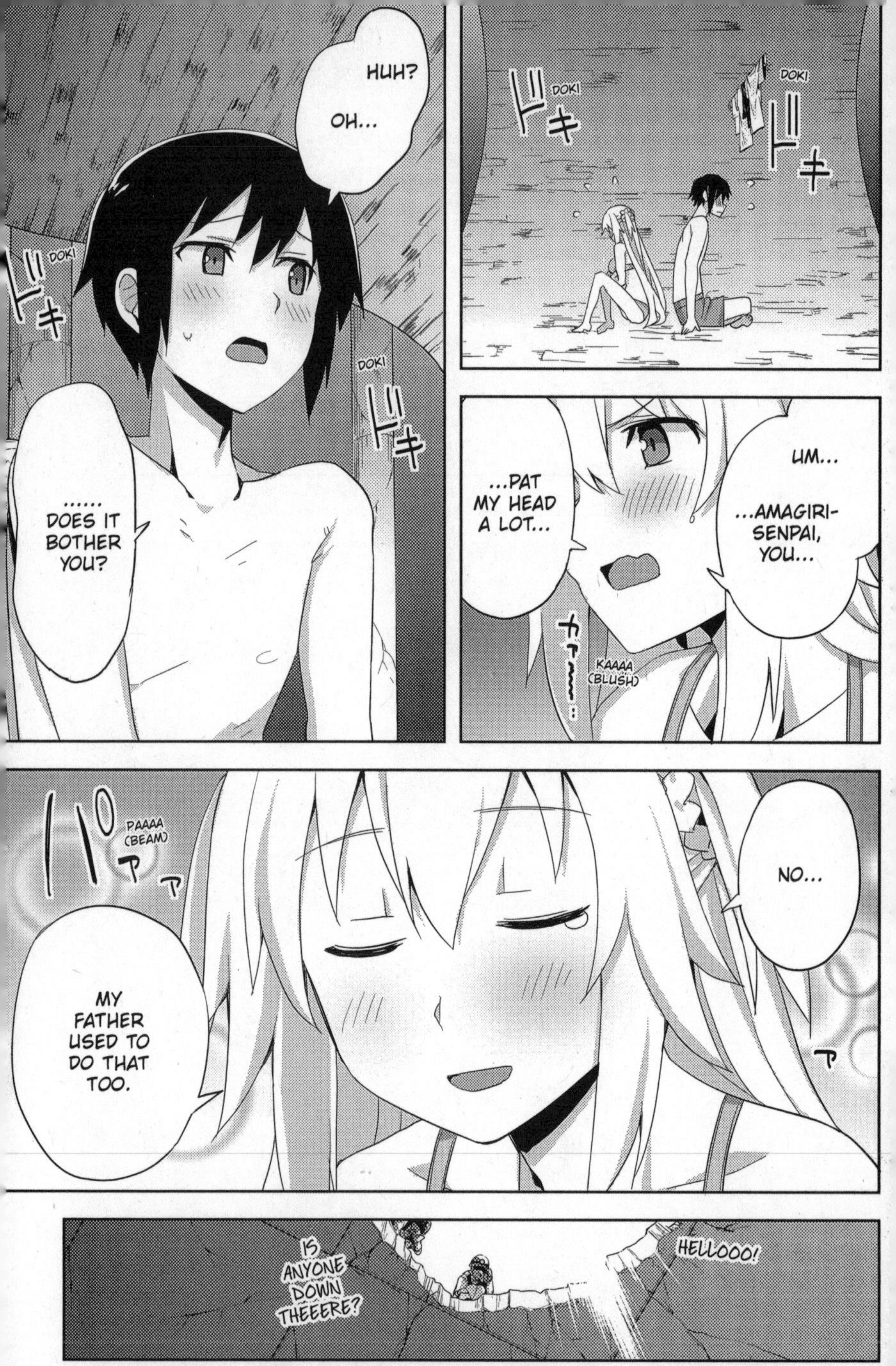

ドキ
DOKI
ドキ
DOKI
UM...
...AMAGIRI-SENPAI, YOU...
...PAT MY HEAD A LOT...
カァ〜〜…
KAAAA (BLUSH)
HUH?
OH...
ドキ
DOKI
ドキ
DOKI
...... DOES IT BOTHER YOU?
NO...
パァァ
PAAAA (BEAM)
MY FATHER USED TO DO THAT TOO.
HELLOOO!
IS ANYONE DOWN THEEERE?

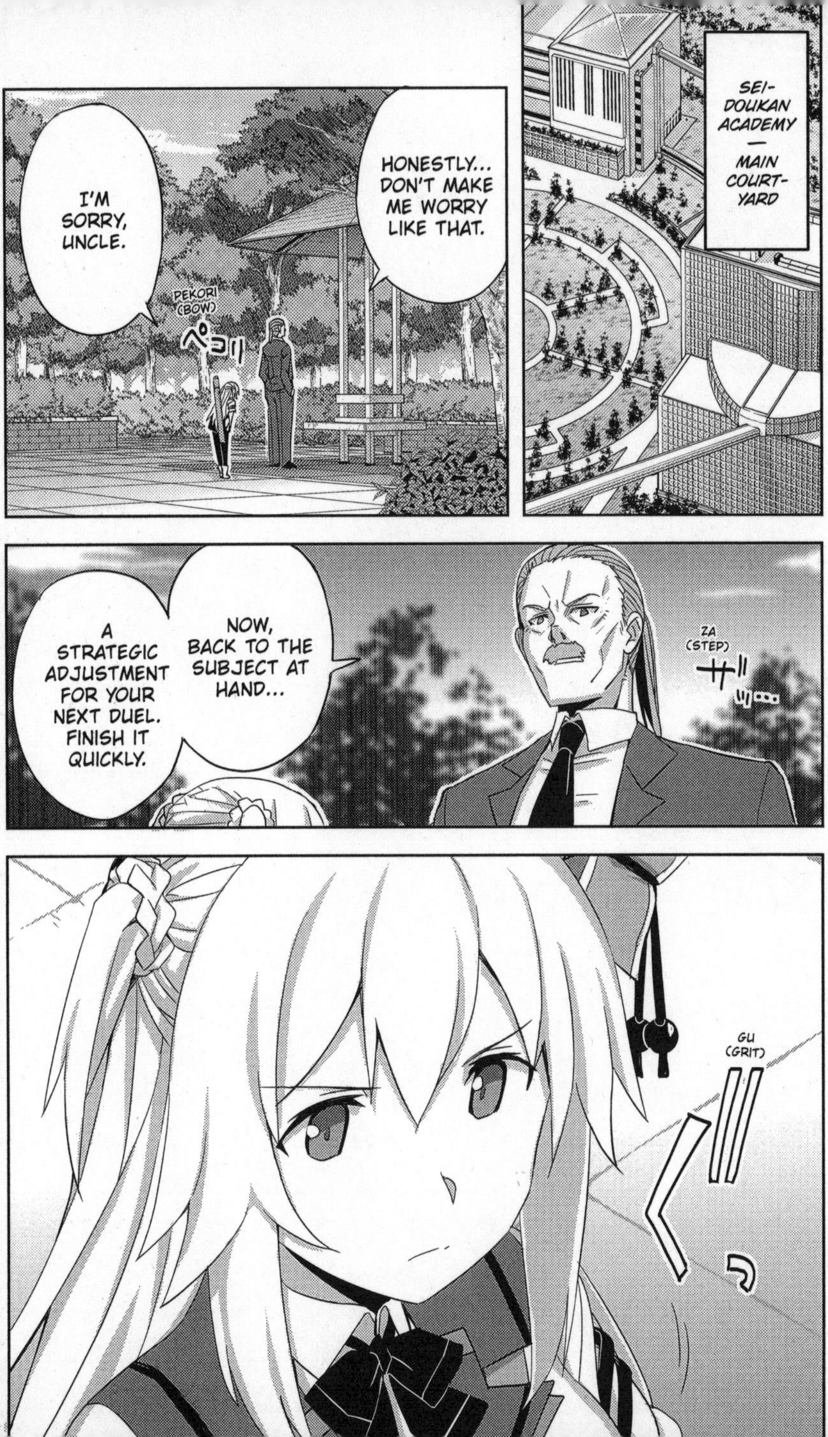

SEI-DOUKAN ACADEMY — MAIN COURTYARD
HONESTLY... DON'T MAKE ME WORRY LIKE THAT.
I'M SORRY, UNCLE.
PEKORI (BOW)
ZA (STEP)
NOW, BACK TO THE SUBJECT AT HAND...
A STRATEGIC ADJUSTMENT FOR YOUR NEXT DUEL. FINISH IT QUICKLY.
GU (GRIT)

THE ASTERISK WAR

DRAGON ON STANDBY

......

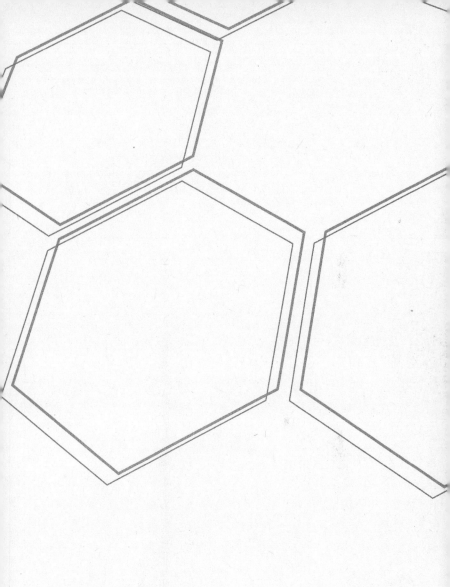

THE
ASTERISK WAR

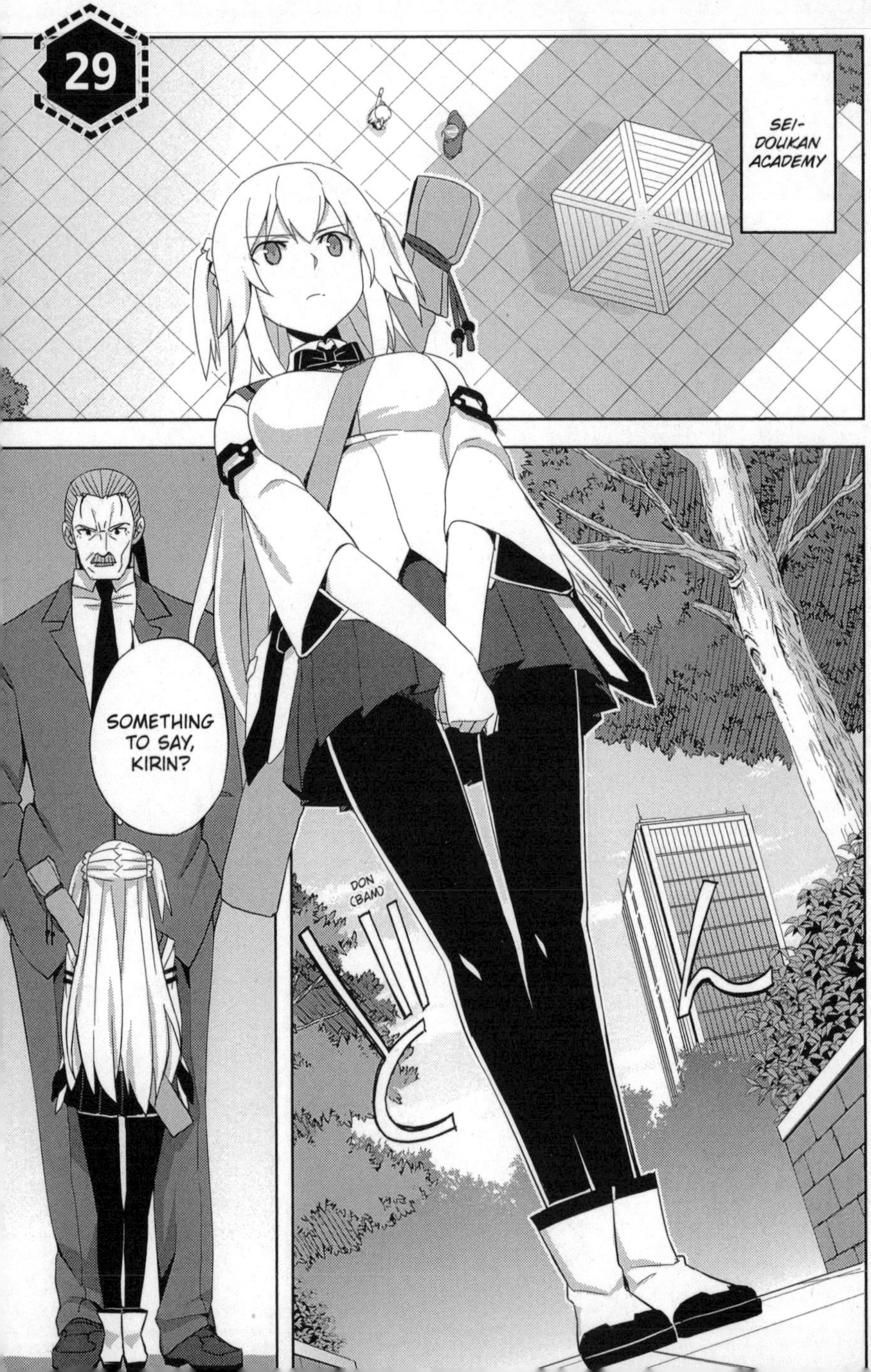
29
SEI-DOUKAN ACADEMY
SOMETHING TO SAY, KIRIN?
DON (BAM)

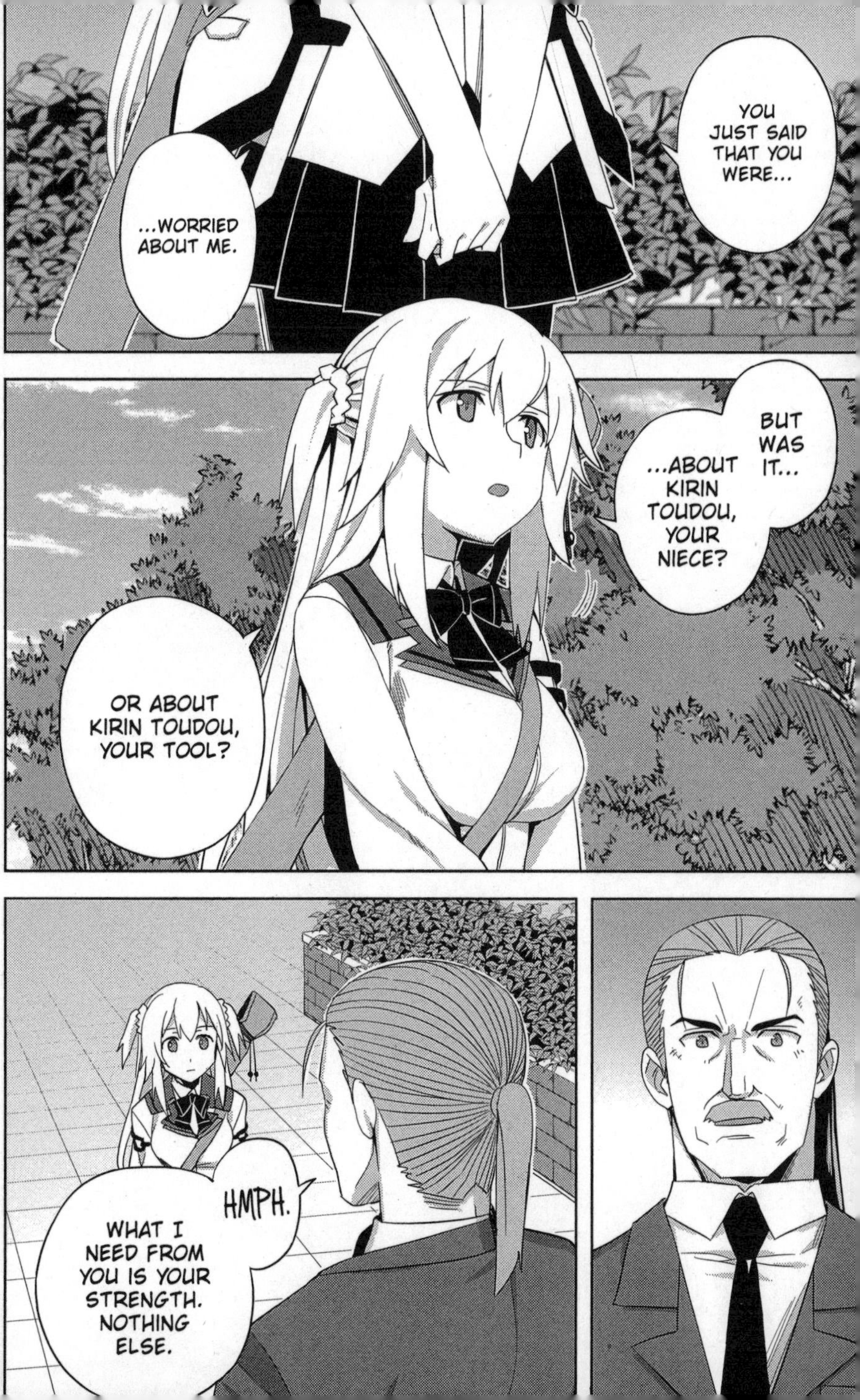
YOU JUST SAID THAT YOU WERE...
...WORRIED ABOUT ME.
BUT WAS IT...
...ABOUT KIRIN TOUDOU, YOUR NIECE?
OR ABOUT KIRIN TOUDOU, YOUR TOOL?
HMPH.
WHAT I NEED FROM YOU IS YOUR STRENGTH. NOTHING ELSE.

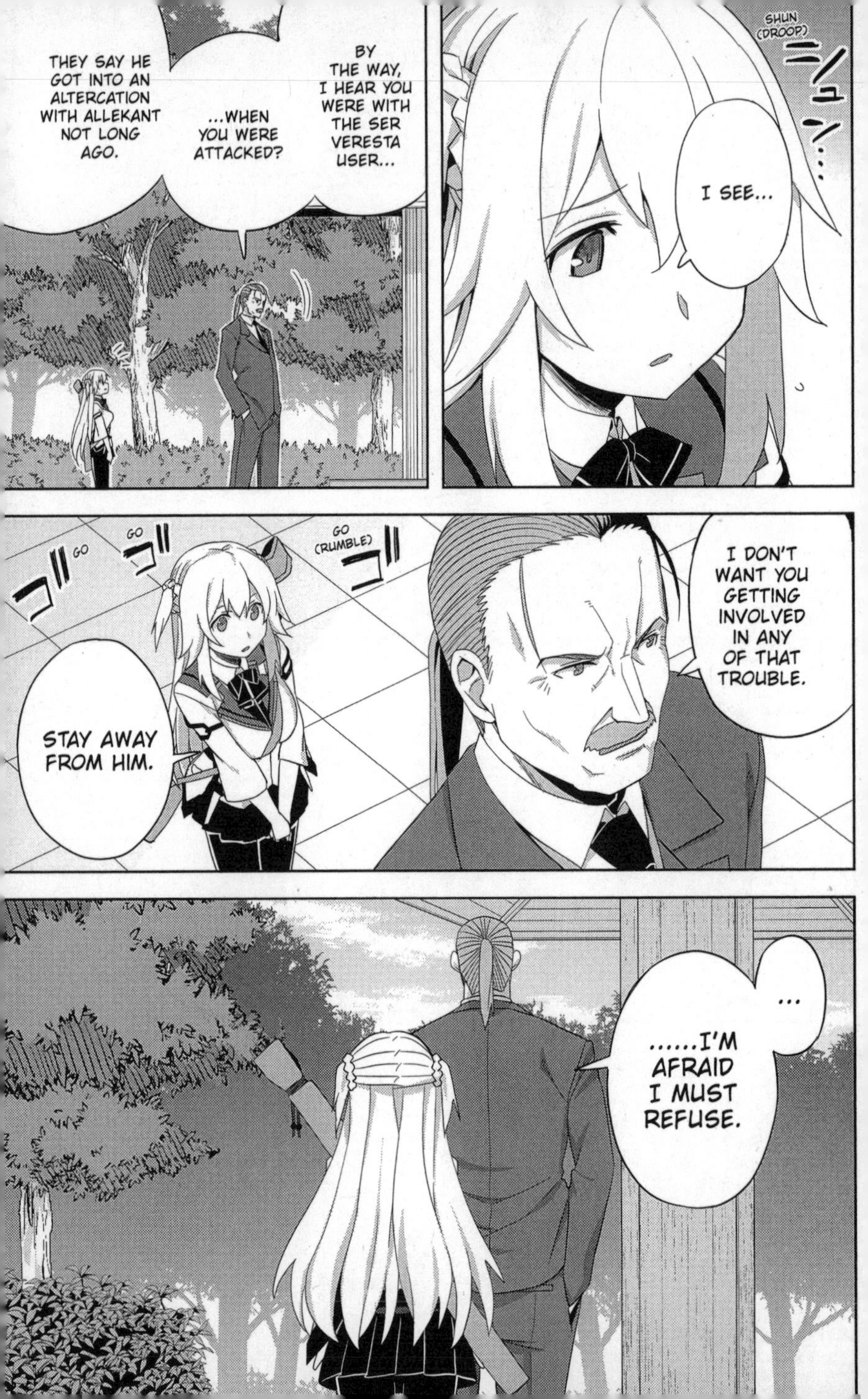
SHUN (DROOP)
I SEE...
BY THE WAY, I HEAR YOU WERE WITH THE SER VERESTA USER...
...WHEN YOU WERE ATTACKED?
THEY SAY HE GOT INTO AN ALTERCATION WITH ALLEKANT NOT LONG AGO.
GO (RUMBLE)
I DON'T WANT YOU GETTING INVOLVED IN ANY OF THAT TROUBLE.
GO
GO
STAY AWAY FROM HIM.
...
......I'M AFRAID I MUST REFUSE.

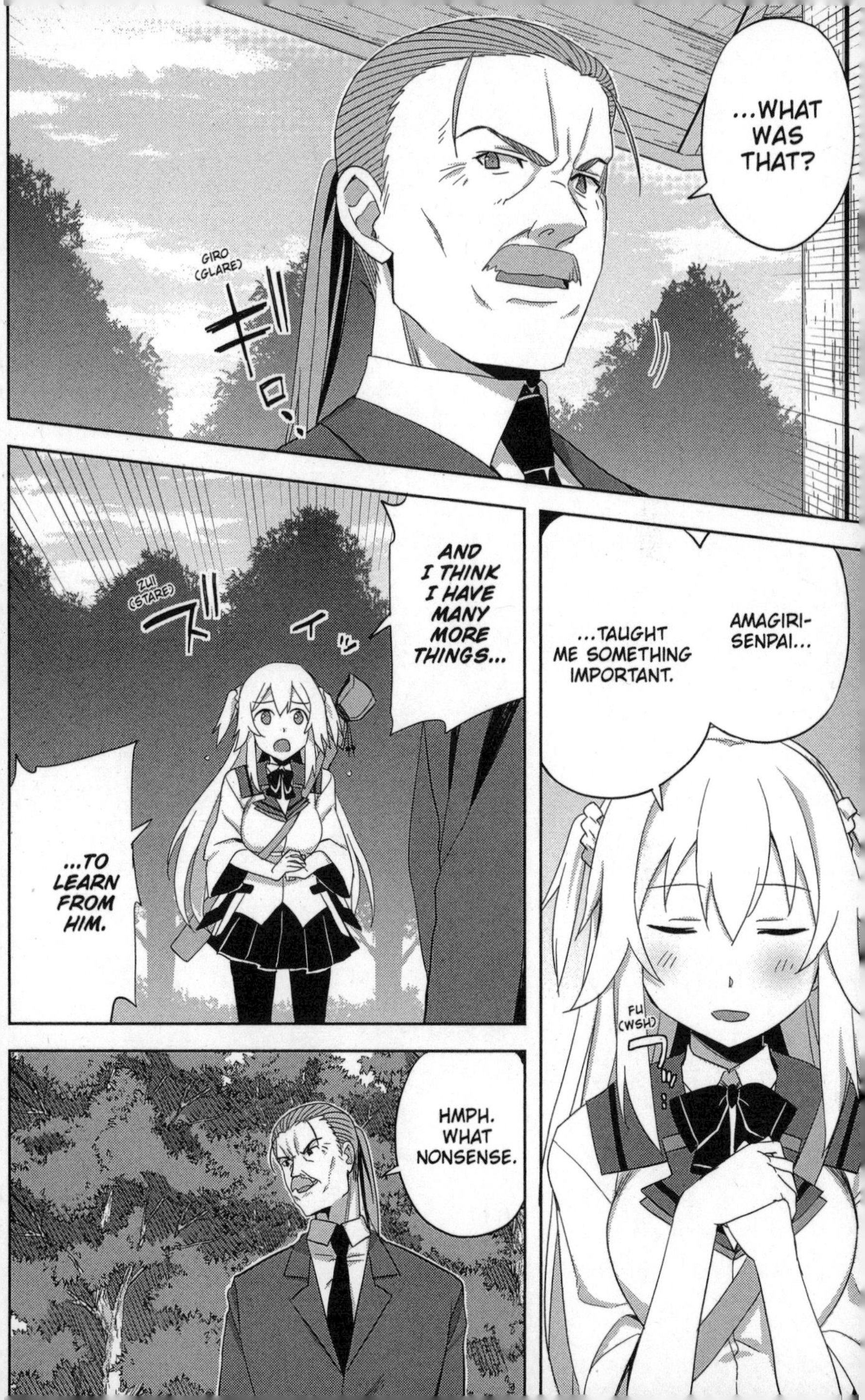
...WHAT WAS THAT?
GIRO (GLARE)
AMAGIRI-SENPAI...
...TAUGHT ME SOMETHING IMPORTANT.
FU (WSH)
AND I THINK I HAVE MANY MORE THINGS...
ZUI (STARE)
...TO LEARN FROM HIM.
HMPH. WHAT NONSENSE.

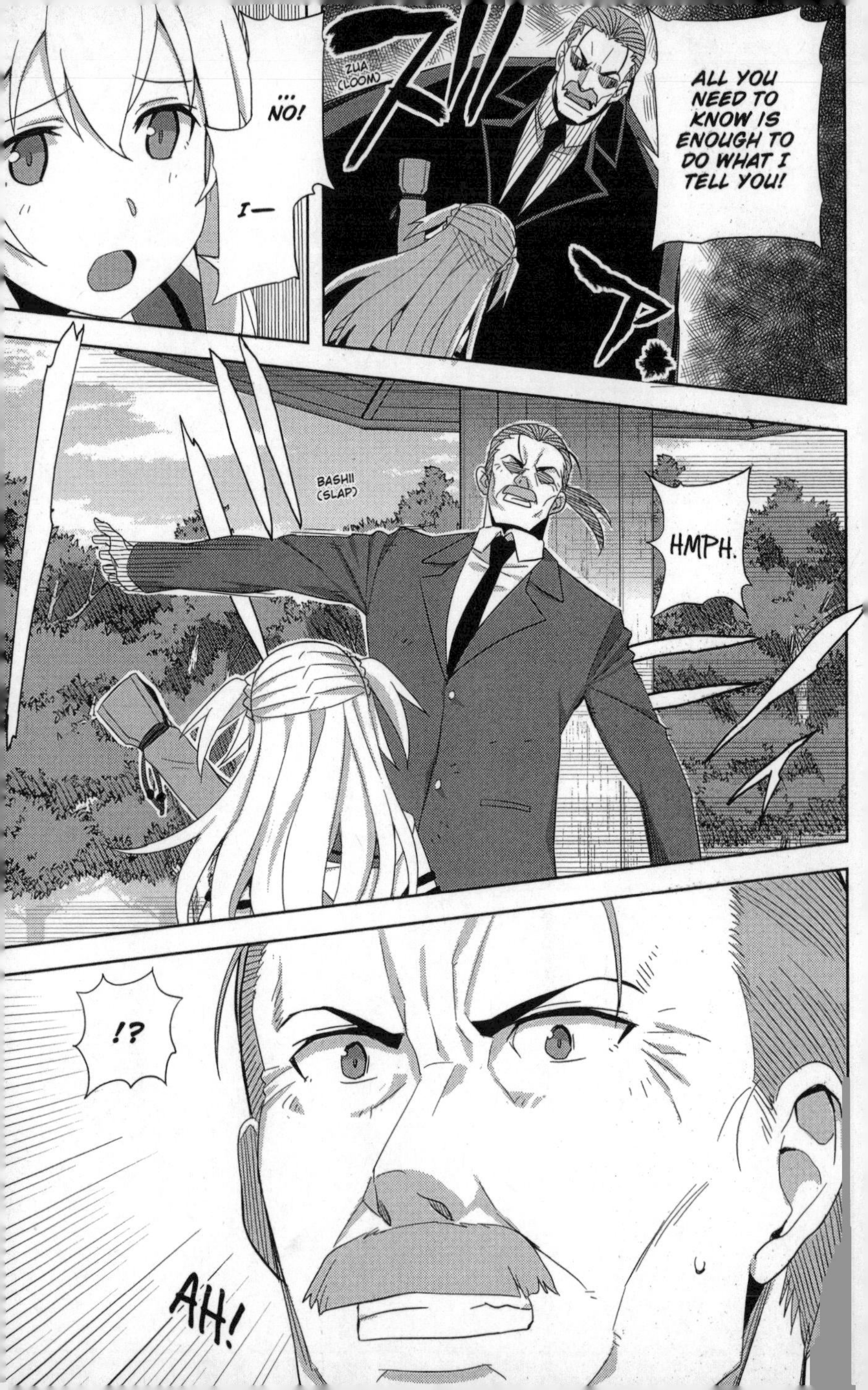
ALL YOU NEED TO KNOW IS ENOUGH TO DO WHAT I TELL YOU!
ZUA (LOOM)
... NO!
I—
HMPH.
BASHII (SLAP)
!?
AH!

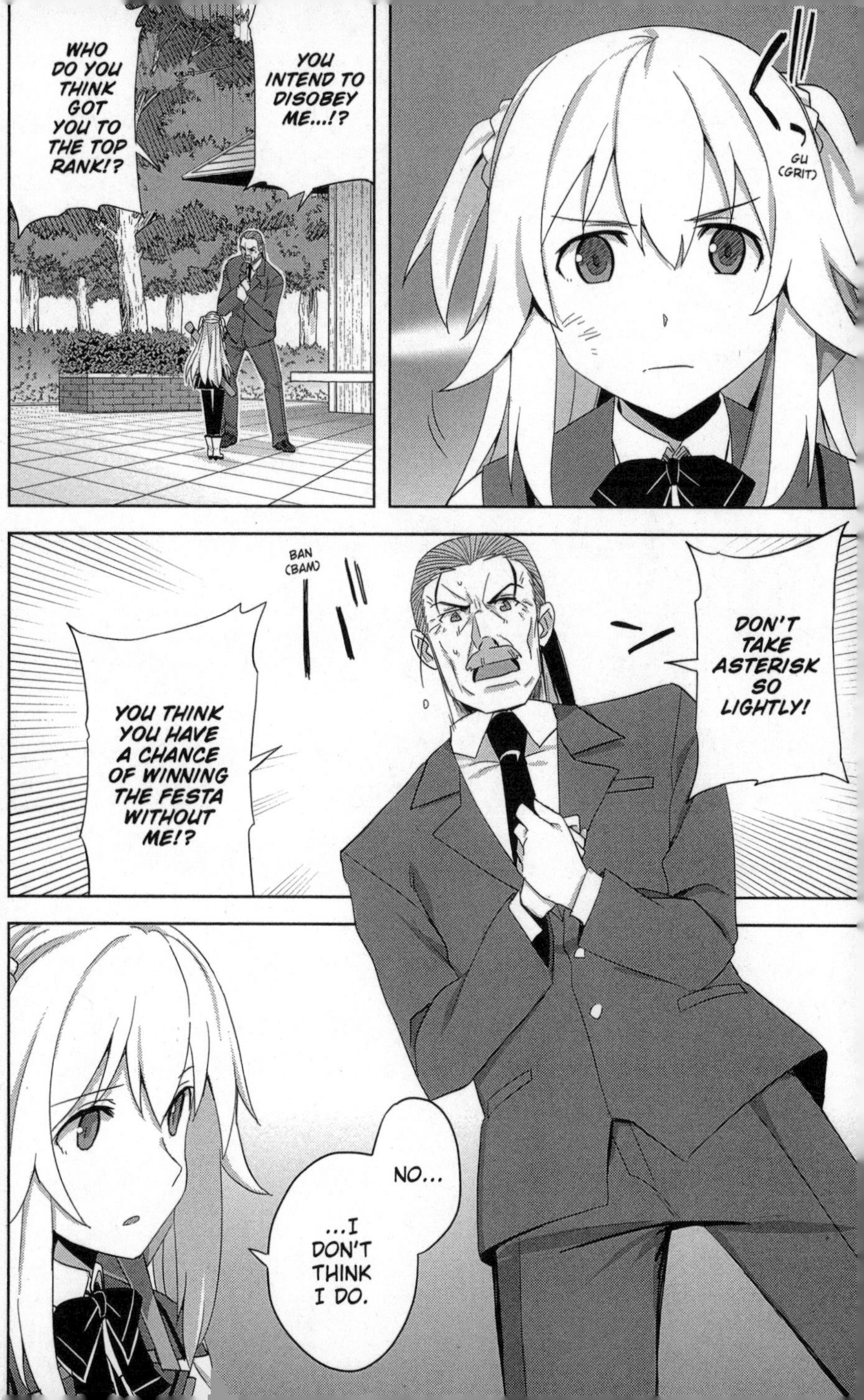
GU (GRIT)
YOU INTEND TO DISOBEY ME...!?
WHO DO YOU THINK GOT YOU TO THE TOP RANK!?
DON'T TAKE ASTERISK SO LIGHTLY!
BAN (BAM)
YOU THINK YOU HAVE A CHANCE OF WINNING THE FESTA WITHOUT ME!?
NO...
...I DON'T THINK I DO.

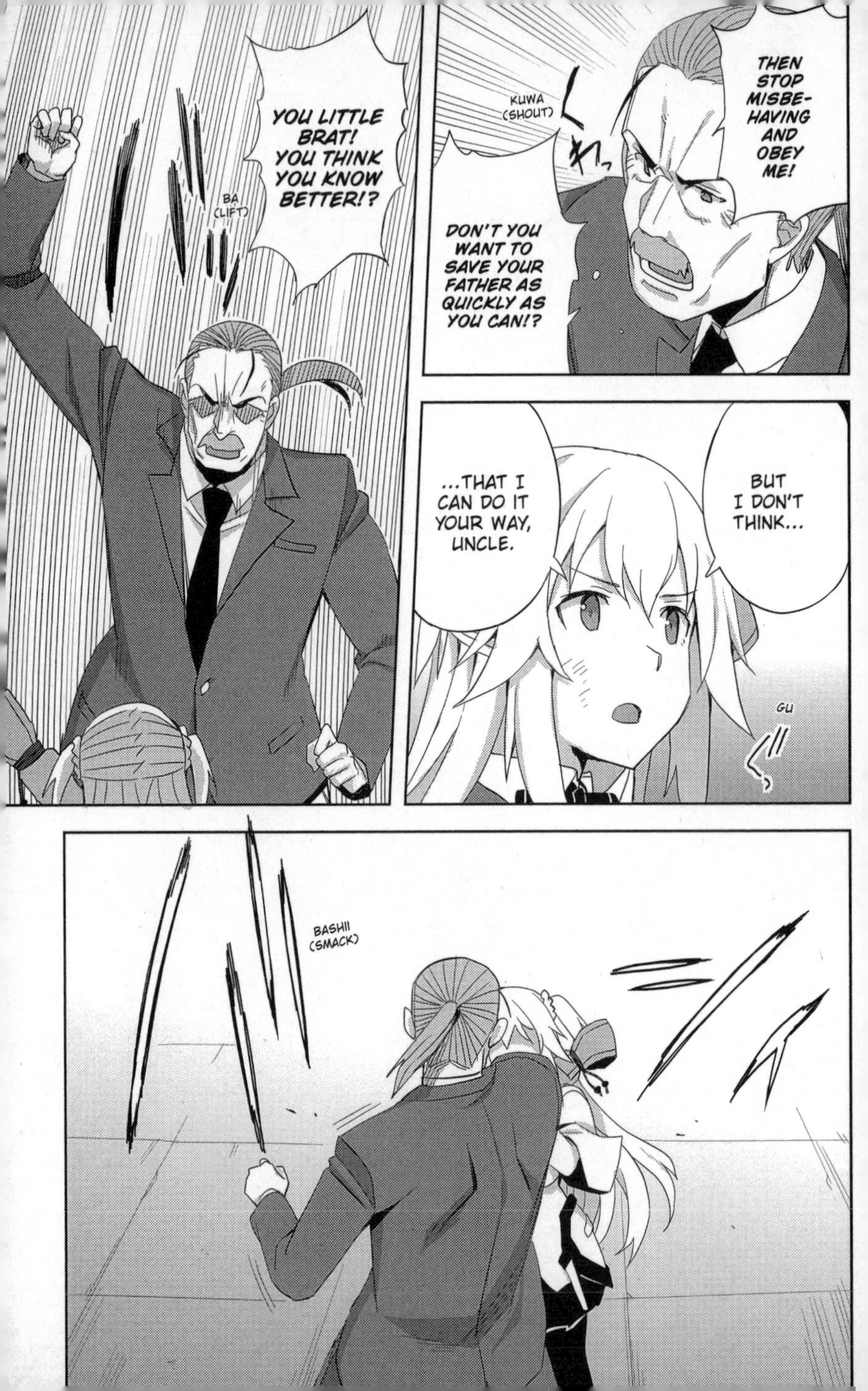
THEN STOP MISBE-HAVING AND OBEY ME!
KUWA (SHOUT)
DON'T YOU WANT TO SAVE YOUR FATHER AS QUICKLY AS YOU CAN!?
BUT I DON'T THINK...
...THAT I CAN DO IT YOUR WAY, UNCLE.
GU
YOU LITTLE BRAT! YOU THINK YOU KNOW BETTER!?
BA (LIFT)
BASHII (SMACK)

DON
(BOOM)

GU
(STRAIN)
GU

I'M SORRY,
UNCLE...

GU
GU
GU

NGH...!

ZO
(FLINCH)

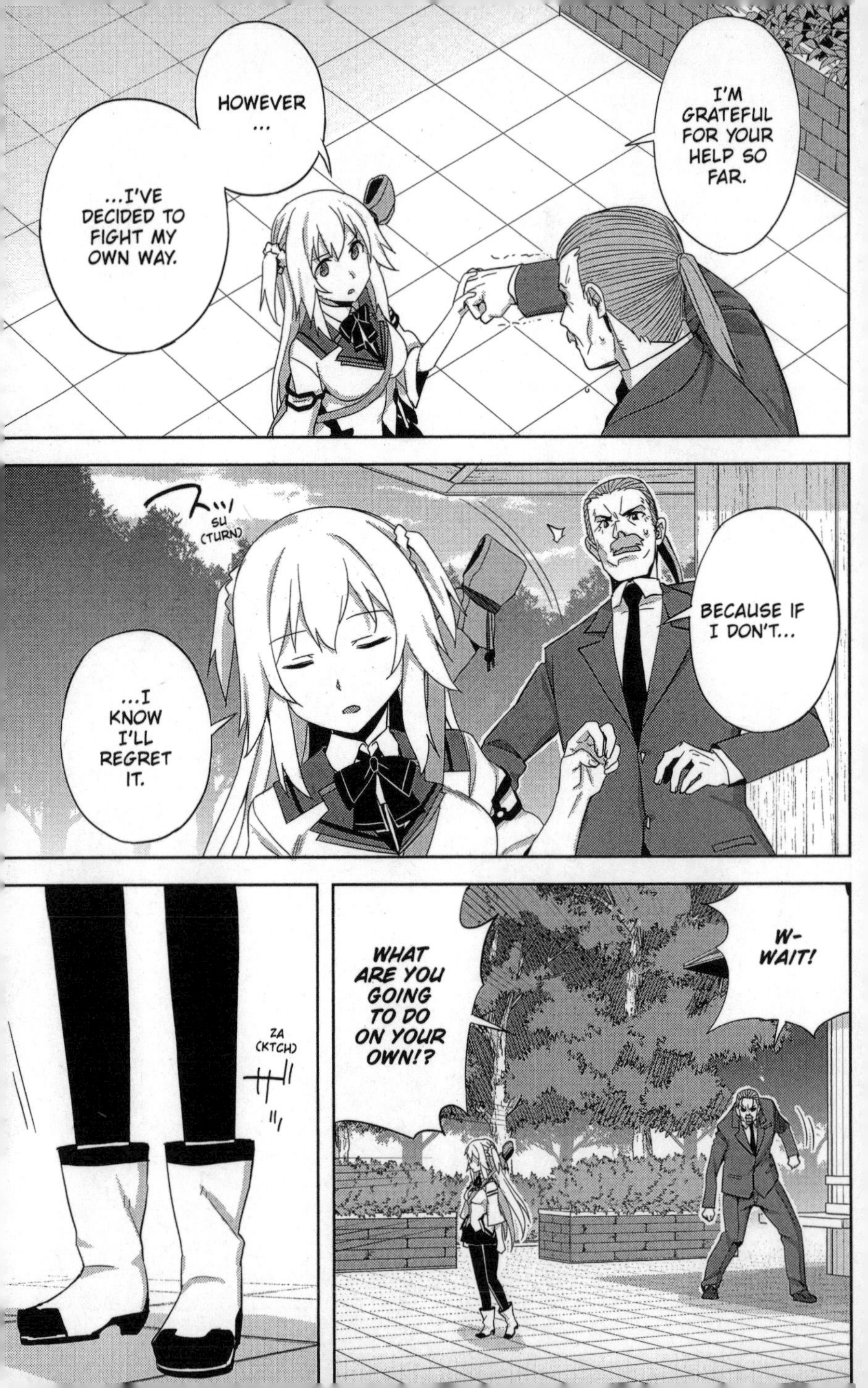

I'M GRATEFUL FOR YOUR HELP SO FAR.
HOWEVER ...
...I'VE DECIDED TO FIGHT MY OWN WAY.
BECAUSE IF I DON'T...
SU (TURN)
...I KNOW I'LL REGRET IT.
W-WAIT!
WHAT ARE YOU GOING TO DO ON YOUR OWN!?
ZA (KTCH)

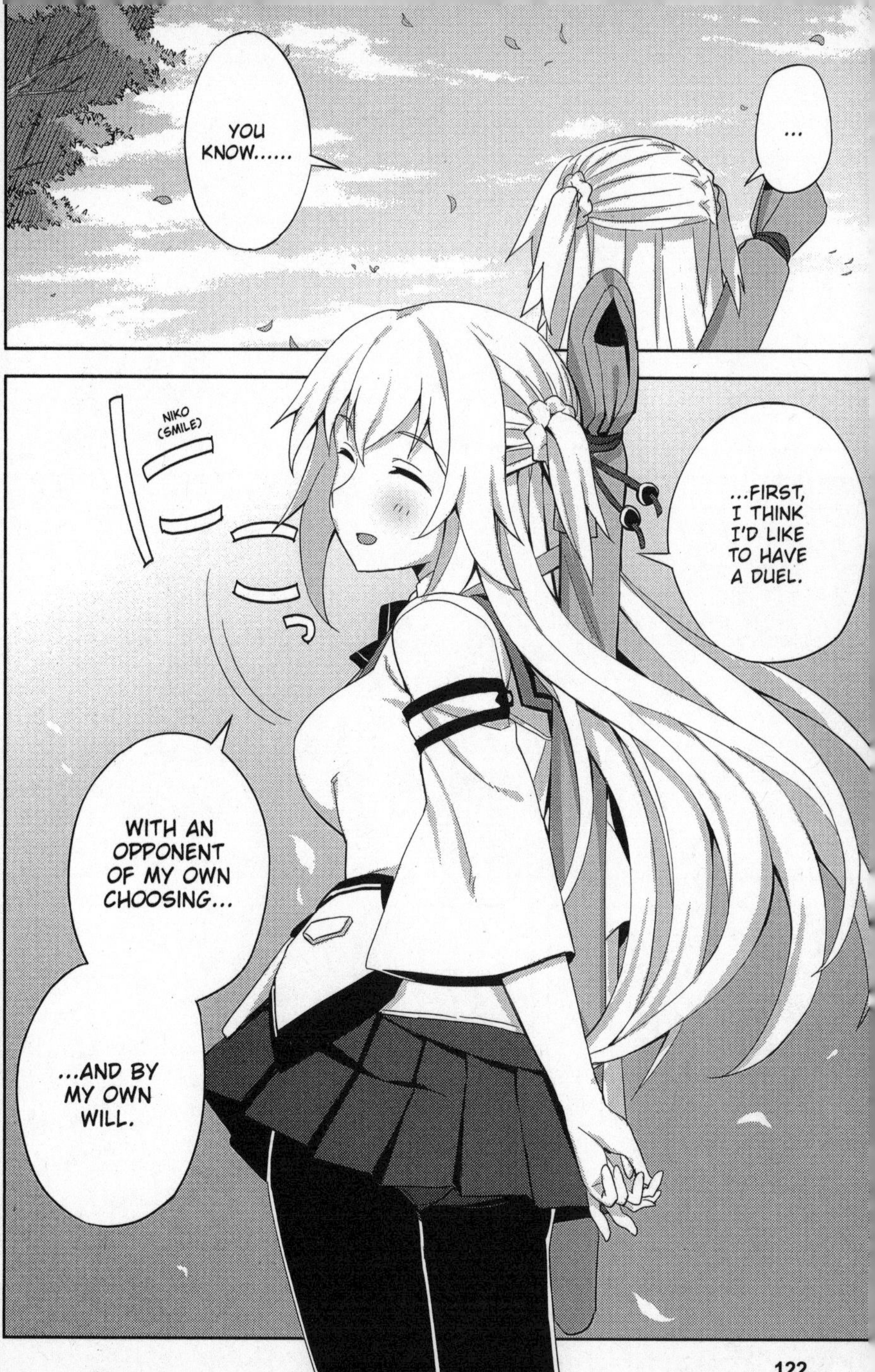
...
YOU KNOW......
...FIRST, I THINK I'D LIKE TO HAVE A DUEL.
NIKO (SMILE)
WITH AN OPPONENT OF MY OWN CHOOSING...
...AND BY MY OWN WILL.

THE ASTERISK WAR

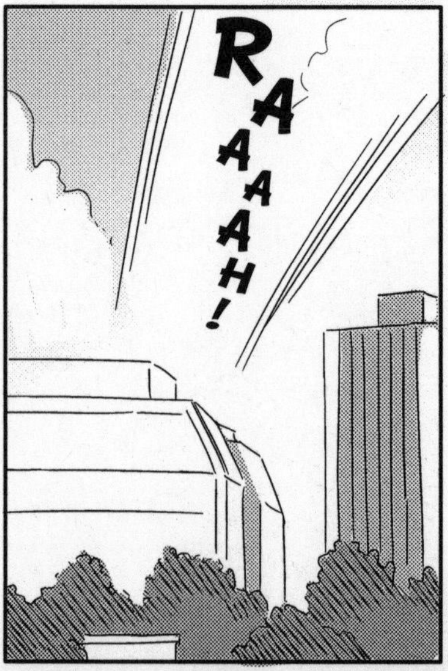
RAAAAAH!

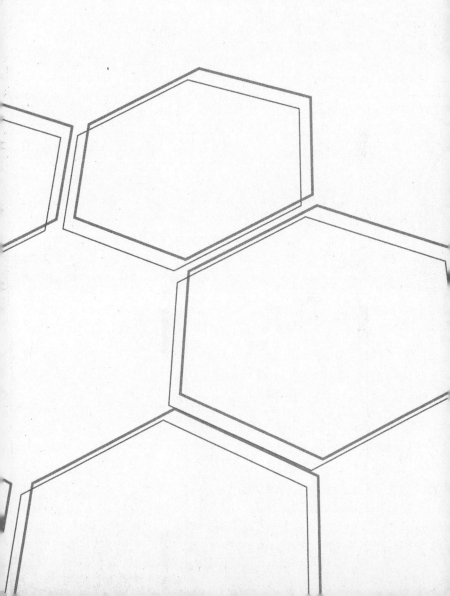

THE
ASTERISK WAR

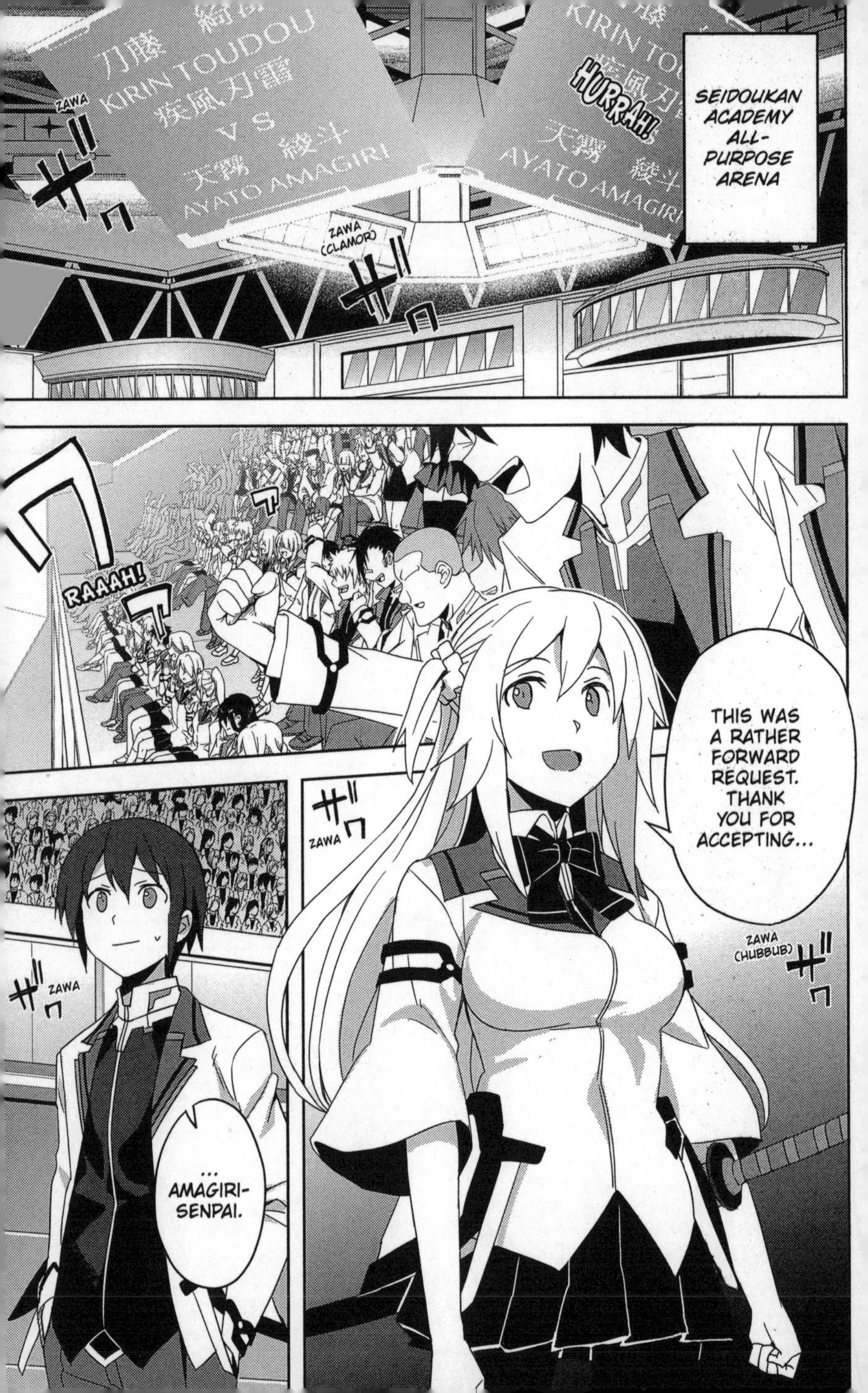
SEIDOUKAN ACADEMY ALL-PURPOSE ARENA
HURRAH!
KIRIN TOUDOU
疾風刃雷
VS
天霧 綾斗
AYATO AMAGIRI
ZAWA (CLAMOR)
ZAWA
RAAAH!
THIS WAS A RATHER FORWARD REQUEST. THANK YOU FOR ACCEPTING...
ZAWA (HUBBUB)
ZAWA
...AMAGIRI-SENPAI.
ZAWA

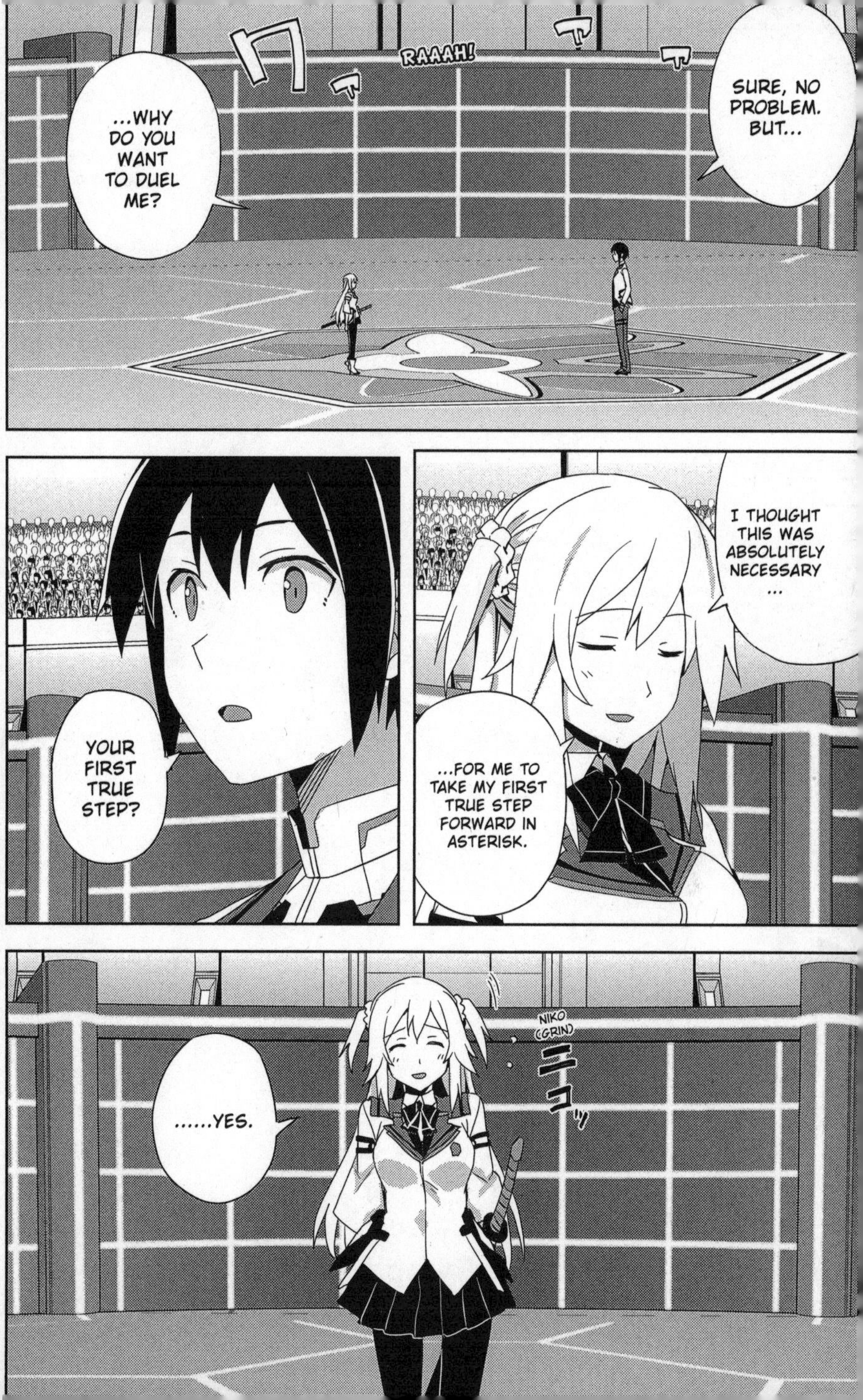
SURE, NO PROBLEM. BUT...
RAAAH!
...WHY DO YOU WANT TO DUEL ME?
I THOUGHT THIS WAS ABSOLUTELY NECESSARY ...
...FOR ME TO TAKE MY FIRST TRUE STEP FORWARD IN ASTERISK.
YOUR FIRST TRUE STEP?
NIKO (GRIN)
......YES.

YES!

BUT IF WE'RE GOING TO DO THIS...

...I WON'T HOLD BACK!

OKAY.

CHA (KCHK)

WELL, IT'S NOT LIKE I DID BEFORE EITHER.

GUN (SHAMM)

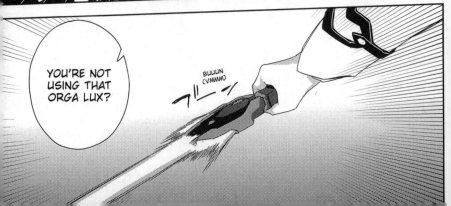

YOU'RE NOT USING THAT ORGA LUX?

BUUUN (VMMMM)

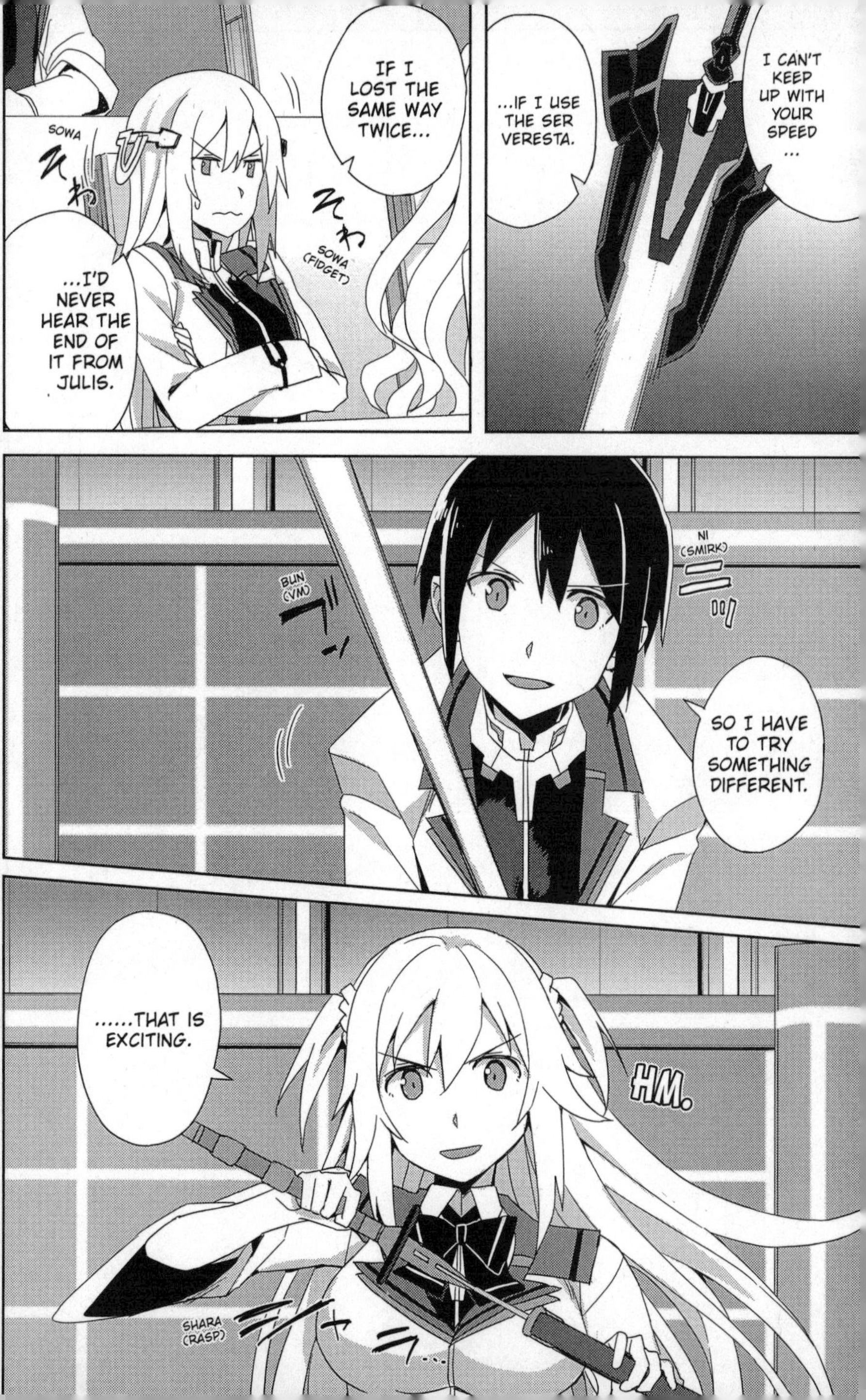
I CAN'T KEEP UP WITH YOUR SPEED...
...IF I USE THE SER VERESTA.
IF I LOST THE SAME WAY TWICE...
SOWA
SOWA (FIDGET)
...I'D NEVER HEAR THE END OF IT FROM JULIS.
NI (SMIRK)
BUN (VM)
SO I HAVE TO TRY SOMETHING DIFFERENT.
......THAT IS EXCITING.
HM.
SHARA (RASP)

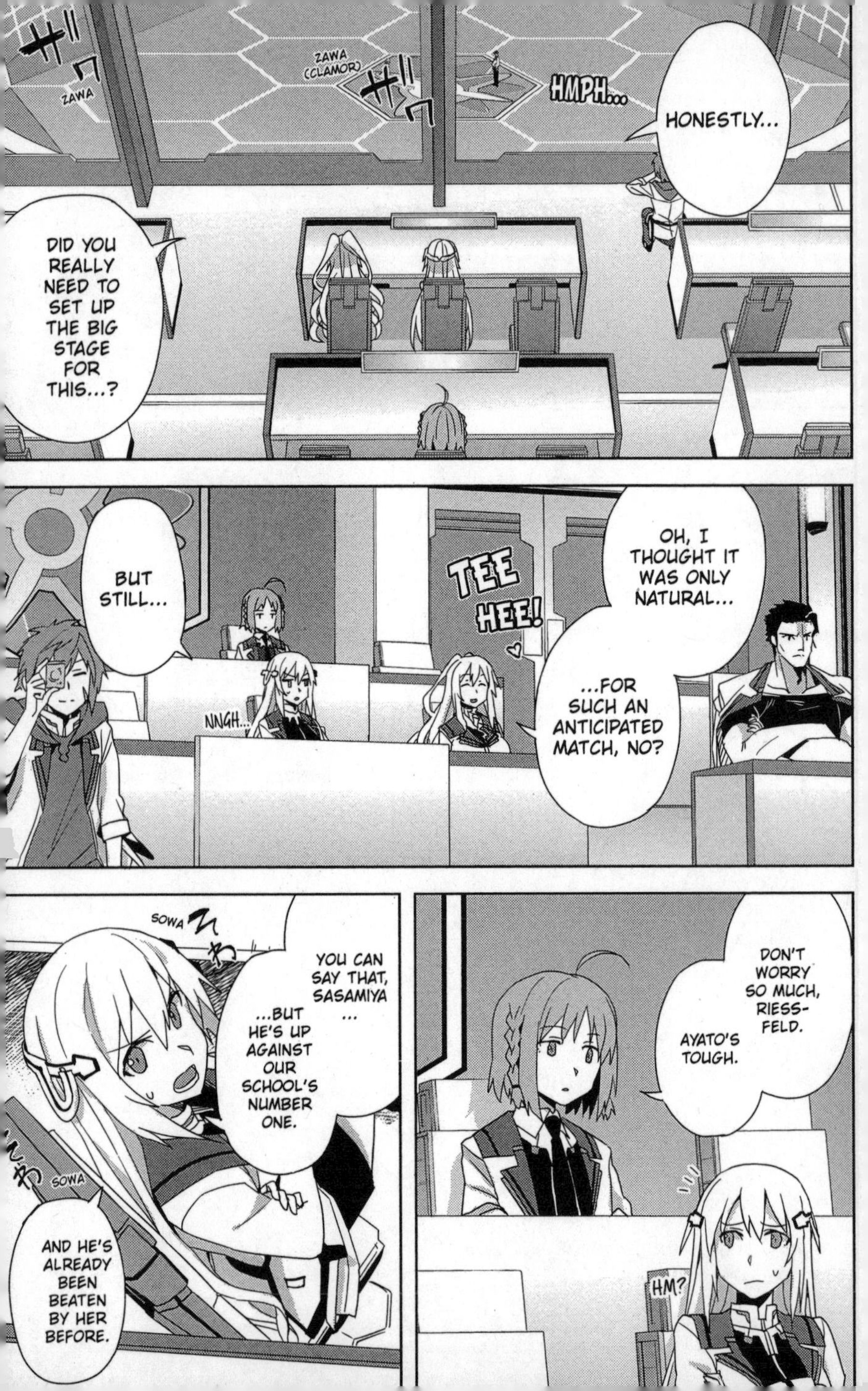
HONESTLY...
HMPH...
ZAWA (CLAMOR)
ZAWA
DID YOU REALLY NEED TO SET UP THE BIG STAGE FOR THIS...?
OH, I THOUGHT IT WAS ONLY NATURAL...
TEE HEE!
...FOR SUCH AN ANTICIPATED MATCH, NO?
BUT STILL...
NNGH...
DON'T WORRY SO MUCH, RIESSFELD.
AYATO'S TOUGH.
HM?
SOWA
YOU CAN SAY THAT, SASAMIYA...
...BUT HE'S UP AGAINST OUR SCHOOL'S NUMBER ONE.
SOWA
AND HE'S ALREADY BEEN BEATEN BY HER BEFORE.

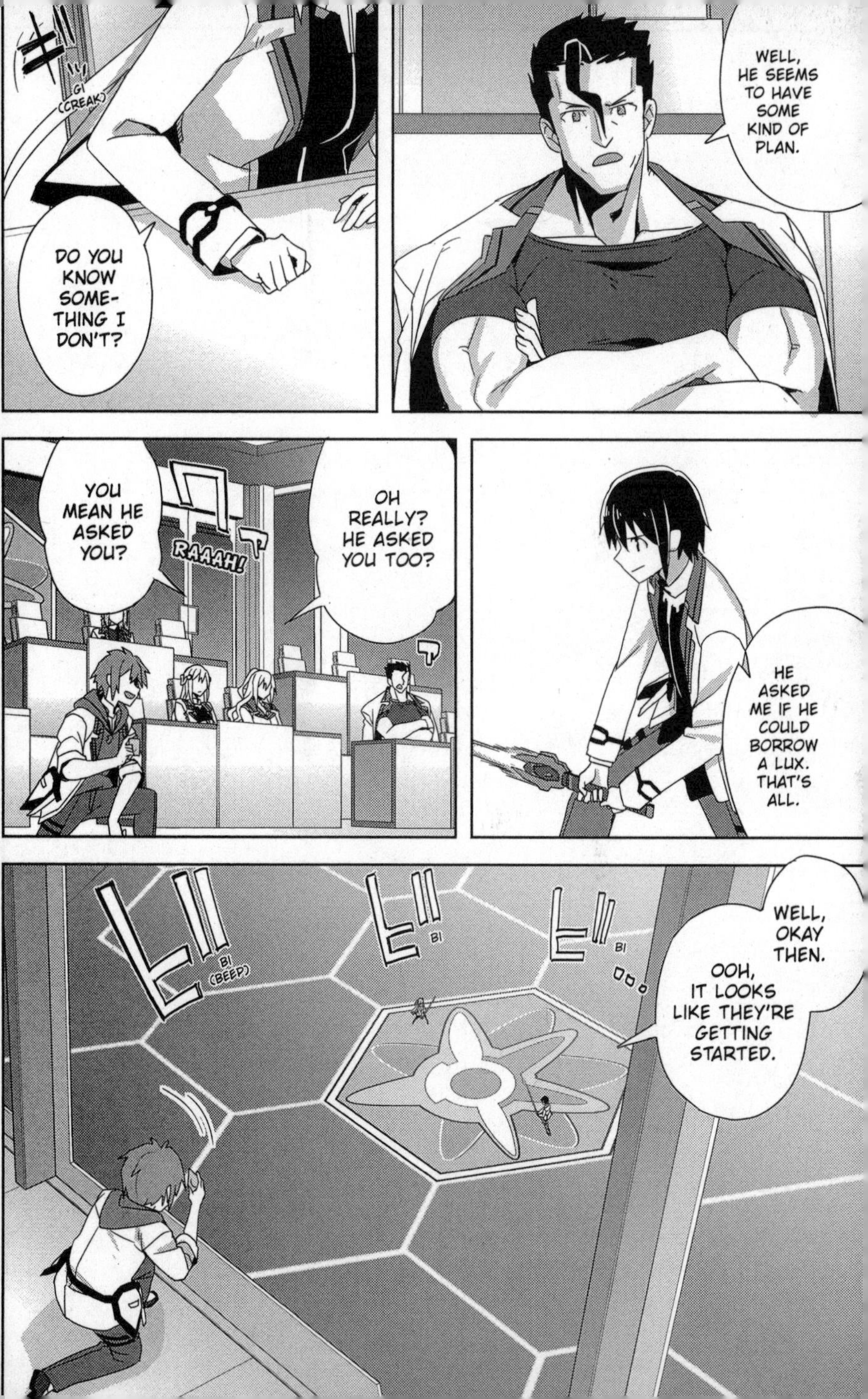
WELL, HE SEEMS TO HAVE SOME KIND OF PLAN.
GI (CREAK)
DO YOU KNOW SOME-THING I DON'T?
HE ASKED ME IF HE COULD BORROW A LUX. THAT'S ALL.
OH REALLY? HE ASKED YOU TOO?
RAAAH!
YOU MEAN HE ASKED YOU?
WELL, OKAY THEN.
OOH, IT LOOKS LIKE THEY'RE GETTING STARTED.
BI
BI
BI (BEEP)

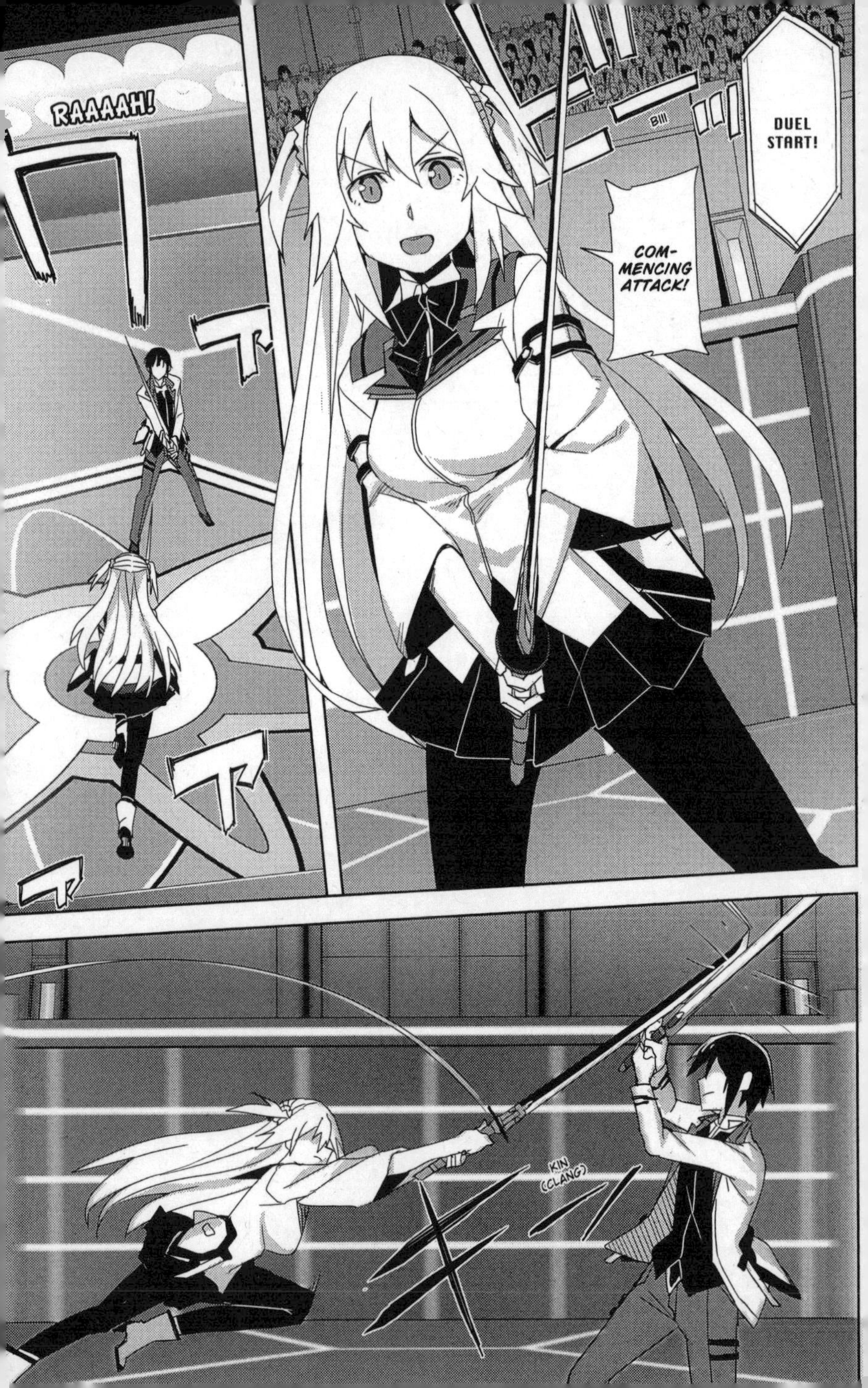
DUEL START!
BIII
COM-MENCING ATTACK!
RAAAAH!
KIN (CLANG)

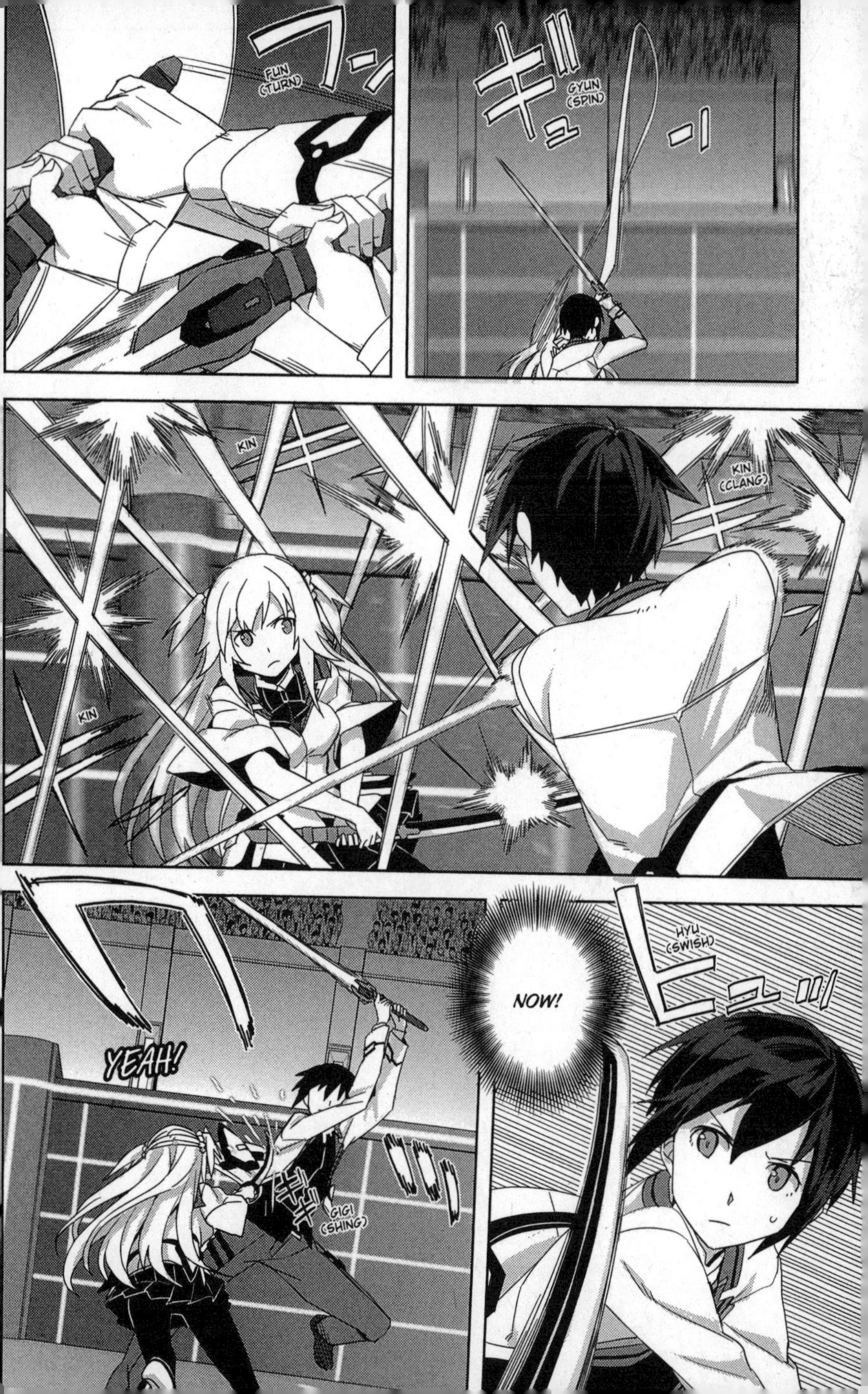
GYUN (SPIN)
FUN (TURN)
KIN (CLANG)
KIN
KIN
HYU (SWISH)
NOW!
YEAH!
GIGI (SHING)

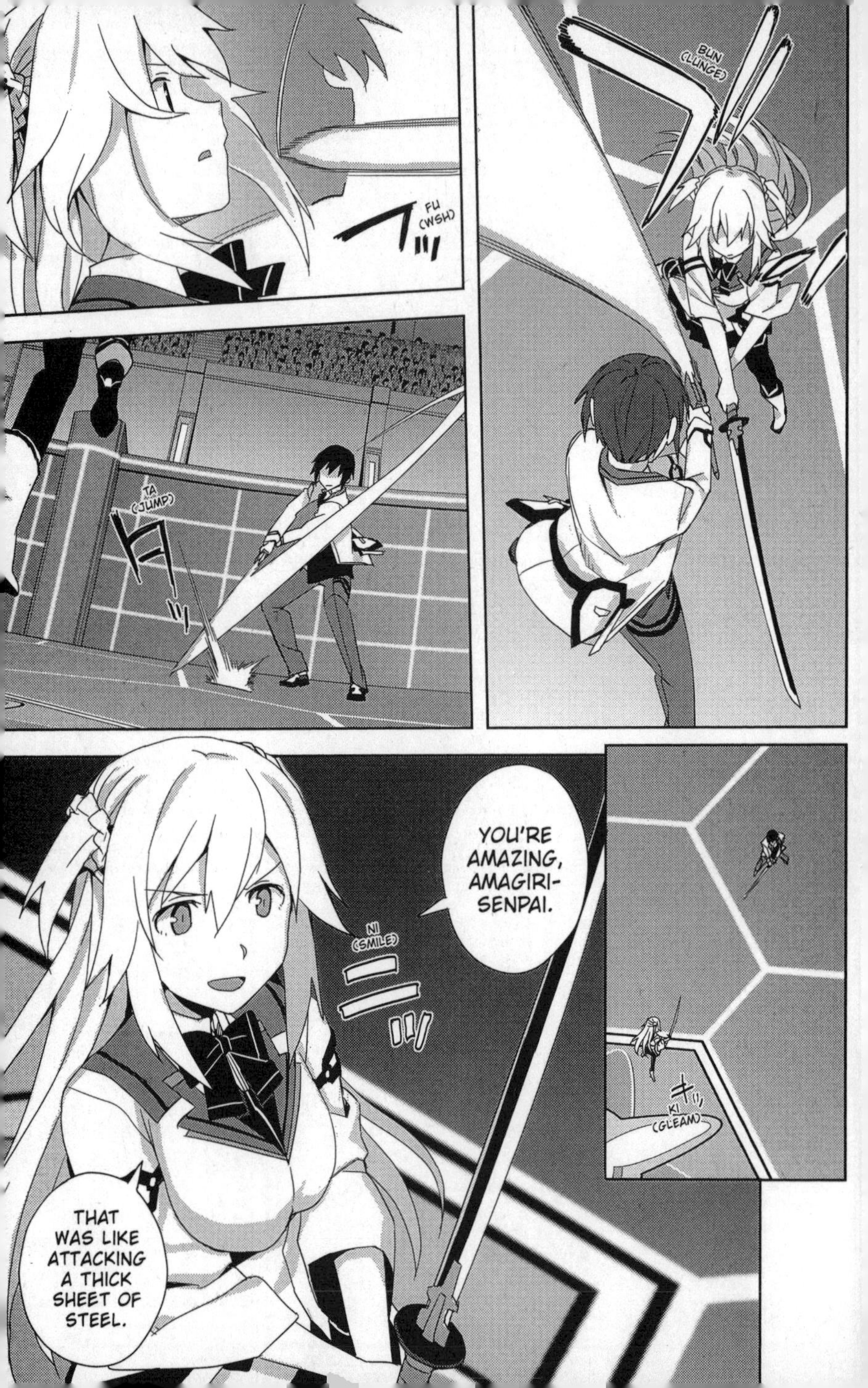
BUN (LUNGE)
FU (WSH)
TA (JUMP)
KI (GLEAM)
YOU'RE AMAZING, AMAGIRI-SENPAI.
NI (SMILE)
THAT WAS LIKE ATTACKING A THICK SHEET OF STEEL.

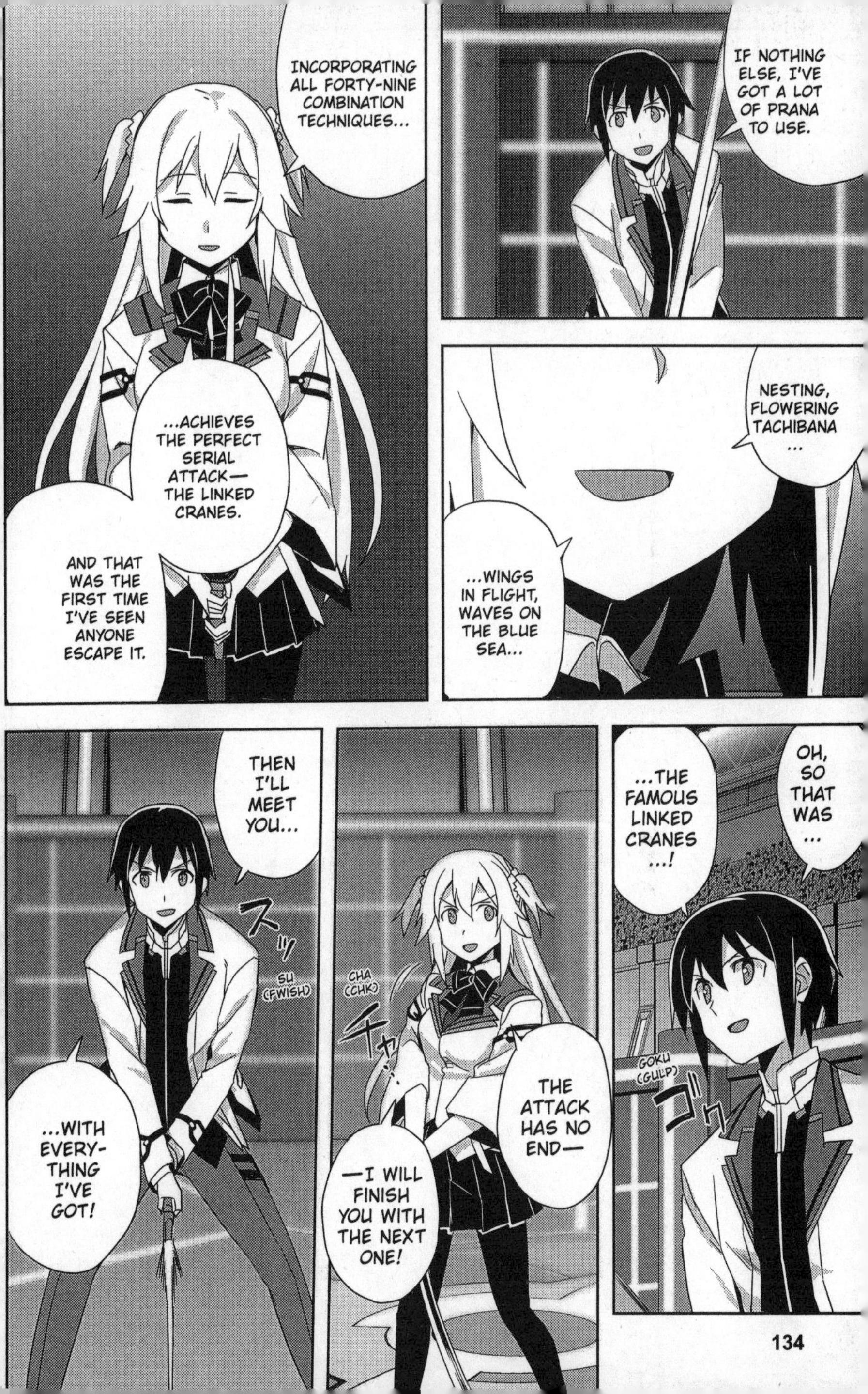
IF NOTHING ELSE, I'VE GOT A LOT OF PRANA TO USE.
NESTING, FLOWERING TACHIBANA...
...WINGS IN FLIGHT, WAVES ON THE BLUE SEA...
INCORPORATING ALL FORTY-NINE COMBINATION TECHNIQUES...
...ACHIEVES THE PERFECT SERIAL ATTACK—THE LINKED CRANES.
AND THAT WAS THE FIRST TIME I'VE SEEN ANYONE ESCAPE IT.
OH, SO THAT WAS...
...THE FAMOUS LINKED CRANES...!
GOKU (GULP)
THE ATTACK HAS NO END—
—I WILL FINISH YOU WITH THE NEXT ONE!
CHA (CHK)
THEN I'LL MEET YOU...
SU (FWISH)
...WITH EVERY-THING I'VE GOT!

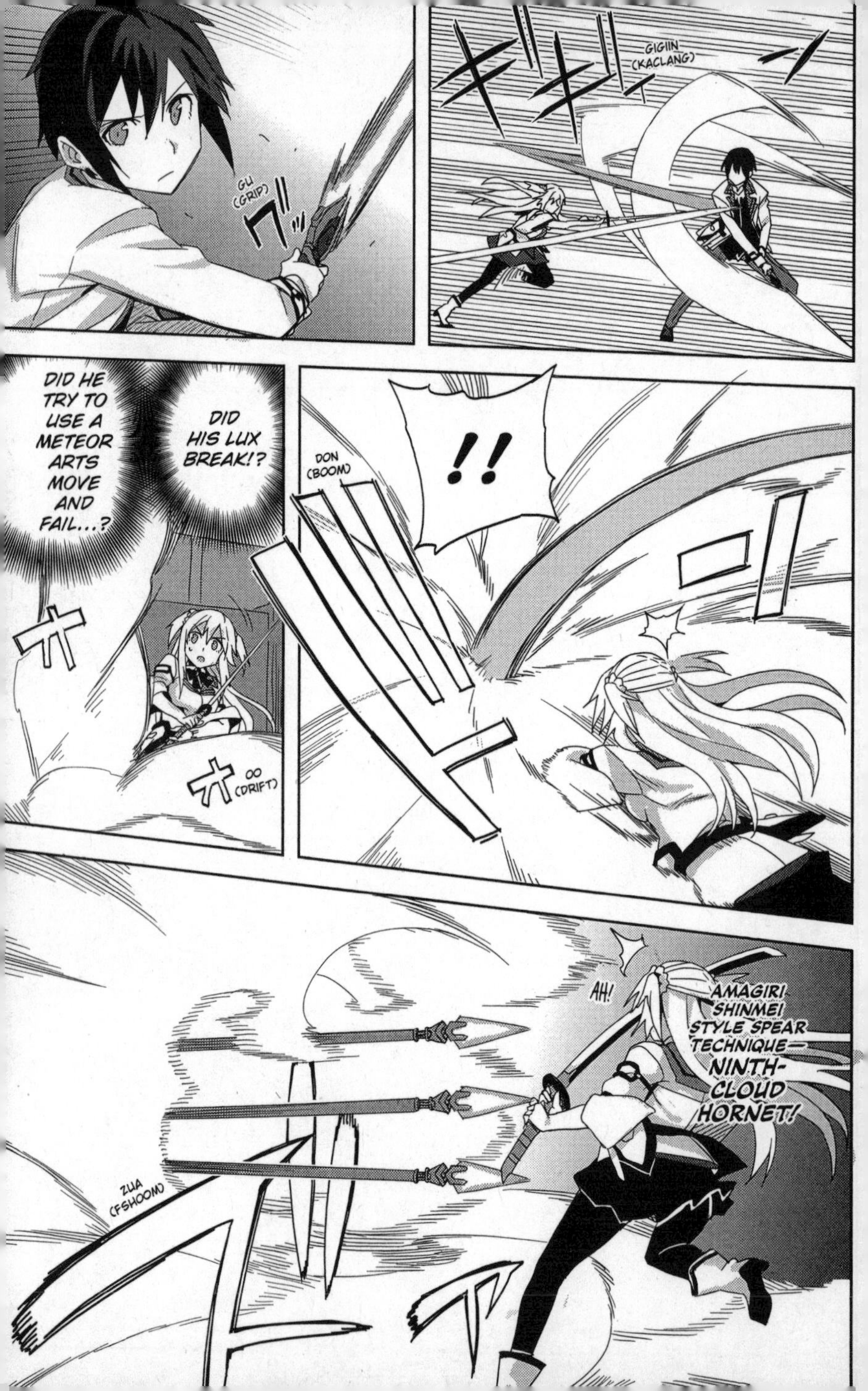
GIGIIN (KACLANG)
GU (GRIP)
DON (BOOM)
!!
DID HIS LUX BREAK!?
DID HE TRY TO USE A METEOR ARTS MOVE AND FAIL...?
OO (DRIFT)
AH!
AMAGIRI SHINMEI STYLE SPEAR TECHNIQUE— NINTH-CLOUD HORNET!
ZUA (FSHOOM)

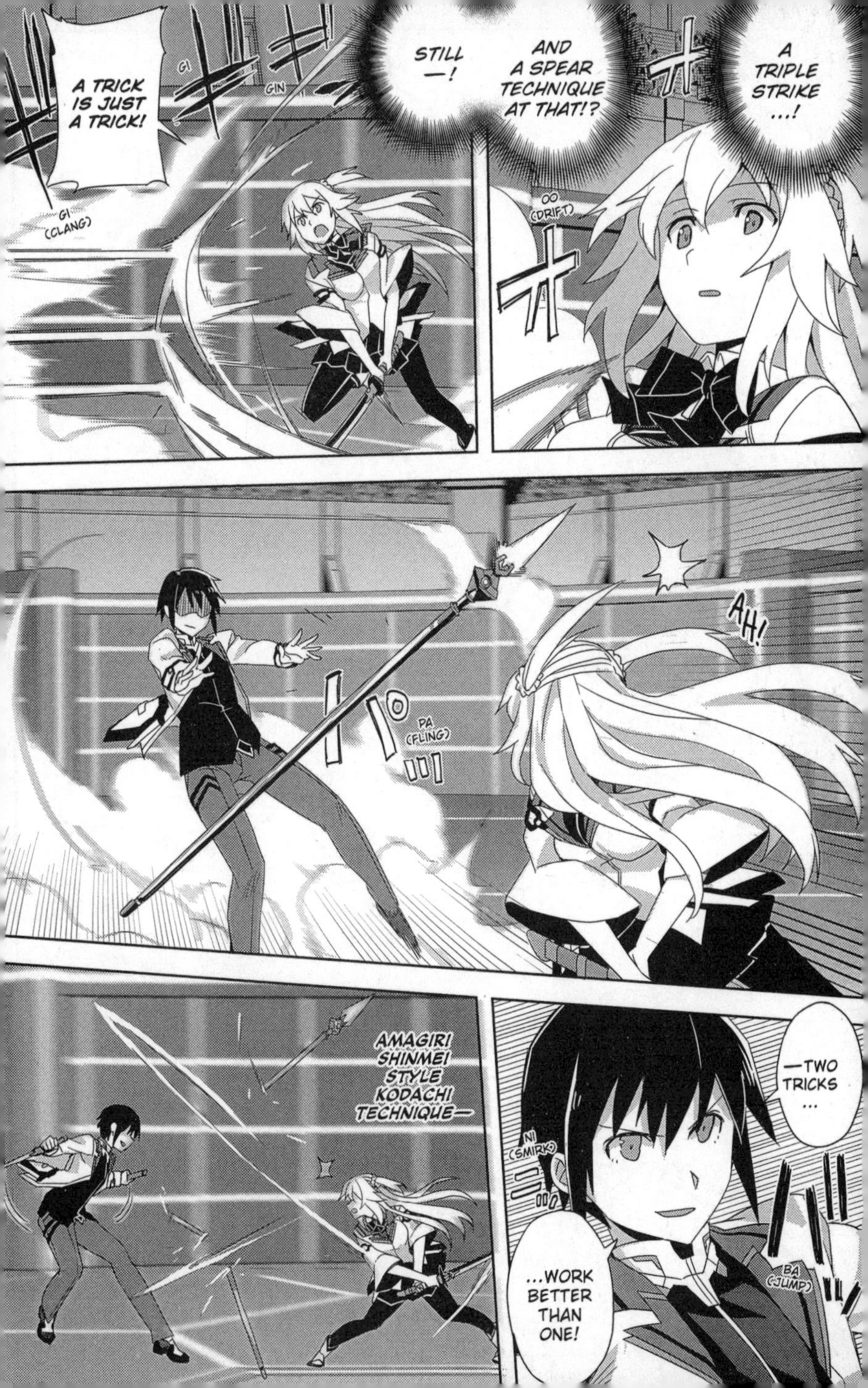
A TRIPLE STRIKE ...!
AND A SPEAR TECHNIQUE AT THAT!?
STILL —!
OO (DRIFT)
A TRICK IS JUST A TRICK!
GI
GIN
GI (CLANG)
AH!
PA (FLING)
—TWO TRICKS ...
NI (SMIRK)
...WORK BETTER THAN ONE!
BA (JUMP)
AMAGIRI SHINMEI STYLE KODACHI TECHNIQUE—

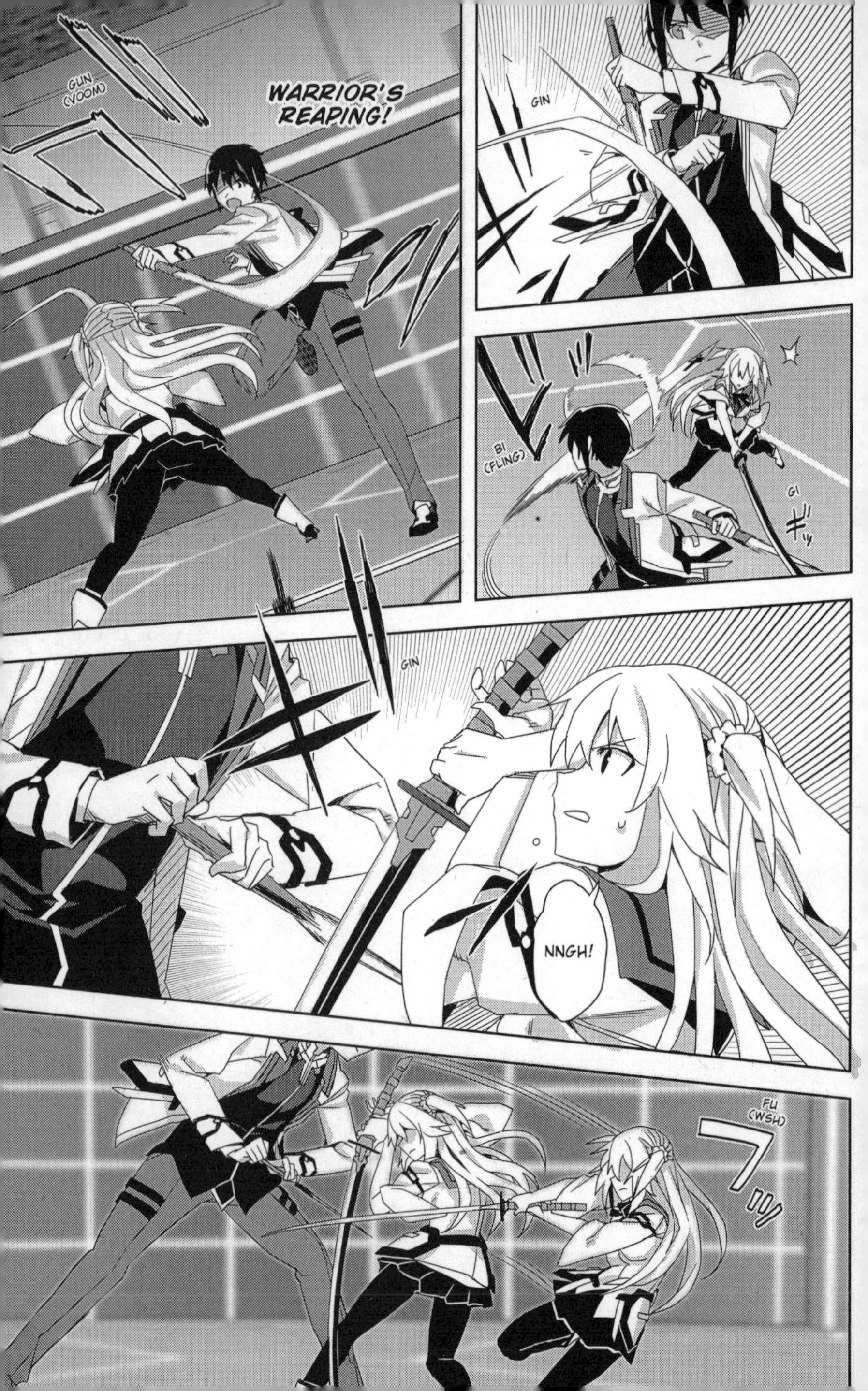
GIN
BI
(FLING)
GI
ギッ
GUN
(VOOM)
WARRIOR'S REAPING!
GIN
NNGH!
FU
(WSH)
フッ

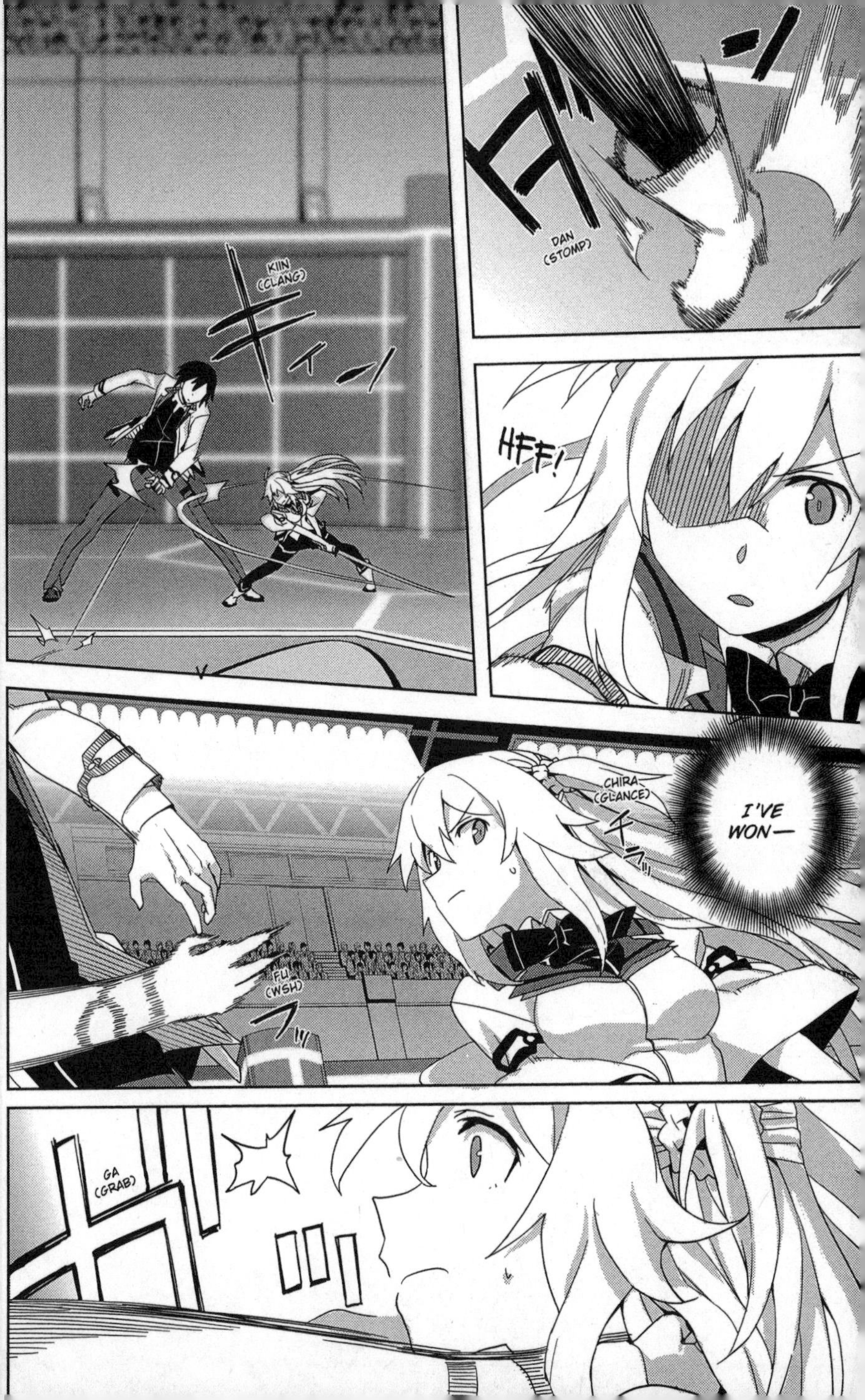

DAN (STOMP)
HFF!
KIIN (CLANG)
I'VE WON—
CHIRA (GLANCE)
FU (WSH)
GA (GRAB)

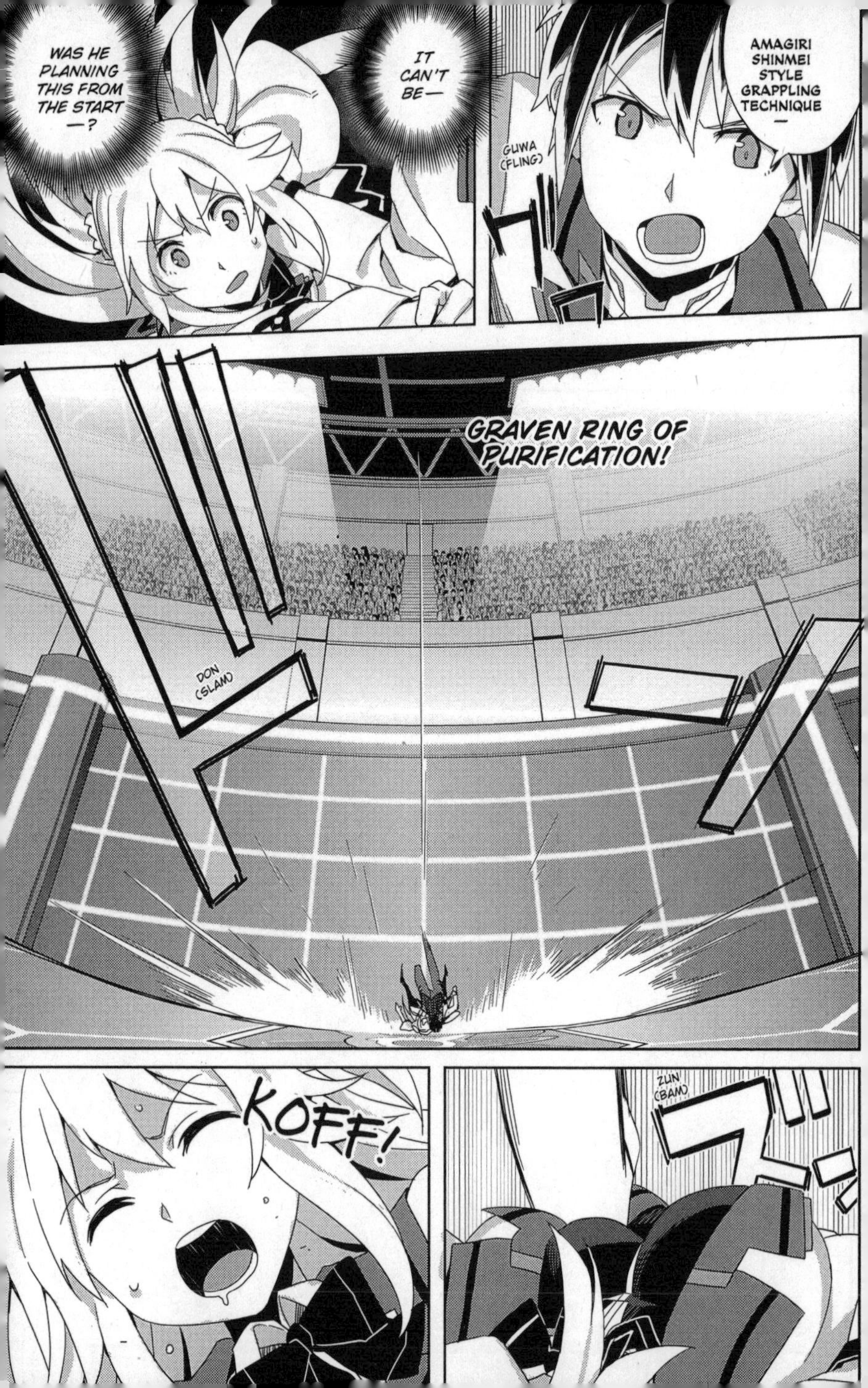
AMAGIRI SHINMEI STYLE GRAPPLING TECHNIQUE —
GUWA (FLING)
IT CAN'T BE—
WAS HE PLANNING THIS FROM THE START —?
GRAVEN RING OF PURIFICATION!
DON (SLAM)
ZUN (BAM)
KOFF!

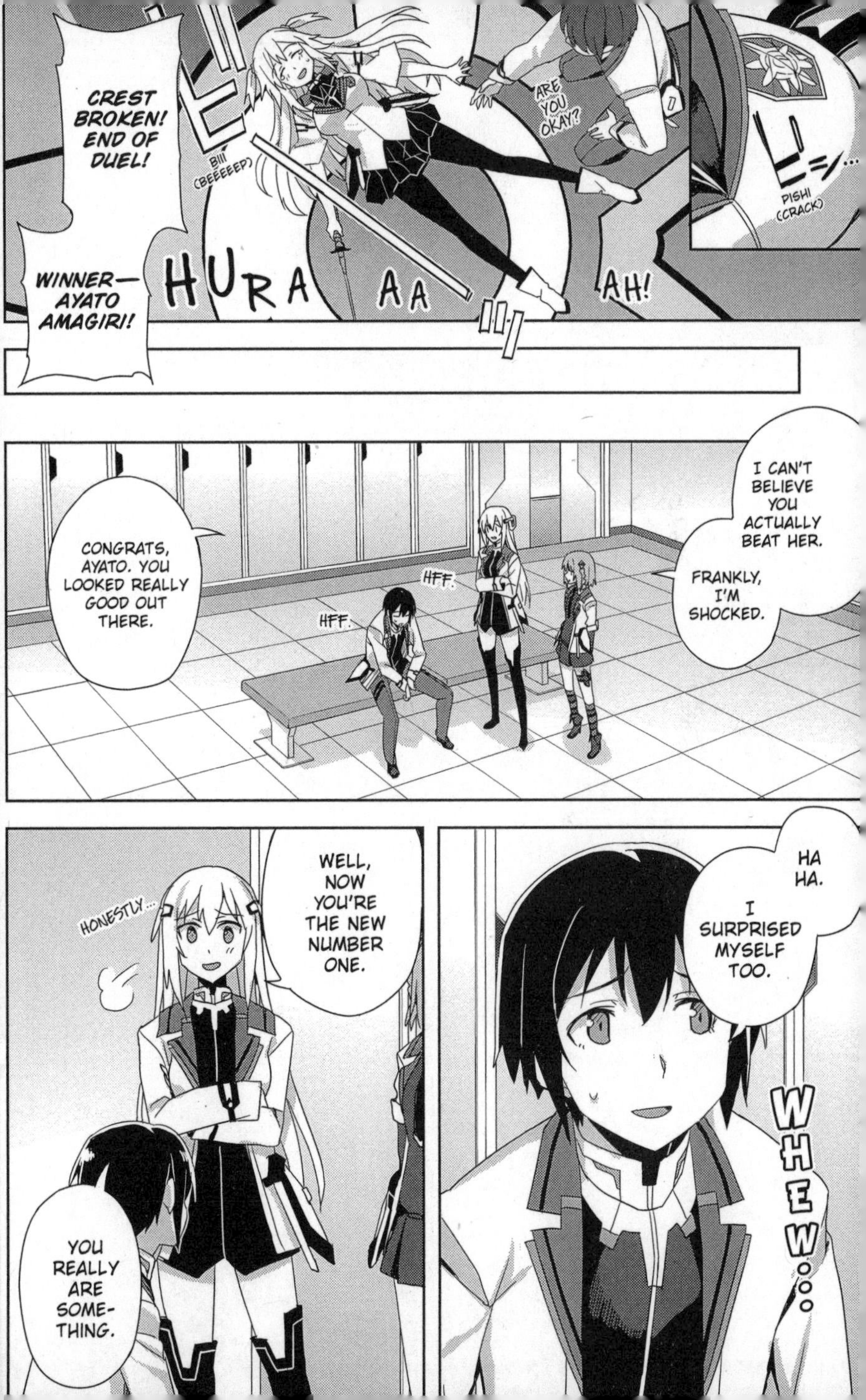
PISHI (CRACK)
ARE YOU OKAY?
CREST BROKEN! END OF DUEL!
BIII (BEEEEEEP)
HURAAAAH!
WINNER—AYATO AMAGIRI!
I CAN'T BELIEVE YOU ACTUALLY BEAT HER.
FRANKLY, I'M SHOCKED.
HFF.
HFF.
CONGRATS, AYATO. YOU LOOKED REALLY GOOD OUT THERE.
HA HA.
I SURPRISED MYSELF TOO.
WHEW...
WELL, NOW YOU'RE THE NEW NUMBER ONE.
HONESTLY...
YOU REALLY ARE SOME-THING.

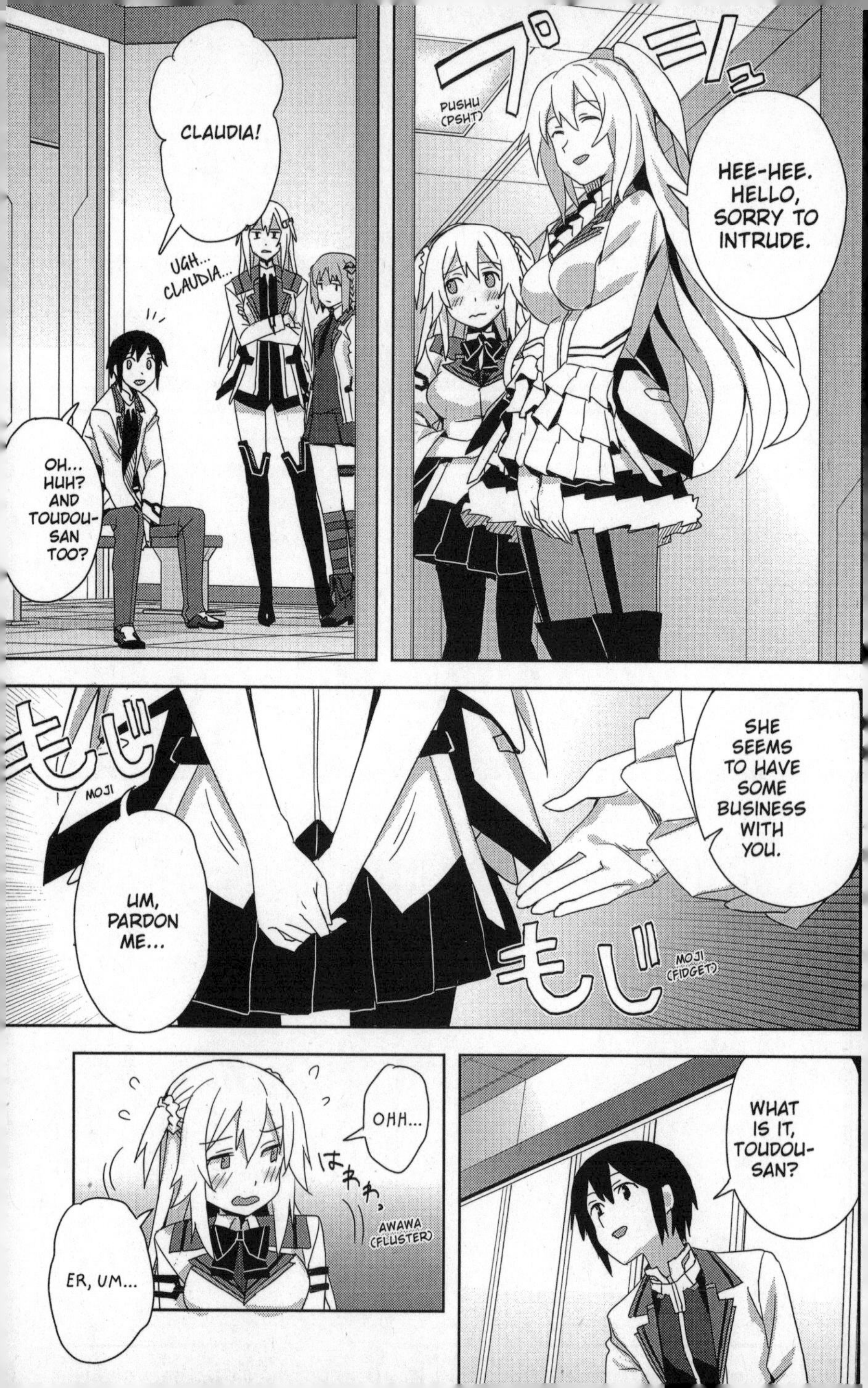
プシュ
PUSHU (PSHT)
HEE-HEE. HELLO, SORRY TO INTRUDE.
CLAUDIA!
UGH... CLAUDIA...
OH... HUH? AND TOUDOU-SAN TOO?
SHE SEEMS TO HAVE SOME BUSINESS WITH YOU.
もじ
MOJI (FIDGET)
もじ
MOJI
UM, PARDON ME...
WHAT IS IT, TOUDOU-SAN?
OHH...
はわわ
AWAWA (FLUSTER)
ER, UM...

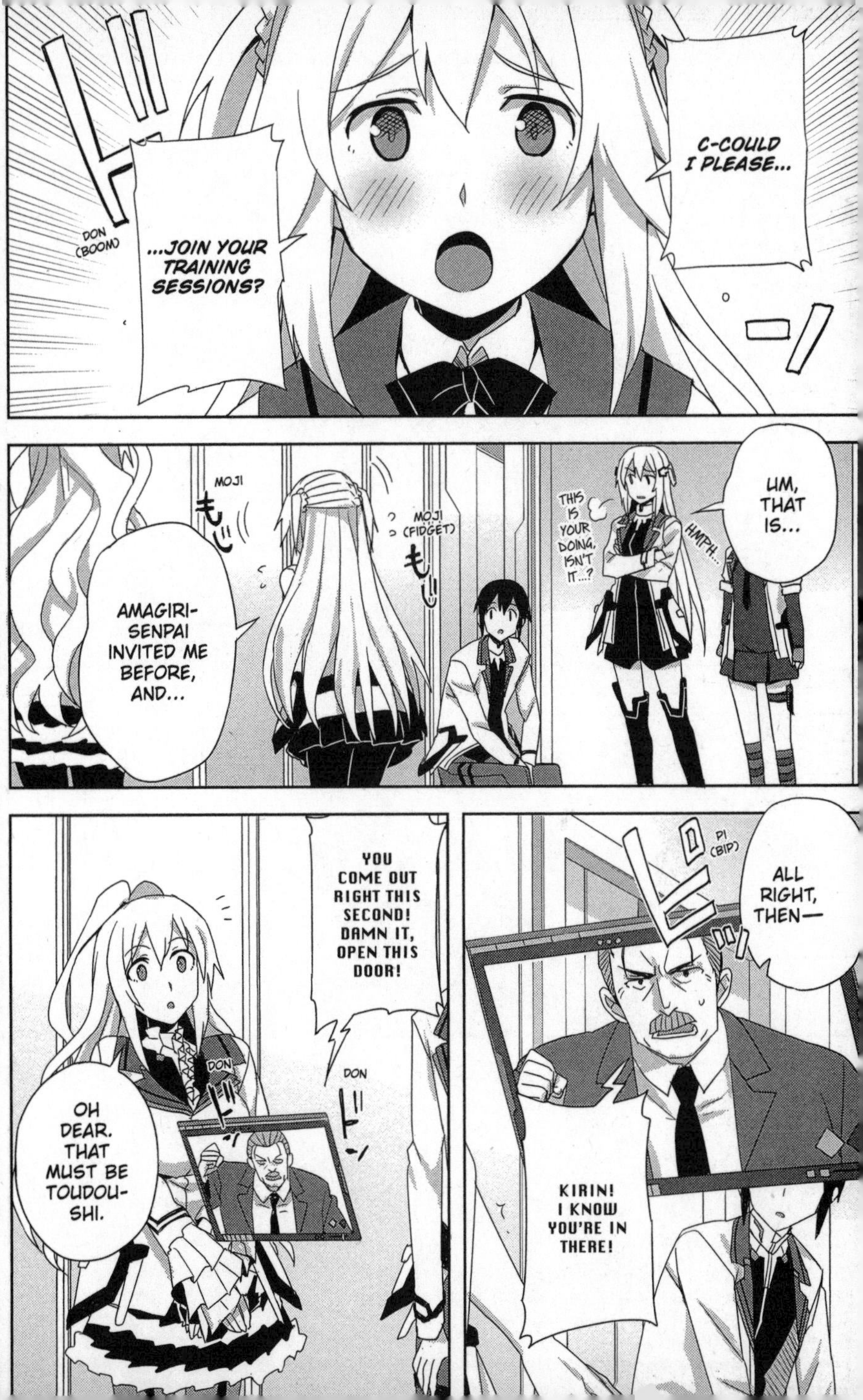
C-COULD I PLEASE...
...JOIN YOUR TRAINING SESSIONS?
DON (BOOM)
UM, THAT IS...
HMPH...
THIS IS YOUR DOING, ISN'T IT...?
MOJI (FIDGET)
MOJI
AMAGIRI-SENPAI INVITED ME BEFORE, AND...
PI (BIP)
ALL RIGHT, THEN—
KIRIN! I KNOW YOU'RE IN THERE!
YOU COME OUT RIGHT THIS SECOND! DAMN IT, OPEN THIS DOOR!
DON
DON
OH DEAR. THAT MUST BE TOUDOU-SHI.

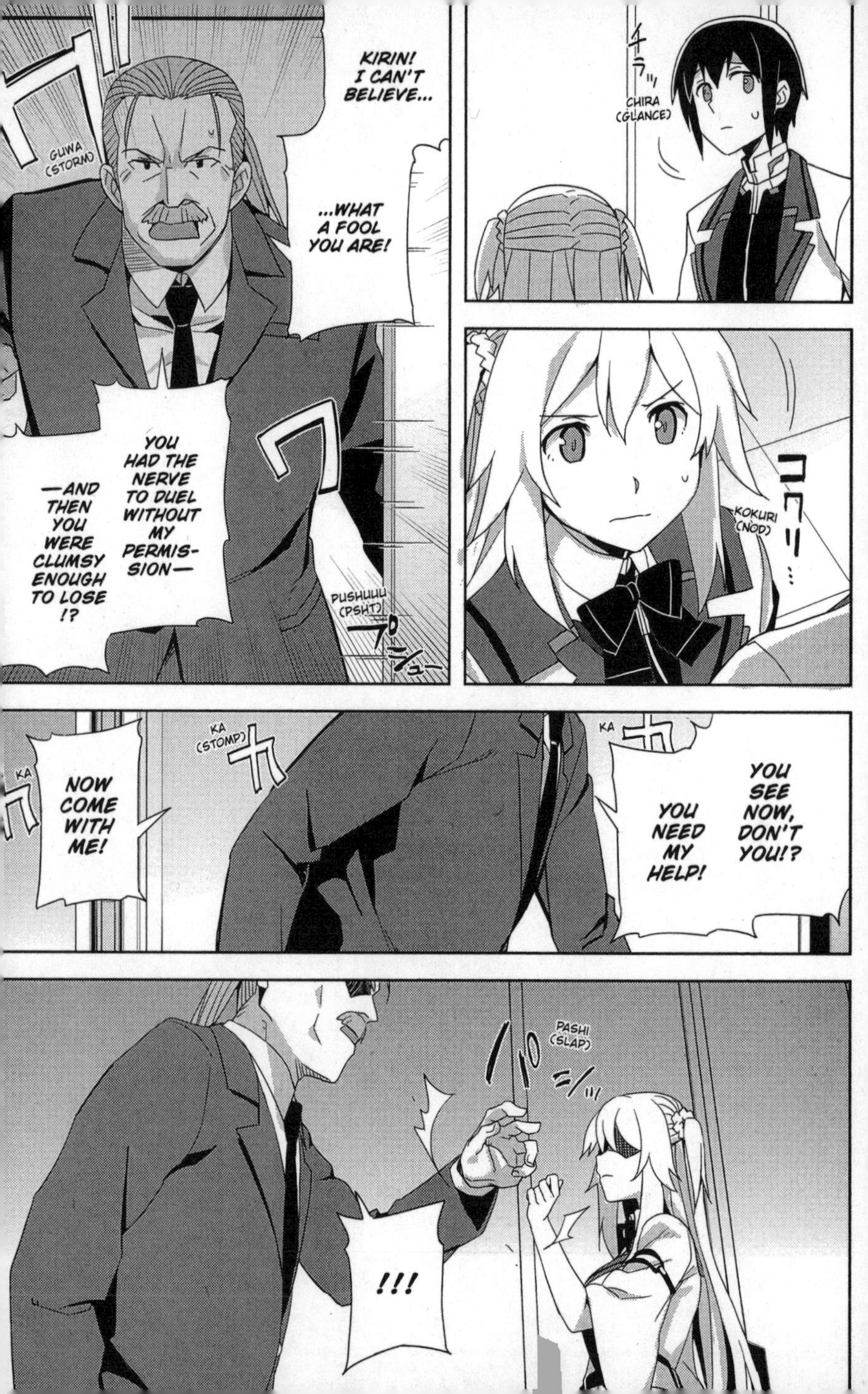
イラッ
CHIRA (GLANCE)
コクリ…
KOKURI (NOD)
KIRIN! I CAN'T BELIEVE...
...WHAT A FOOL YOU ARE!
GUWA (STORM)
YOU HAD THE NERVE TO DUEL WITHOUT MY PERMISSION—
—AND THEN YOU WERE CLUMSY ENOUGH TO LOSE!?
PUSHUUU (PSHT)
プシュー
KA
カ
YOU SEE NOW, DON'T YOU!?
YOU NEED MY HELP!
KA (STOMP)
カ
KA
カ
NOW COME WITH ME!
PASHI (SLAP)
パシッ
!!!

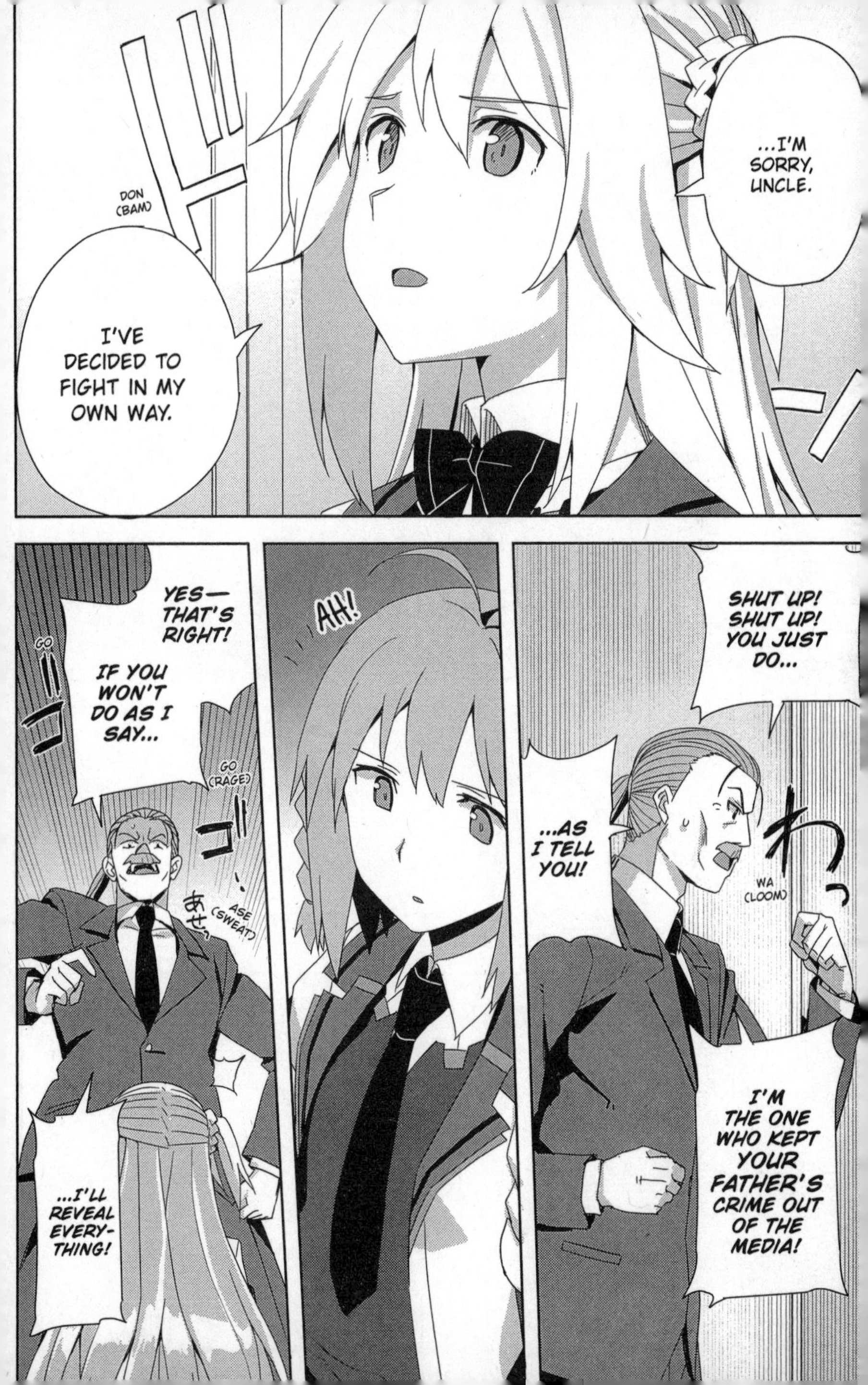
...I'M SORRY, UNCLE.
DON (BAM)
I'VE DECIDED TO FIGHT IN MY OWN WAY.
SHUT UP! SHUT UP! YOU JUST DO...
...AS I TELL YOU!
WA (LOOM)
I'M THE ONE WHO KEPT YOUR FATHER'S CRIME OUT OF THE MEDIA!
AH!
YES— THAT'S RIGHT!
IF YOU WON'T DO AS I SAY...
GO
GO (RAGE)
あせっ
ASE (SWEAT)
...I'LL REVEAL EVERY-THING!

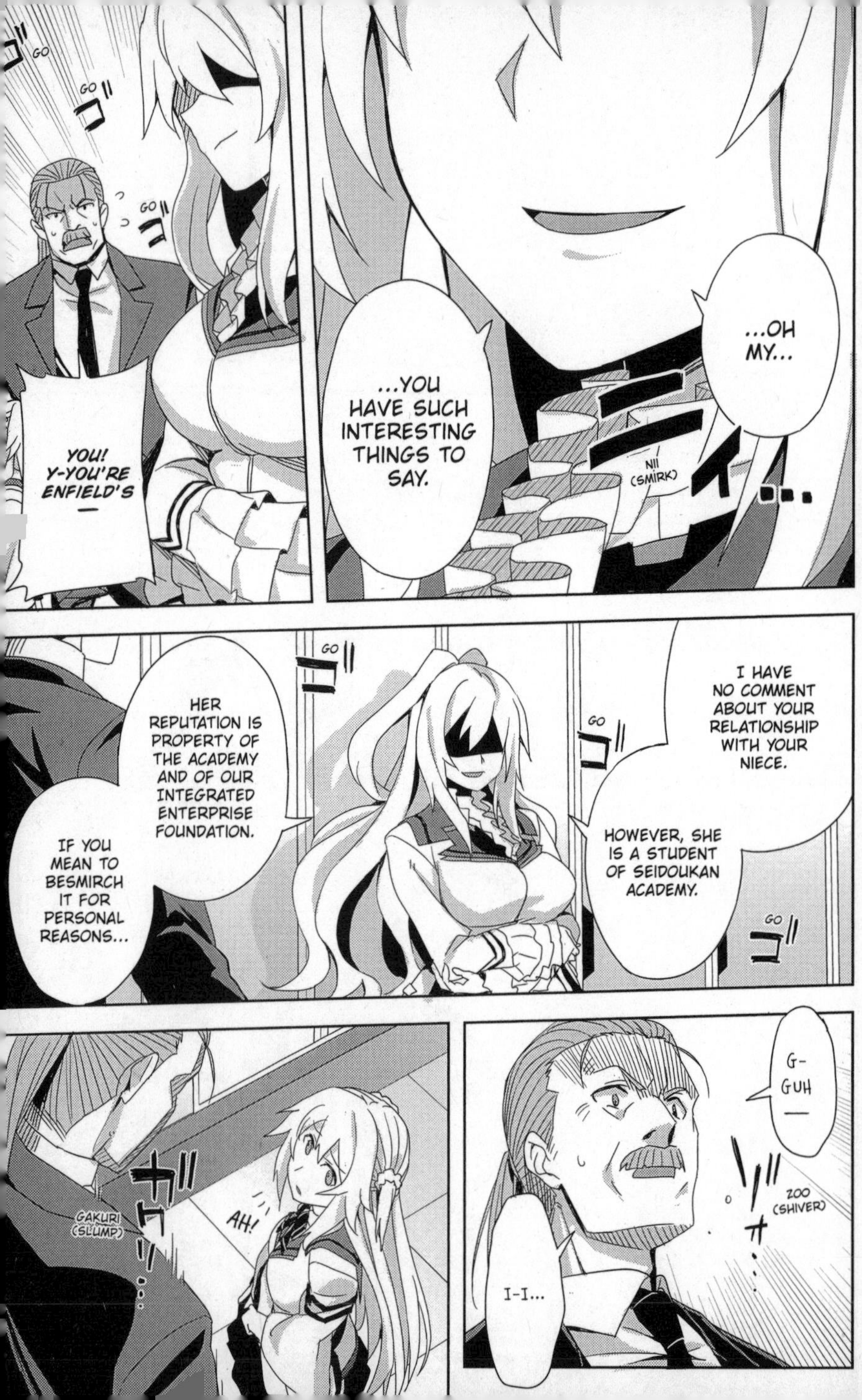
...OH MY...
NII (SMIRK)
...YOU HAVE SUCH INTERESTING THINGS TO SAY.
GO
GO
GO
YOU! Y-YOU'RE ENFIELD'S —
I HAVE NO COMMENT ABOUT YOUR RELATIONSHIP WITH YOUR NIECE.
HOWEVER, SHE IS A STUDENT OF SEIDOUKAN ACADEMY.
GO
GO
GO
HER REPUTATION IS PROPERTY OF THE ACADEMY AND OF OUR INTEGRATED ENTERPRISE FOUNDATION.
IF YOU MEAN TO BESMIRCH IT FOR PERSONAL REASONS...
G-GUH —
ZOO (SHIVER)
I-I...
AH!
GAKURI (SLUMP)

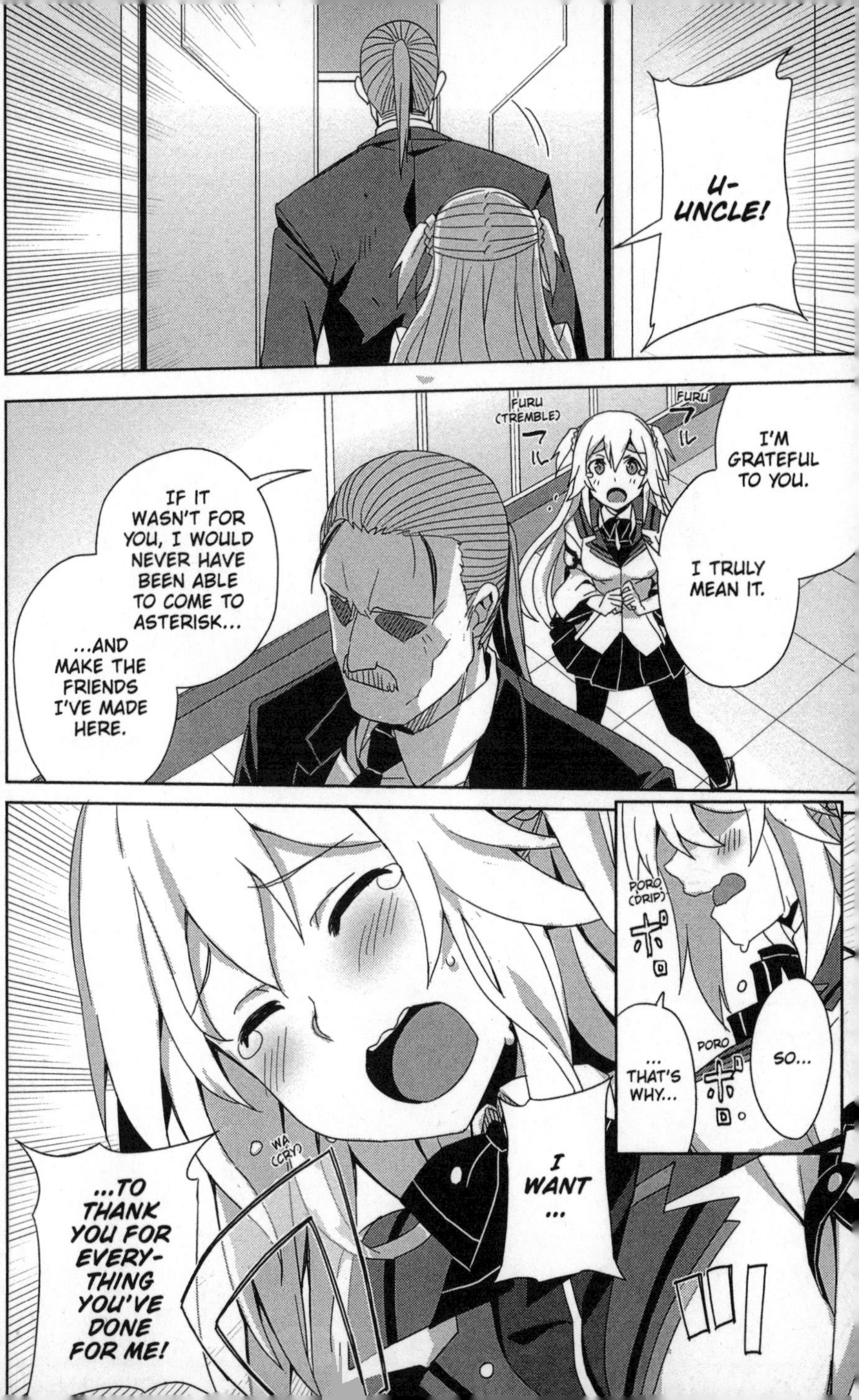
U-UNCLE!
FURU
FURU (TREMBLE)
I'M GRATEFUL TO YOU.
I TRULY MEAN IT.
IF IT WASN'T FOR YOU, I WOULD NEVER HAVE BEEN ABLE TO COME TO ASTERISK...
...AND MAKE THE FRIENDS I'VE MADE HERE.
PORO (DRIP)
SO...
PORO
...THAT'S WHY...
I WANT...
WA (CRY)
...TO THANK YOU FOR EVERY-THING YOU'VE DONE FOR ME!

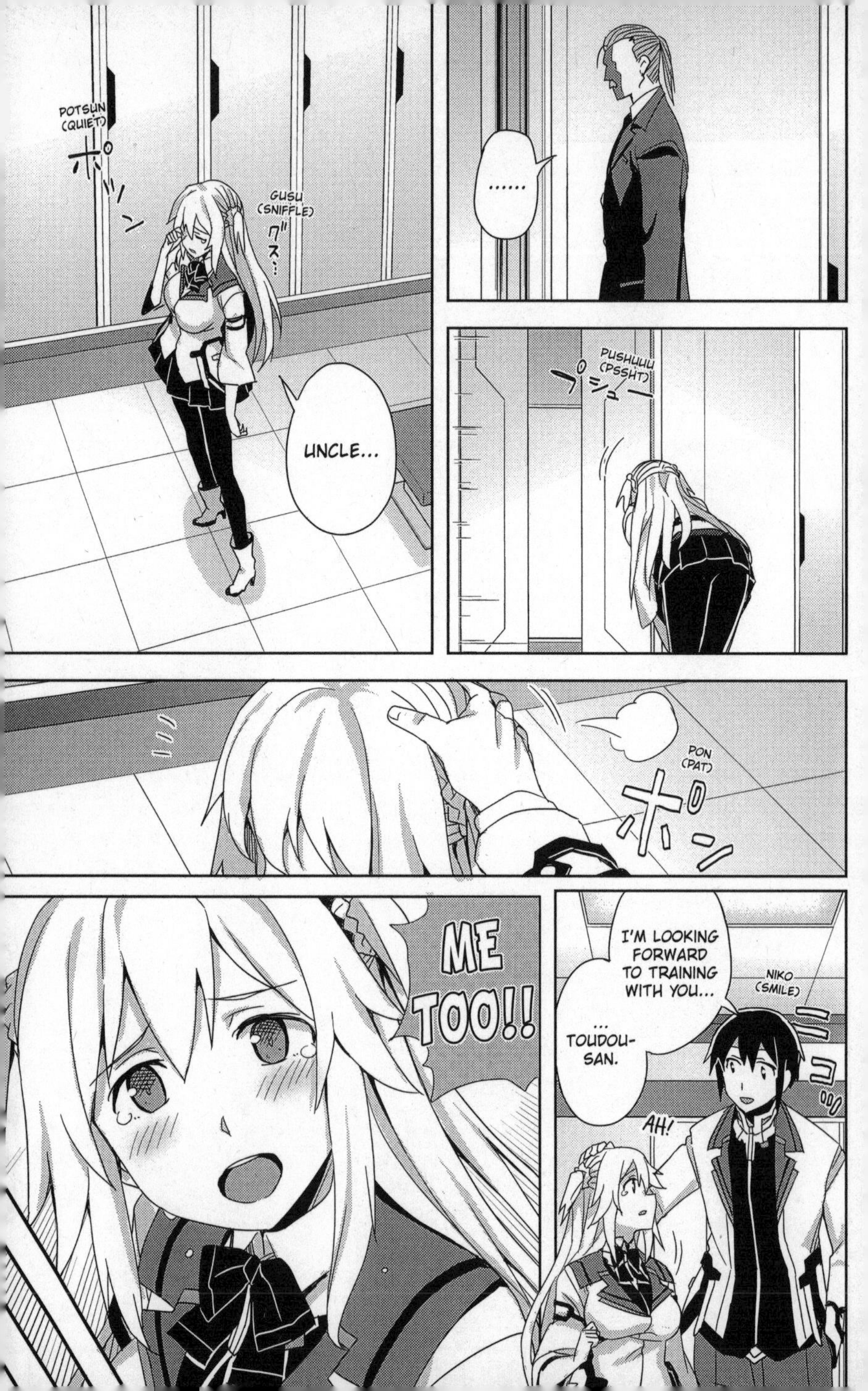
......
PUSHUUU (PSSHT)
POTSUN (QUIET)
GUSU (SNIFFLE)
UNCLE...
PON (PAT)
I'M LOOKING FORWARD TO TRAINING WITH YOU...
... TOUDOU-SAN.
NIKO (SMILE)
AH!
ME TOO!!

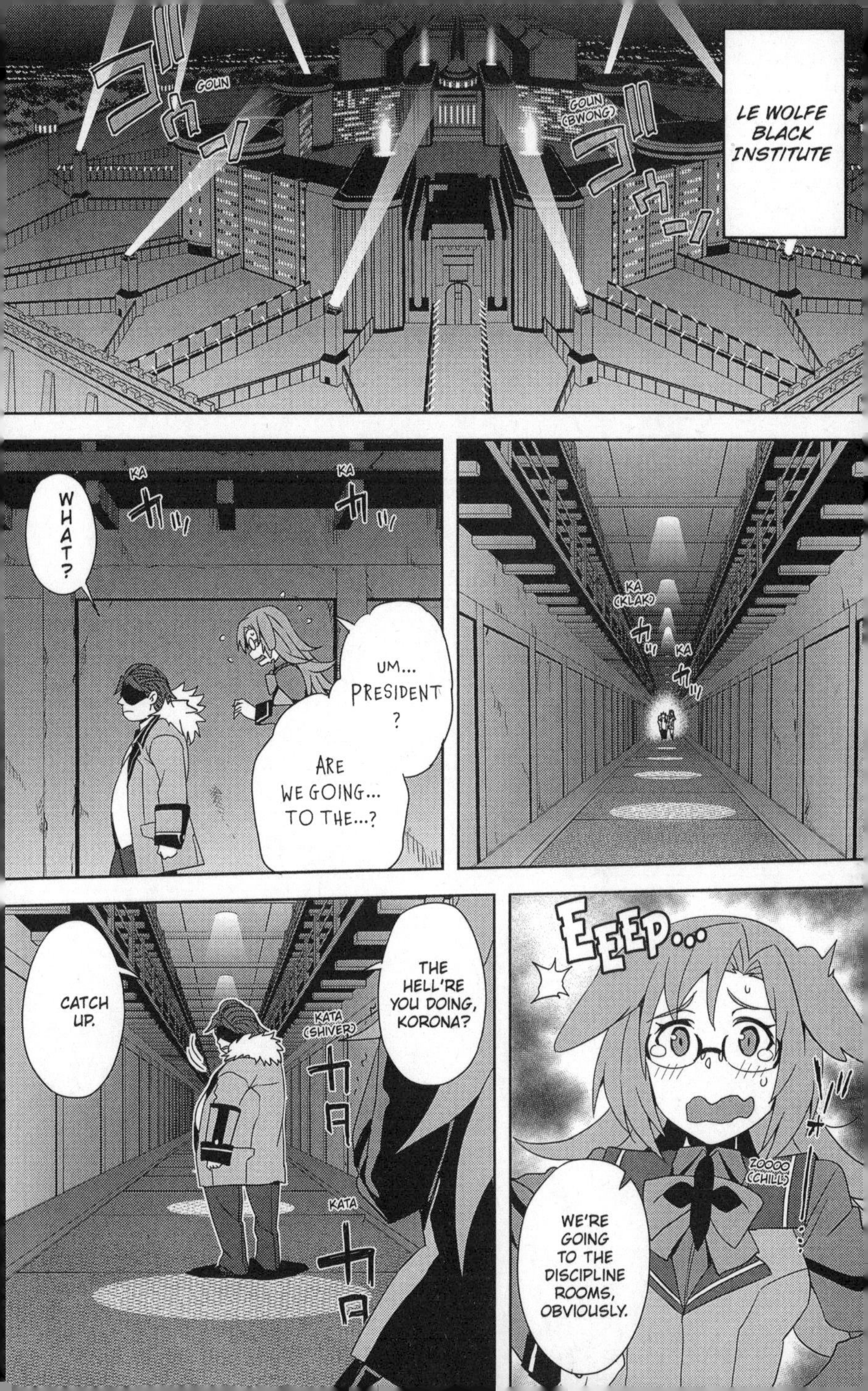
LE WOLFE BLACK INSTITUTE
GOUN (BWONG)
GOUN
KA (KLAK)
KA
KA
KA
WHAT?
UM... PRESIDENT?
ARE WE GOING... TO THE...?
EEEP...
ZOOOO (CHILL)
WE'RE GOING TO THE DISCIPLINE ROOMS, OBVIOUSLY.
THE HELL'RE YOU DOING, KORONA?
CATCH UP.
KATA (SHIVER)
KATA

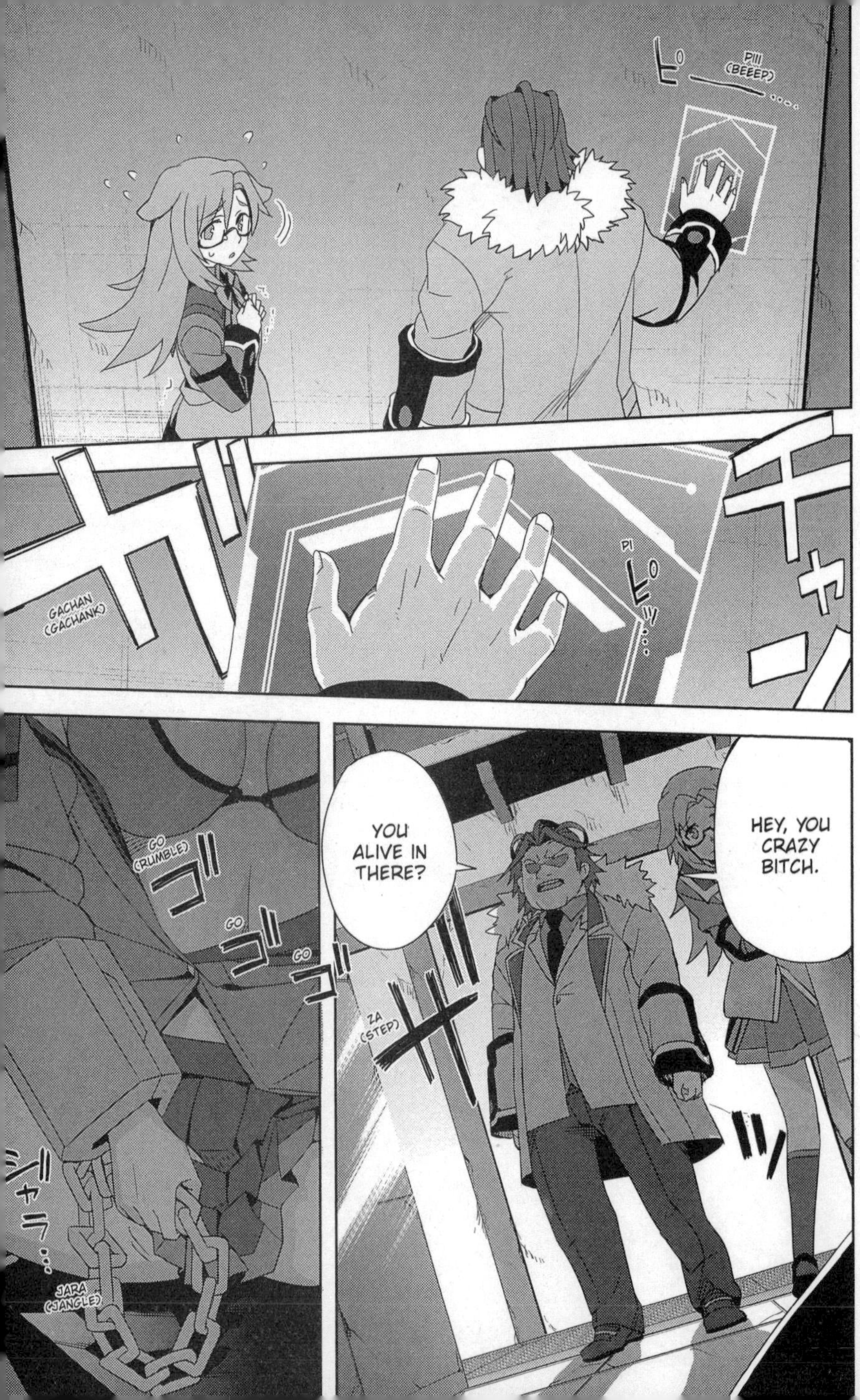
PIII (BEEEP)
PI
GACHAN (GACHANK)
HEY, YOU CRAZY BITCH.
YOU ALIVE IN THERE?
ZA (STEP)
GO (CRUMBLE)
GO
GO
JARA (JANGLE)

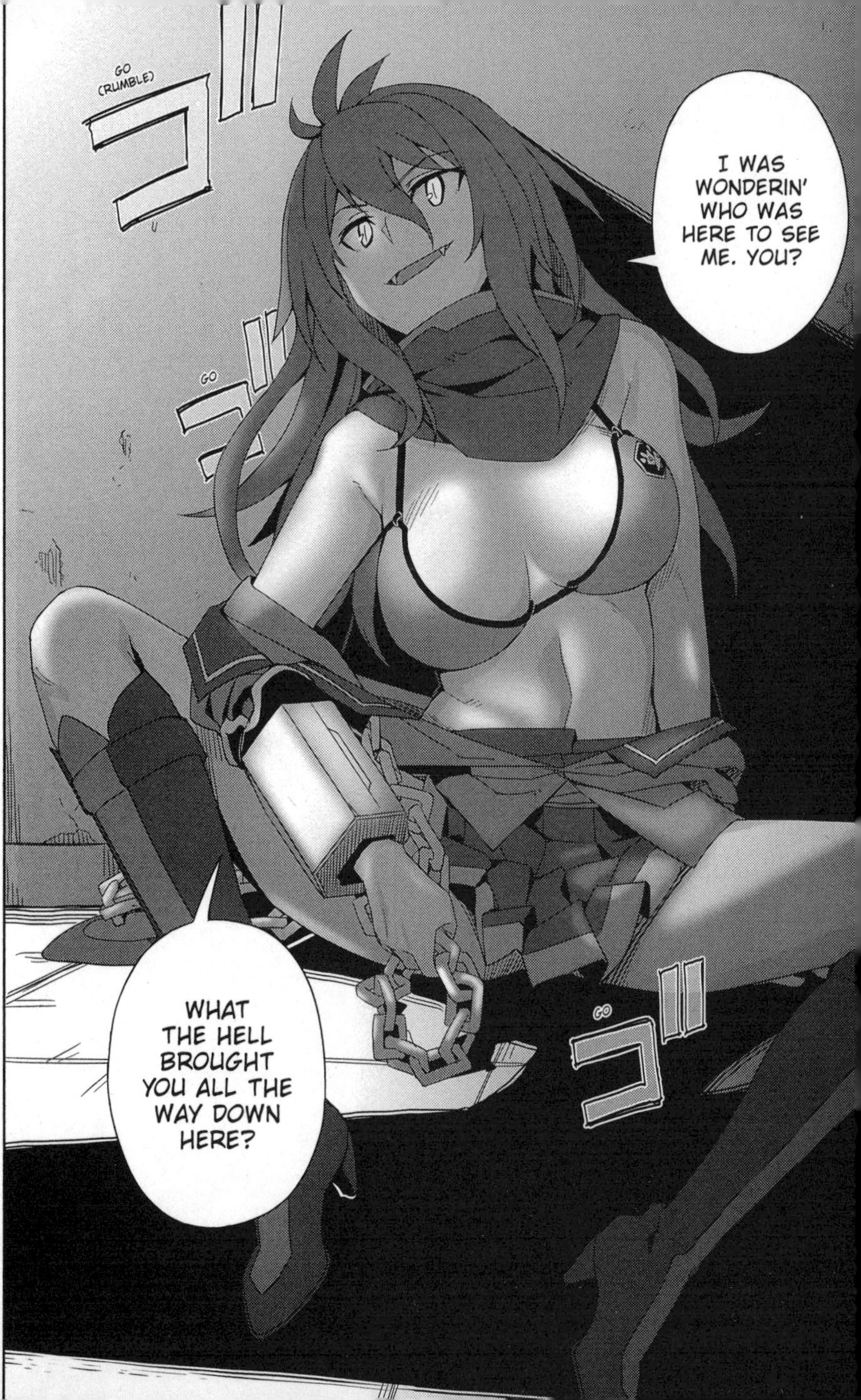
I WAS WONDERIN' WHO WAS HERE TO SEE ME. YOU?
GO (RUMBLE)
GO
GO
WHAT THE HELL BROUGHT YOU ALL THE WAY DOWN HERE?

— TO BE CONTINUED...

Afterword

Hi, it's Ningen again.
Thanks to all your support, here's the fourth volume!

The first season of the anime aired, and there's a game out too—the world of *The Asterisk War* just keeps getting more exciting. I hope this manga series adds to the fun at least a little bit.

Once again, thank you so much to Yuu Miyazaki-sensei and okiura-sensei, who brought us the original novels and their illustrations; to the *Comic Alive* editorial staff; and to Shimada-kun and Jou Yukino-sama for all your help!

See you next time in Volume 5!

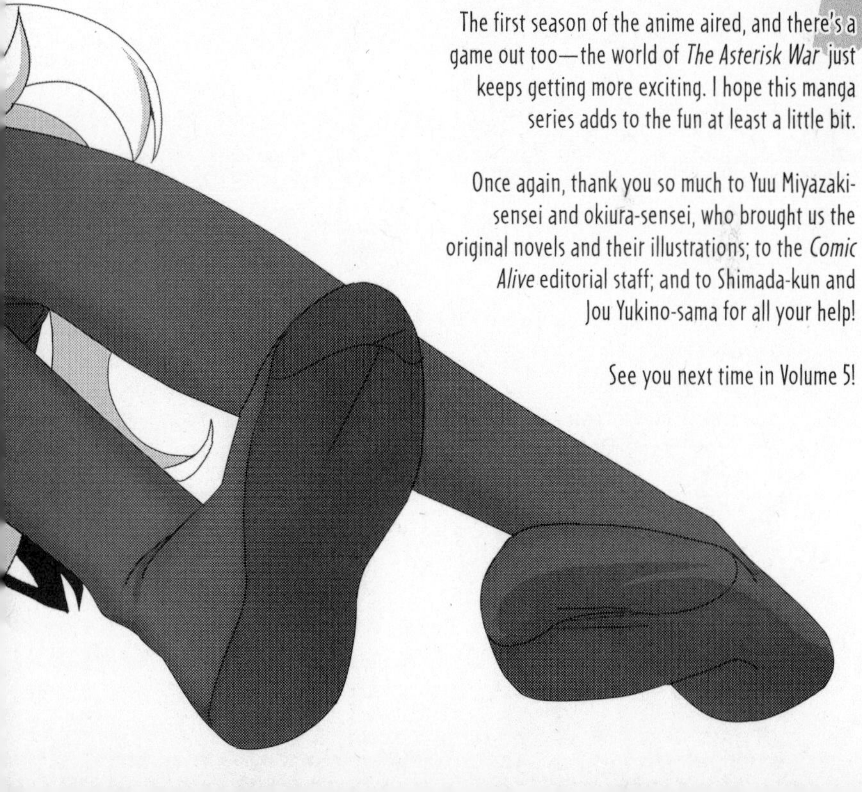

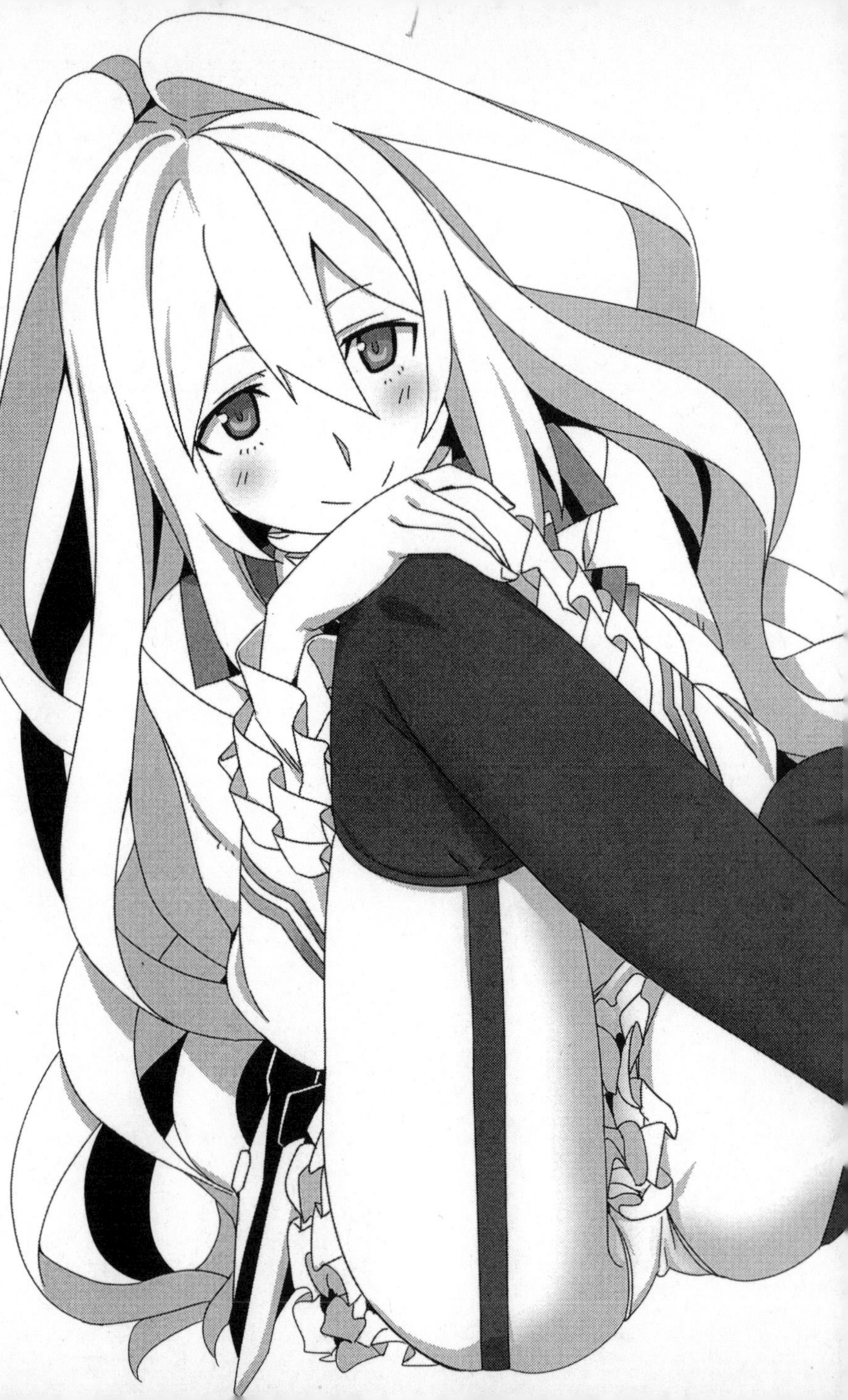

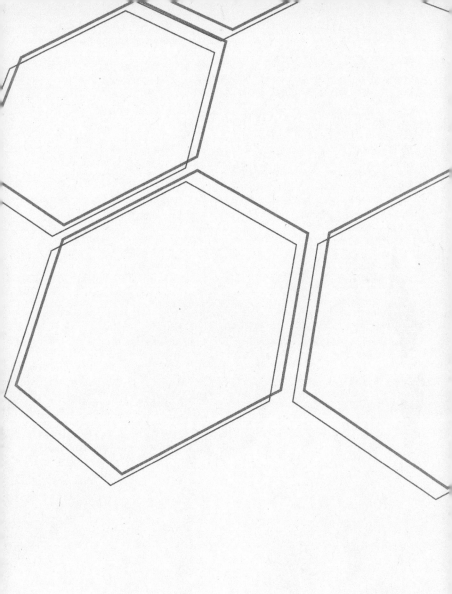

THE
ASTERISK WAR